The Emergence of
African Fiction

Charles R. Larson

The Emergence of
African Fiction

Indiana University Press

BLOOMINGTON / LONDON

ACKNOWLEDGMENTS

To the Macmillan Company, 866 Third Avenue,
New York, New York, for permission to quote from
Camara Laye's *The Radiance of the King* (1971).
To Librairie Plon, 8, Rue Garancière, Paris, for per-
mission to quote from Camara Laye's *Le regard du
roi* (1953).

*Published in Canada by Fitzhenry & Whiteside Limited,
Don Mills, Ontario*

Library of Congress catalog card number: 71-180489

ISBN: 0-253-31945-5 (cl.)

0-253-20149-7 (paper)

Manufactured in the United States of America

FOR

RICHARD M. DORSON,
EMILE SNYDER,
ALAN R. TAYLOR,
and, especially,

NEWTON P. STALLKNECHT

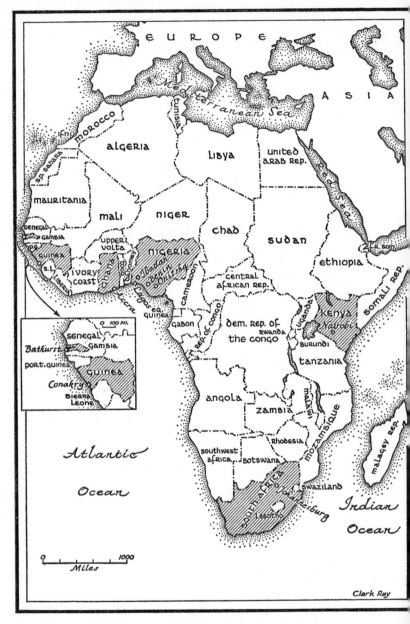

Africa Today: shaded areas indicate the countries
of the writers examined in this study.

Contents

Foreword

WITH ADMIRABLE FRANKNESS, DR. LARSON HAS warned his readers that African literature has in the last quarter century surpassed the limits of clear-cut definition. Indeed, the term "African" can now apply only in a geographical sense to many recent publications, especially in the field of fiction, that challenge the attention of the critic. African literature is rapidly assuming a cosmopolitan aspect so that interpretation can no longer center directly upon racial or cultural considerations. In many cases, a concept such as that of *négritude* no longer offers a viable approach, and the reader is at times unable to decide from any internal evidence whether his author is African or European. The very concept of African literature has become an historical one (I would prefer not to call it "obsolete" as Dr. Larson does). It refers, however, to a very recent history that follows upon the Second World War and extends well into the sixties. This history, rich in cultural and literary developments, includes a radical transformation, one might almost say a metamorphosis, of ideas, attitudes, and modes of expression. Such a rapid and continuous process of re-orientation can bewilder the reader, especially if he is no better acquainted with the African scene than are most American readers of fiction. Here, Dr. Larson's contribution will stand many of us in good stead. He has mapped in broad outline the frontiers of thought and feeling along which these changes have taken place.

The student of literature and of ideas may well find these studies of absorbing interest. They describe a confused yet persistent expansion of world-view and of self-knowledge that has accompanied the passage from a naive, oral tradition to a literature capable of absorbing the influence of such writers as Franz Kafka and James Joyce. We may be tempted to compare this rapid movement to other instances of radical transformation more familiar to the student. Roman acceptance of Greek culture, the Gothic adaptation to Roman Christianity, the Western rediscovery of the Classical world, and the Russians' acceptance of the West after Peter the Great offer analogies and contrasts worthy of careful consideration—to say nothing of American encounters with European thought and letters from the time of the Enlightenment to the novels of Henry James. The emergence of an African fiction that responds to European influence and interprets its own world in European terms is a cultural event of prime importance.

Yet we should not allow these marginal considerations, fascinating as they are, to distract our attention from the fact that among the novels that Dr. Larson considers, there are a few of unusual literary power. Among these, Tutuola's *The Palm-Wine Drinkard* stands out in its exuberant fantasy as *sui generis*, a light that never was on sea or land. This romance presents itself as a piece of spontaneous and primitive surrealism, the product of a dream-like imagination nourished by the marvels of traditional folklore and quite naively at ease before the supernatural. Tutuola's attitude is undisciplined by a European sense of reality, yet he seems at times ironically conscious of things European and of the contrast between Europe and Africa. The European may wonder whether these tales have been perhaps conceived in a more or less deliberate effort to escape the drab realities of an uncongenial colonialism or its subsequent dictatorships. In marked contrast to Tutuola's dream world there appears Achebe's unforgettable story, *Things Fall Apart*, as sober and responsible as the *Drinkard* is fantastic and carefree. Achebe describes, often with shrewd anthropological insight, the moral disintegration of an ancestral order and of an heroic leader brought into collision with European power and ideas—all this in cruel reversal of Conrad's famous story.

Although these books are especially memorable, there are others that deserve attention for their own sake. These works remind us that as we study African letters we are in contact with gifted and sensitive people, now for the first time acquiring or having forced upon them, perhaps rather too suddenly, sophisticated habits of self-observation and self-criticism. Here we may witness the gallant and often tragic commitment of human selfhood reshaping itself in opposition to the devious ambiguities of the modern world and assuming the burden of a conscious autonomy. Those of us who look with sympathy upon these crises of the spirit will find Dr. Larson's exposition a rewarding interpretation.

NEWTON P. STALLKNECHT

The Emergence of
African Fiction

1

Critical Approaches to African Fiction

LATE IN 1951, AN UNKNOWN NIGERIAN WRITER with six years of primary school education submitted the manuscript of his first novel to the British publishing house of Faber and Faber. The manuscript, which was called *The Palm-Wine Drinkard*, was accepted, and the following spring when the book was published, Amos Tutuola became the first "novelist" from tropical Africa to gain extensive exposure among Western literary audiences. Tutuola was not, however, the first novelist from Africa to be published by a European house. There had been earlier writers, almost as far back as the turn of the century, who had gained recognition of one kind or another for their pioneer literary endeavors. In 1906, the South African, Thomas Mofolo, had written a novel in his native language, Sesuto, which was later translated into English under the title *The Traveller of the East* and published in London by the Society for Promoting Christian Knowledge (1934).[1] Mofolo's first novel was followed by two others: *Pitseng* (1910) and *Chaka* (1925), the latter an account of the great South African warrior, translated into English in 1931. Two later writers of historical interest were both from Ghana. In 1911, E. Casely-Hayford published a novel which (in a later English translation) was called *Ethiopia Unbound*. Much later, in 1943, R. E. Obeng's *Eighteenpence* (written in English) was published by Arthur H. Stockwell, Ltd. (London).[2]

These three early African novelists shared one common bond: a certain reverence and awe for Christianity, which had led them along the pathway to Western education in the first place. Mofolo's novels were published by the church mission from which he had received his education. Tutuola, however, was strikingly different from these earlier novelists in that he broke away from Christianity.

Moreover, his use of the English language was notably original. Purists were shocked by Tutuola's irreverent use of the English language, and, as we shall see, the novel as a genre took on a slightly different shape because of Tutuola's imaginative use of Yoruba folk materials.

Tutuola's novel begins as follows:

> I was a palm-wine drinkard since I was a boy of ten years of age. I had no other work more than to drink palm-wine in my life. In those days we did not know other money, except COWRIES, so that everything was very cheap, and my father was the richest man in our town.
>
> My father got eight children and I was the eldest among them, all of the rest were hard workers, but I myself was an expert palm-wine drinkard. I was drinking palm-wine from morning till night and from night till morning. By that time I could not drink ordinary water at all except palm-wine.
>
> But when my father noticed that I could not do any work more than to drink, he engaged an expert palm-wine tapster for me; he had no other work more than to tap palm-wine every day.
>
> So my father gave me a palm-tree farm which was nine miles square and it contained 560,000 palm-trees, and this palm-wine tapster was tapping one hundred and fifty kegs of palm-wine every morning, but before 2 o'clock p.m., I would

have drunk all of it; after that he would go and tap another 75 kegs in the evening which I would be drinking till morning. So my friends were uncountable by that time and they were drinking palm-wine with me from morning till a late hour in the night. But when my palm-wine tapster completed the period of 15 years that he was tapping the palm-wine for me, then my father died suddenly, and when it was the 6th month after my father had died, the tapster went to the palm-tree farm on a Sunday evening to tap palm-wine for me. When he reached the farm, he climbed one of the tallest palm-trees in the farm to tap palm-wine but as he was tapping on, he fell down unexpectedly and died at the foot of the palm-tree as a result of injuries. As I was waiting for him to bring the palm-wine, when I saw that he did not return in time, because he was not keeping me long like that before, then I called two of my friends to accompany me to the farm. When we reached the farm, we began to look at every palm-tree, after a while we found him under the palm-tree, where he fell down and died.[3]

It was undoubtedly the language itself which first struck the non-African reader of Tutuola's work. In a certain sense, Tutuola has been fighting a battle ever since then with his fellow Africans, who have been embarrassed by what they have regarded as Tutuola's "irregular" use of English. And the *Drinkard* misled a number of Western literary critics into believing that Tutuola's language would be the language future Anglophone African writers would employ in their writing. Dylan Thomas, in a now famous review of *The Palm-Wine Drinkard*, referred to Tutuola's language as "young English by a West African. . . ."[4] He was not alone. Anthony West, reviewing the American edition of the *Drinkard*, commented to much the same effect: "One catches a glimpse of the very beginning of literature, that moment when writing at last seizes and pins down the myths and legends of an analphabetic culture."[5] West further added, *The Palm-Wine Drinkard* must be valued for its own freakish sake, and as an unrepeatable happy hit."[6]

Yet, Tutuola has repeated his "hit" no less than five times

since the publication of the *Drinkard*, publishing four later novels and a collection of short stories in essentially the same Tutuolan style. And the critics—who if they are a little less awed now than they were in the early 1950's—have continued to contradict one another in their attempts to make his works fit into some pigeonhole of Western literature. Reviewing the *Drinkard* for the *Saturday Review*, Lee Rogow referred to the work as a "fantastic primitive . . . written in English, but . . . an English with inflections and phrasings which make it seem like a new-born language. . . ." [7] Rogow, who appears to be amazed that Africans can write, adds, "The interest lies in the primitive play of language," [8] a statement which in retrospect appears to be completely erroneous. For, if anything, the interest in Tutuola should be in his original use of mythology and folklore, that is, in what he has carried over from the oral tradition into a non-African literary genre known as the novel.

Several years after the appearance of his first novel, with American publication of Tutuola's fourth work, *The Brave African Huntress*, the critics' enthusiasm for Tutuola's English seemed considerably subdued. The opening paragraph of Rye Vervaet's review of the book in the *New York Times Book Review* clearly indicates that by 1958, Tutuola's language, which Dylan Thomas had referred to as terse, direct, and savory, has become at least for Vervaet something less than communicative.

> If Amos Tutuola were a native New Yorker instead of a native West African, his dreams would no doubt be exorcised on an analyst's couch. In that case, they would be lost to the rest of us, which would be too bad. But in a sense they are lost anyway because the author has not really learned to communicate. [9]

And Vervaet further notes of Tutuola's style: the "flat, matter-of-fact tone . . . robs the story of suspense and dramatic effect. The ungrammatical, misspelled style, so obviously inadvertent, lends a certain picturesque quality to the book, but does not help to illuminate its meaning." [10] Tutuola's language, it appears, has prevented Vervaet from noticing much else —especially Tutuola's reshaping of the novel form.

More recently, Tutuola has begun to gain the recognition he deserves including a respect among his fellow Africans, who no longer seem to be quite as embarrassed about his presence as they were in the early 1950's. He is still, however, at the center of a continuous debate about his true stature in African literature, a debate which has still not decided exactly what it is that Tutuola has been writing for twenty years, to what genre his works belong. Tutuola is only an archetype in this instance, only one of a number of pioneer African writers who have frequently been misunderstood by non-African critics in their passion for place and order. Again and again, reading Western criticism of African writers one has the impression that the critic has noticed that something is different in African literature; yet this "differentness" is something the critic all too frequently has failed to put his finger on.

The case can be further illustrated with Tutuola. Although the term "novel" has often been used in evaluations of his work, one senses that critics have not been quite certain if this is exactly what Tutuola has written. In a generally fine study called *Amos Tutuola*, Harold R. Collins struggles with the problem of categorization, yet never quite comes to the crux of the issue: the African writer's penchant for "bending" the novel form. Collins writes,

> Most reviewers of Tutuola's books have taken for granted that they are meant to be novels, and this misconception has made for a good deal of critical clumsiness in judgment and some unfairness. If we suppose that the novel proper is a piece of prose fiction that has realistic characters, that deals with man in social relations, usually in a more or less contemporary setting, then surely the Tutuola works are something else again and are not fairly judged as novels.[11]

This is a rather large qualification, especially when one realizes that any number of contemporary Western novelists would not fit in Collins' definition at all (Kafka, Nathanael West, Robbe-Grillet, among others.) Collins goes on to say,

> A really accurate genre-name for Tutuola's works would be "naive romances"; "naive" to distinguish them from the more sophisticated romances of William Morris or perhaps Hawthorne. The romance genre has been brilliantly distinguished and analyzed by Northrop Frye in his *Anatomy of Criticism*. Frye's placing of the "romance mode of fiction" by the degree of the "hero's power of action" seems exactly pertinent to Tutuola's ghost novels. . . .[12]

The error here appears to be that Collins is attempting to categorize Tutuola as an eighteenth or nineteenth century novelist, is trying to force him into a literary tradition dead both in the West and in Africa. Nevertheless, and perhaps almost accidentally, Collins has stumbled upon a description which admits that, at least on one level, Tutuola's books are novels: "ghost novels." But what are the characteristics of the African novel, since Tutuola is only one among any number of African writers who have altered for their own purposes the shape of the Western genre?

It is impossible to leave Tutuola without referring to one critic of African literature who, in spite of his brevity, has made a number of singularly important comments about Tutuola's highly individualized style. In his slim pioneer volume, *Seven African Writers*, Gerald Moore begins his chapter on Tutuola by stating:

> Amos Tutuola was unfortunate enough to be the first famous Nigerian writer. He is still suffering for it. Countless white readers have found his books "amusing" and "quaint." Countless black readers have been pained and embarrassed by his incorrect English. Amid this welter of misguided admiration and abuse, few readers of any color have penetrated to the sources of his real merit and distinction.[13]

The problem with Tutuola, as Moore notes, is indeed the problem of the African writer in general today. The latter has long been caught in the curious dilemma of on the one hand being praised for the wrong reasons, and on the other hand tormented and attacked—again, usually for the wrong reasons. Moore also, it seems to me, has said the last word on the future of Tutuola's "curious form." No, Tutuola's novels are not the typical form of African fiction, (nor has his language been imitated by later writers) and as twenty years have shown, the African novel has not fallen into the Tutuolan pattern. Moore concludes: "Tutuola's books are far more like a fascinating cul-de-sac than the beginning of anything directly useful to other writers. The cul-de-sac is full of wonders, but is nevertheless a dead end." [14]

The problem of the African novel in regard to its reception in the West might more realistically be called a problem of comparative aesthetics. Non-African literary critics were the first to evaluate African writers simply because there were no African critics. For the most part, these critics have applied Western literary terms to something which at base may have its roots in Western literature but which has also had a healthy injection of distinct Africanisms added to the "traditional" Western literary form. Expressed in another way, the African writer has been confronted down through the years with the Western critic and reviewer whose point of view has been solely Western. While it is true that for the most part the Western critic has been sympathetic toward the African writer, it is also true that a certain amount of his criticism has been condescending and singularly removed from any attempt to look at African writing from an African point of view, to establish, as it were, the reasons African writing is frequently different from Western writing.

What are the differences, and to what are they due? And if these novels are often so widely at variance with the Western form of the novel, is this simply a matter of cultural backgrounds, or is it something else? The problem, it would seem, would be, first, to determine exactly what these differences are, and second, to determine if these alterations are related to differences between African and Western cultures. What is it, finally, that gives the African novel its pattern and form? First, however, let us go back a step.

The reception of African literature by the West has, for the most part, been sympathetic. To a great extent the African writer has been praised for his literary undertakings. One wonders, however, if in large part this criticism has not been simply a form of patronage due to the critic's lack of any suitable criteria for evaluating a typically Western literary form written by someone who is not from the West. The critics of African literature, in short, have praised African writers without making any serious attempt to tell us why this praise is justified. They have frequently said that a certain work is good, imaginative, and so forth—the usual string of adjectives applied to all writing, without really telling us very much —a type of criticism which seems to have done as much harm as good, for as anyone who has read many African novels knows, the proportion of poor African novels is just as great as of poor Western ones. More often than not, one gets the impression that the critic has reacted favorably to an African novel if he has learned something about the "dark continent" by reading it.

Let us return to Tutuola again to illustrate this premise, beginning with Tutuola's language. We have noted the initial reactions to what the critics referred to as Tutuola's simplistic style. Dylan Thomas' comment "young English" (whatever that means); Anthony West's comment about "the very beginning of literature"; Lee Rogow's statements "a new-born language" and a "primitive play of language." The total result of these similar comments is that they actually say very little about Tutuola's writing abilities—as a novelist. After quoting a section of Tutuola's *Drinkard*, West says, "This sounds naïve and barbaric, and it is." [15] One wonders exactly what

West means by his statement. "Naïve" and "barbaric" are loaded words, or seem to be used as such here. Is the Western critic, by calling Tutuola's style "young English," "primitive," and "barbaric," simply saying that the writing isn't very good? Is he simply saying that the novel is poorly written but he will let it pass by, because, after all, it was written by an African writing in a second language? The question would seem to be one of the subtle manipulation of euphemisms used by the Western critic who does not want to come right out and say that he thinks an African novel is inferior to a Western one. Thus, the terms we have already noted, and too many others such as "quaint," "picturesque," and "local color-ish."

It should be pointed out before we continue further that the African writer who writes in a European language has chosen to do so out of expediency rather than from any real desire to communicate in a non-African tongue. Because Africa is a continent with so many different ethnic groups, with somewhere around a thousand different languages and dialects, the African writer has had little option in choosing the language for his writing. If he should choose to write in his native tongue (and there is at present a growing amount of writing all over the continent in the vernacular languages), he seriously limits the size of his reading audience. For better or for worse, because of the colonial era, English and French seem fated to be the two major languages of communication on the African continent. In a country such as Nigeria, where there are nearly 250 languages and dialects, there can be little doubt of the practicality of writing in the colonial language—English. The result is bound to affect the use of this English in a variety of ways, and certainly Tutuola's use of English has been as highly influenced by his vernacular tongue (Yoruba) as by the brief amount of time he was exposed to Western education and formal training in English.

Mannerisms of language, then, constitute one of the basic

differences (and barriers) immediately recognizable in the African novel written in a European language. A Yoruba writer of English handles the language somewhat differently than does an Ibo writer, although the two are probably closer in usage than has formerly been noted. It is simply that there is something known as "West African English," just as there is "Indian English," "Australian English," and "American English."

But the Western critic has not been completely fair in his evaluation of African writing if he has been content to limit his approach to linguistics alone and relegate African writing into a category known as "young" or "quaint" or "picturesque."

"Simplicity" has been a quality commonly attributed by Western critics to African fiction. The term has been used in a variety of ways. About Chinua Achebe's first novel, *Things Fall Apart*, the reviewer in the *Times Literary Supplement* said: "His literary method is apparently simple, but a vivid imagination illuminates every page, and his style is a model of clarity." [16] About Achebe's second novel, *No Longer at Ease*, Milton S. Byam in the *Library Journal* wrote, "The plot is almost juvenile in its simplicity . . ."; [17] and in a much more direct reference to Achebe's style in *No Longer at Ease*, Keith Waterhouse asserted in the *New Statesman:*

> It is usual, almost traditional, to pay tribute to the simplicity of style of novels such as this. We tend to harp on about it, as if short words were something new in fiction. I suppose the fact of the matter is that simplicity is all we ask for in the African novel. We want a lucid, uncluttered account of the way life is changing in these territories. We want sound, competent craftsmen to put up the framework; later when the chronicles of change are more or less complete, some very fortunate writers indeed will be able to fill the framework in, wallowing in the new luxuries of characterisation, motivation, depth, psychology and all the rest of it.[18]

Waterhouse's review is a classic example of condescension. If nothing good can be said about Achebe's novel, Waterhouse implies, it is still an excellent example of simplicity. His comment that "simplicity is all we ask for in the African novel" is a blatant ignoring of the merits of Achebe's novel, though I must agree that *No Longer at Ease* is a lesser work than *Things Fall Apart*. By implication, Waterhouse is saying that African writing is not very good at all and that for the time being the Western reader will simply have to put up with a lack of "characterisation, motivation, depth, psychology and all the rest of it." Apparently without realizing it, Waterhouse has pointed out some of the major differences between the African and the Western novel; what he and others have not attempted to do is to analyze why they are often so distinctly different.

The reviewing of books is always erratic. In the case of African novels, the pattern has generally been that the reviewers have spent some time in Africa—as missionaries, anthropologists, or more recently Peace Corps Volunteers. This has, of course, accounted for much of the sympathetic criticism of African fiction. But at the same time, all too often African fiction has been reviewed by the "Africanist" trained in some discipline other than literature: political science, sociology, or, very frequently, anthropology; and this kind of reviewer, someone who may be naive about literature itself, has written as much erroneous criticism as has been produced by the few actual literary critics (generally completely unfamiliar with non-Western writing) who have occasionally reviewed and written articles about African literature. One might generalize by saying that the anthropologists have reviewed African writers favorably because they have been interested in African cultures *per se*, and the literary-trained critics have been unsympathetic simply because they have attempted to force the African writer into a Western literary tradition to which he does not always belong. The anthropologist wants to learn about another culture when he reads an African novel. The literary critic is more often concerned with style, plot, and characterization. Neither critic appears to appreciate the other's tools.

A particularly devastating example of a reviewer's approach to African fiction may be noticed if we examine a few of the statements made in a review of Chinua Achebe's third novel (but his fourth in the order in which they were published in the United States). The novel is *Arrow of God* and the critic is Ronald Christ, whose stance is literary, not anthropological. The opening of his review—which appeared in the *New York Times Book Review*—illustrates the fact that Mr. Christ is aware of the differing approaches which have been made toward African fiction:

> Before he opens this book, the American reader will be well advised to ask himself two basic questions. Is he about to read it because it's a new novel—or because it's written by a prominent Nigerian about Nigeria? Will he judge it as fiction, or as ethnic reporting of ancient customs in conflict with new politics? In both cases, the second approach will prove more rewarding—though even then the rewards will be on the meager side.[19]

The questions Christ asks are loaded against Achebe right from the beginning. One wonders if someone without a specific interest in Africa would continue reading the review.

Christ continues his review by commenting on Achebe's three other novels, *Things Fall Apart, No Longer at Ease,* and *A Man of the People.* The first two of these, he states, "were long on native customs and idiom, and short on narrative interest." Then Christ continues along the same lines with his analysis of *Arrow of God*, stating, ". . . the slender story-line is soon lost in a plethora of local color—and local color alone, whether Nigerian or Californian, is no longer adequate stuff for novels, now that the anthropologists are doing the job so much better." It is in a statement such as this that Christ begins to force the African novel into a Western pattern. He is particularly annoyed by Achebe's "local color," (his use of ethnological materials), obviously because local color is no longer the vogue in Western literature; and he continues his review by severely criticizing Achebe's use of proverbs, saying one must go back as far as Cervantes to find "anyone else as meaninglessly proverbial." Christ continues:

> No American or English novelist could have written such sentences; unfortunately, they are even more abundant in "Arrow of God." Perhaps no Nigerian, at the present state of his culture and ours, can tell us what we need to know about that country, in a way that is available to our understanding— not, at least, in the way W. H. Hudson made South America real to us, or T. E. Lawrence brought Arabia to life on the printed page.

Clearly, Christ's view of the novel as a literary form is ethnocentrically limited. He is disappointed that an American or an Englishman did not write *Arrow of God*. He would rather read what an anthropologist has written about African culture, and he prefers W. H. Hudson's picture of South America and T. E. Lawrence's vision of Arabia to fictional accounts by the indigenous writers from these areas.

When Christ's statements are placed next to those of others, we come almost full circle. No anthropologist whom I know has yet said that he has a better view of a culture that he is looking at from outside than a writer recording it from within. It should be noted that the anthropologists were the first to look at African literature from a serious point of view —albeit ethnological and not literary. Many of the first courses which made extensive use of African literature were taught in anthropology departments under the catch-all name "area studies," simply because of the anthropologists' belief that African literature is an excellent way to gain insight into African culture. This cultural approach has often been supported by other reviewers of African fiction, as two brief examples will illustrate. In Hassoldt Davis's review of Achebe's first novel, *Things Fall Apart*, he states, "No European ethnologist could so intimately present this medley of mores of the Ibo tribe, so detail the intricate formalities of life in the clan." [20] About Achebe's *A Man of the People*, the reviewer for *Time* said, "His book is worth a ton of documentary journalism." [21] What is clearly needed is the reviewer equipped to examine African fiction both from a cultural (anthropological) and an aesthetic (literary) point of view, though I am not trying to suggest that the two are ever totally separated.

It should be clear by now that a number of traditional techniques and conventions are often missing from the African novel or noticeably altered. With Tutuola and Achebe we noted the use of language—whether that be Tutuola's own African English or Achebe's reliance on traditional Ibo speech patterns in the form of proverbs and other oral literary materials. The anthropological, which Christ is correct in equating with local color in Western literature, is another convention typical of many contemporary African novels— especially of the first generation of Anglophone African writers—and I am in no sense attempting to suggest that an anthropological background can be fully justified in all African writing. Gerald Moore has already pointed out the classic misuse of the ethnological in African fiction. In an article in *Présence Africaine* entitled "English Words, African Lives," Moore has illustrated—by citing the Ibo novelist Onuora Nzekwu—the disasters which can result when a writer attempts to rely too much on anthropology for "atmosphere." Of Nzekwu, Moore writes:

> His interest is in ideas and institutions. A few years ago, he wrote a draft of a book of Ibo custom and tradition, containing a good deal of the very interesting anthropological material which has since been worked, somewhat laboriously, into his two novels. A misguided English friend advised him to recast the material in novel form, a blunder for which we are still

paying the price. Nzekwu has not yet grasped that the retailing of anthropological matter for its own sake is mere exoticism in a work of creative art. It can be used only as Achebe uses it, to make the life before us more actual, to surround it with its own dignity, beauty or cruelty in its own moment of time and place.[22]

A factor which still remains to be considered, however, is the African writer's frequent use of ethnological material instead of description. Description, as we tend to think of it in the Western novel, is frequently missing from the African novelist who writes in English, though his French-writing counterpart (Camara Laye, for example) has made extensive use of description for conveying mood and atmosphere.

Perhaps the most striking difference the reader of African fiction immediately notices is the often limited importance of characterization. From a Western point of view, many African novels are almost totally devoid of characterization—especially character introspection and character development—and yet, these novels may still be emotionally gripping, fully capable of drawing in the reader. Gerald Moore noted Nzekwu's reliance on the anthropological while at the same time noting the weakness of his characters. Moore wrote of Nzekwu: "Added to this weakness of language and penchant for curious information is an inability to develop character in any significant relationship to events. . . . All these violent switches of character are inadequately motivated and prepared." [23] Reviewing James Ngugi's *Weep Not, Child*, Toban lo Liyong complained that Ngugi "rarely uses dialogue to help characterization. What is one who does not know the type to make of this: 'In physical appearance at least, he [Mr. Howlands] was a typical Kenya settler'?" [24] Liyong answers his question himself: "Although traditional African sense of respect perhaps prohibits an author from 'staring another in the face like a river snake,' African writers must be as alert with their eyes, nose, and other senses, as they are with their ears." [25] Liyong, it should be noted, is an African. An unnamed reviewer of William Conton's novel, *The African*, also pointed out the novel's weak characters: ". . . the motivation of characters is not really probed, and becomes increasingly thin in the final chapters." [26] Similar statements about weaknesses of characterization have been made about almost all of the Anglophone African writers who began their writing careers in the 1950's or early 1960's, though their French counterparts have, again, fared considerably better.

Closely aligned to differences in characterization are the African writer's frequent difficulties in writing convincing dialogue. Indeed, in many African novels dialogue is quite sparse, and in others it appears to have nothing beyond a functional purpose. Gerald Moore notes a dialogue deficiency in the novels of Onuora Nzekwu and states that "Dialogue is also a central weakness with another Nigerian writer, Cyprian Ekwensi." [27] John Hughes has noted a similar weakness in William Conton's *The African*, saying, "Some of the dialogue is laden with Churchillian vocabulary, sometimes quite out of character with everyday settings either in England or Africa." [28] All one need do to notice the drastic difference between characterization and dialogue in African fiction and the Western novel is compare a work set in Africa but written by a European, such as Joyce Cary's *Mister Johnson*, with an African novel: the contrast is almost immediately obvious, but the reasons for the differences have yet to be fully explored.

Plot, the conception of a well-made story in Western critical terms, takes on a widely different importance in much contemporary African fiction, whether this be in the situational plots of Chinua Achebe or the Cameroonian, Mongo Beti, or even of the highly-skilled experimentalist, Wole Soyinka, whose story in *The Interpreters* bears little affinity to the works of his fellow African writers or even of his contemporaries outside of Africa. The plot structure of a great number of African novels usually falls into one of these two categories: (1) the loose narration of separate events, stories, and tales; or (2) the situational construction wherein not one person but an entire group of people (a village, a tribe, a clan) becomes ultimately affected (usually for the worse) by the major event of the narration. The novels of Amos Tutuola, which often read as if they were a series of short tales strung together by a main character's quest, clearly belong to the first category. The Cameroonian writer, Mbelle Sonne Dipoko has noted this loose structure in Elechi Amadi's *The Concubine* which he says "at times reads like a collection of short stories tied together. . . ." [29] Toban lo Liyong noted the same looseness in Ngugi's *Weep Not, Child*, stating, "The novel consists of too many unrelated essays and stories. . . ." [30] The same may be said of Chinua Achebe's two traditional novels, *Things Fall Apart* and *Arrow of God*, though Achebe's novels more typically belong in the situational category. Other conventions of narration, as Christ noted with Achebe, are different than we commonly think of their being in Western literature. Hassoldt Davis has complained, for example, of Achebe's *Things Fall Apart* that "The flashbacks of the book are confusing, the narration undisciplined. . . ." [31] Milton S. Byam wrote of *Things Fall Apart*: "This is a tale grounded in folklore rather than a novel. . . ." [32]

Another major difference commonly noted in the fiction of African writers is the frequent occurrence of the didactic ending. The following novelists especially belong in this category, though in a certain sense, there are few African novelists among the first generation whose works are not somehow related to this moral overtone: Cyprian Ekwensi, Chinua Achebe, William Conton, Ferdinand Oyono, Camara Laye, Amos Tutuola, and James Ngugi. The Western reader is especially conscious of the high frequency of didactic endings because our own literary tastes have changed so considerably since the nineteenth century.

Other aspects of African fiction also should be noted. The

conception of time, for example, is often widely different than we think of its being in the West. In Yambo Ouologuem's *Le devoir de violence* (*Bound to Violence*), the story begins in 1202 and ends in the year 1947, yet the novel's mode is not fantasy, as one might expect, but stark realism. Tutuola's novels reveal a world strange in both time and space; they are often near perfect examples of the surreal.

To be sure, in attempting to identify the defining characteristics of African fiction one major difficulty is the Western novel itself. The concept of the novel in the West has altered considerably down through the ages, and it will certainly make a difference whether we compare African fiction to a novel by Henry Fielding, Thomas Hardy, or Virginia Woolf. Since the nature of the "typical" Western novel depends decidedly on the period in which the work was written, it may be more practical to make a number of generalizations and simply note, as I have already tried to do, that a number of aspects of the Western novel which have been identified in the last three hundred years are often noticeably absent in African fiction. To make the statement that description is frequently missing in the works of a great many African novelists, when description is also missing in certain Western novelists of the twentieth century (in Ivy Compton-Burnett's novels, for instance), obviously amounts to saying nothing at all. It may be more fitting to make a kind of reverse generalization such as the following: description to create mood and atmosphere, such as in the manner of Thomas Hardy and Joseph Conrad or even Charles Dickens, is, in large part, missing in the African novel in English.

Ultimately, the question which must be asked is why the African novel should be required to be the same as the Western novel. And, if we accept the premise that it frequently is not, what then is the essence of the African novel? The two following conclusions will constitute the working basis of this study: (1) that the African novel is frequently different from its Western counterpart and that the differences can be attributed to cultural backgrounds; and (2) that in spite of the lack of several typical unities which are generally considered to hold the Western novel together, that is, to give it its structural background, the African writer has created new unities which give his fiction form and pattern. Our focus will be especially upon the first generation of Anglophone African novelists—with a contrastive analysis of the Francophone Camara Laye—whose works most frequently illustrate these factors.

In his preface to Léopold Sédar Senghor's now famous *Anthologie de la nouvelle poésie nègre et malgache de langue française,* Jean-Paul Sartre questions how long the West will continue to look at Africa through jaundiced eyes. Sartre's preface begins by posing several crucial questions:

Qu'est-ce donc que vous espériez, quand vous ôtiez le bâillon qui fermait ces bouches noires? Qu'elles allaient entonner vos louanges? Ces têtes que nos pères avaient courbées jusqu'à terre par la force, pensiez-vous, quand elles se relèveraient, lire l'adoration dans leurs yeux? Voici des hommes noirs debout qui nous regardent et je vous souhaite de ressentir comme moi le saisissement d'être vus. Car le blanc a joui trois mille ans du privilège de voir sans qu'on le voie; il était regard pur, la lumière de ses yeux tirait toute chose de l'ombre natale, la blancheur de sa peau c'était un regard encore, de la lumière condensée. L'homme blanc, blanc parce qu'il était homme, blanc comme le jour, blanc comme la vérité, blanc comme la vertu, éclairait la création comme une torche, dévoilait l'essense secrète et blance des êtres. Aujourd'hui ces hommes noirs nous regardent et notre regard rentre dans nos yeux; des torches noires, à leur tour, éclairent le monde et nos têtes blanches ne sont plus que de petits lampions balancés par le vent.

[What would you expect to find, when the muzzle that has silenced the voices of black men is removed? That they would thunder your praise? When these heads that our fathers have forced to the very ground are risen, do you expect to read adoration in their eyes? Here, in this anthology, are black men standing, black men who examine us; and I want you to feel, as I, the sensation of being seen. For the white man has enjoyed for three thousand years the privilege of seeing without being seen. It was a seeing pure and uncomplicated; the light of his eyes drew all things from their primeval darkness. The whiteness of his skin was a further aspect of vision, a light condensed. The white man, white because he was man, white like the day, white as truth is white, white like virtue, lighted like a torch all creation; he unfolded the essence, secret and white, of existence. Today, these black men have fixed their gaze upon us and our gaze is thrown back in our eyes; black torches, in their turn, light the world and our white heads are only small lanterns balanced in the wind.] [33]

Sartre's essay has a sharp ring of latent reality and his assertions probe the very nature of Western man's ethnocentrically sealed world. The white man has looked too long at Africa through Western eyes, too long given only a superficial glance at African culture and African aesthetic values; and black poetry he concludes could only be expected to be aesthetically different. Sartre states, "Et la poésie noire n'a rien de commun avec les effusions de coeur: elle est fonctionnelle, elle répond à un besoin qui la définit exactement." ("Black poetry has nothing in common with the effusions of the heart; it is functional, it answers a need which exactly defines it.") [34] Sartre's comment might just as well be taken as a manifesto of the black man's privilege to change, alter, and re-shape Western artistic standards, for Sartre is telling us that we in the West are naive in believing that the African writer will be content to keep the forms of Western literature as he found them. The black artist has a culturally defined right to take what he needs from the West, set aside what he finds unsatisfactory, and combine it with that which most suits his writing from his own culture. Out of this a new art will be born.

Sartre states, "Ainsi la négritude, en sa source la plus profonde, est une androgynie." ("Thus négritude, in its most profound origin, is androgyny.") [35] Sartre applies the word "androgyny" to the origins of the poetry of négritude, suggesting a unity of two sexes in one. This merging of two distinctly different worlds into one—a syncretism of two in one—might well be regarded as the key to understanding what Janheinz Jahn has called "neo-African literature." [36] For négritude and a great amount of what is now regarded as contemporary African literature has leaned toward a coupling of the cultural and aesthetic forms of the two worlds of traditional African and traditional Western.

We have already noted the strange language combinations in Amos Tutuola's style, and it is fitting that we conclude this introduction by examining several statements concerning these new artistic forms which have been made by several African writers whose works have already been mentioned.

Chinua Achebe, the foremost African novelist writing in English today, has written the following in an article entitled "The Role of the Writer in a New Nation":

For an African, writing in English is not without its serious set-backs. He often finds himself describing situations and modes of thought which have no direct equivalent in the English way of life. Caught in that situation he can do one of two things. He can try and contain what he wants to say within the limits of conventional English or he can try to push back those limits to accommodate his idea. The first method produces competent, uninspired and rather flat work. The second method will produce something new and valuable to the English language as well as to the material he is trying to put over. *But* it can also get out of hand. It can lead to simply *bad* English being accepted and defended as African or Nigerian. I submit that those who can do the work of extending the frontiers of English so as to accommodate African thought-patterns must do it through their mastery of English and not out of innocence.[37]

Although Achebe's comments are limited almost entirely to the use of language, his statement clearly extends beyond this to an implied use of form. Achebe takes for granted the African writer's responsibility for creating something different which will "produce something new and valuable to the English language as well as to the material he is trying to put over." In another article Achebe has stated even more clearly that "The price a world language [English] must be prepared to pay is submission to many different kinds of use.[38]

Achebe's fellow Nigerian, Cyprian Ekwensi, has also noted the African writer's prerogative for creating new language patterns with English. "African writers in English consciously or unconsciously try to Africanise the English language by colouring it with African idioms or pidgin English or in any other way retaining the speech rhythms of the African language." [39] In another article, Ekwensi has also belabored the African writer's twisting of conventional English: "Nigerian creative writers write in their own brand of English. . . ." [40] Ekwensi, whose own works contain fewer African innovations than those of some of his contemporaries, has also foreseen, if somewhat vaguely, the African writer's contribution to world literature as that of an innovator in new art forms: "Students of literature have forecast that in the next twenty-five years African writers are going to contribute an altogether new form in poetry or in the novel." [41] What Ekwensi has failed to note is that, for the most part, these new art forms have already been achieved, and that a second generation of African writers is now appearing whose works are closer to the Western tradition.

Returning to the novel alone, it is fitting that we look at the critical remarks of two other contemporary black writers, Nigerian John Pepper Clark and Denis Williams from Guiana. Although only Williams is a novelist, both have articulated their beliefs that the African has an almost ingrained obligation to alter those forms of literature that are not typically

African. Clark has said, "the novel is the one genre of art that is not Nigerian . . . the one art that Nigerians have really borrowed. But critics have not so much concerned themselves with what our novelists have done to their derived form as with the amount of traditional ritual and modern rottenness and rheum that is to be found in them." [42] Clark's comment is clearly a slam at the sociological/anthropological approach to African fiction which has failed to look at African writing as literature, although Clark himself gives us no clue as to what his African contemporaries "have done to their derived form."

Expressed in other words, Clark is saying that non-Africans have for too long read African writers solely to see what they could learn about Africa—and not for what they could learn about literature itself. A similar belief is paramount in an article by Denis Williams. Writing about the contemporary African novelist, Williams also sees the necessity for giving new blood to old genres:

> For the novel has developed conventions with which it is not easy to tamper and remain intelligible; it is perhaps the most conservative of all the major arts. Yet it is only through a knowledgeable disrespect for the novel, say, a deliberate tampering with the limits which define it as a form, that the African artist can hope to release that mode of his being which he considers particular to himself, and which will be most deeply *credible* to his people. Certainly nothing can be more alien to the African writer than the form of the novel in its present state; nothing could be more opposed to his sense of time and his penchant for exaltation, for belief, for wrapping himself directly around experience. The novel, and particularly the realistic novel, has developed at the behest of a mind very different from that of the African. [43]

The world of African writing is often distinctly different from what we in the West conceive of its being. Because of multiple problems of literacy, economics, and mass communication, the African writer who has slowly been building up an indigenous reading audience on his own continent has often ignored Western literary demands and relied on his traditional African aesthetic. It is unrewarding, therefore, for the non-African reader and critic to look at any of the three major genres in contemporary African writing—the novel, poetry, and drama—solely from the perspective of Western literary criteria and terminology. This is too much like trying to force a glove with three fingers onto a hand with five. Instead, we must look at African writing not only for whatever its similarities with Western literary forms may be, but also— once we have fully identified these—for what is different, and, therefore, African. The hope for continued existence of a literature rests on its ability to change and develop. As Anaïs Nin has written in *The Novel of the Future*, "The total death of the novel is always being announced, when what should be observed is the death of certain forms of the novel." [44] The novel is very much alive in Africa today; African novelists are creating exciting new patterns in the traditional literary form.

Chinua Achebe's
Things Fall Apart:
The Archetypal African Novel

CHINUA ACHEBE'S *Things Fall Apart* WAS PUB-
lished in England in 1958, two years before Nigerian independence. The price of the book was fifteen shillings, which
placed it out of reach for the average Nigerian whose annual
income in those days did not exceed seventy-five dollars.
Achebe's novel, however, had been written not for a Nigerian
reading audience nor even for an African reading audience,
but, to a large extent, for readers outside of Africa. However,
in 1960, when Nigeria became independent, the educational
system began to reflect a sense of growing national pride; and
in 1964, when the traditionally English-oriented School Certificate Examinations were beginning to be Africanized,
Things Fall Apart became the first novel by an African writer
to be included in the required syllabus for African secondary
school students throughout the English-speaking portions of

the continent. By 1965, Achebe was able to proclaim that his novel in a paperbacked reprint edition priced at a more moderate five shillings had the year before sold some 20,000 copies within Nigeria alone.[1]

In the seven years during which this spectacular change had taken place, Chinua Achebe became recognized as the most original African novelist writing in English. He wrote and published three additional novels (*No Longer at Ease*, 1960; *Arrow of God*, 1964; and *A Man of the People*, 1966), and he became one of the first African writers to build up a reading audience among his fellow Africans. So famous and popular did he become within his own country, that by the time Achebe published his fourth novel it could no longer be said that he was writing for a non-African audience. *Things Fall Apart* during this time became recognized by African and non-African literary critics as the first "classic" in English from tropical Africa. So far did Achebe's influence extend that by the late 1960's his impact on a whole group of younger African novelists could also be demonstrated.*

In the thirteen years which have now passed since its initial publication, *Things Fall Apart* has come to be regarded as more than simply a classic; it is now seen as the archetypal African novel. The situation which the novel itself describes —the coming of the white man and the initial disintegration of traditional African society as a consequence of that—is typical of the breakdown all African societies have experienced at one time or another as a result of their exposure to the West. And, moreover, individual Africans all over the continent may identify with the situation Achebe has portrayed.

Things Fall Apart is the kind of novel that had to be

* Ugandan author, Robert Serumaga, for example, mentions Chinua Achebe in his own first novel, *Return to the Shadows* (London, 1969). Kenyan novelist, James Ngugi, has clearly been influenced by Achebe's work, as have a whole string of later Ibo novelists.

written, and has been continually rewritten in one form or another by later imitators of Achebe all over the African continent. For this reason, too, no matter what Achebe writes during the rest of his literary career, he will be faced with the continual criticism that his first novel is his best one. (This was already being said at the publication of *Arrow of God*, which also paints a picture of early tribal exposure to the West. Although *Arrow of God* is in some ways probably artistically superior to *Things Fall Apart*, it is fated to run a second place in popularity to Achebe's first work.) The novel may also be regarded as archetypal because of Achebe's reshaping of a traditional Western literary genre into something distinctly African in form and pattern. It is with the second of these distinctions that we will be most generally concerned here in the attempt to discover what is African in African fiction.

An initial reading of *Things Fall Apart* exposes one to the basic elements of the story, which takes place in inland Eastern Nigeria (Iboland), in a village called Umuofia, roughly between the years 1890 and 1900. Okonkwo, a middle-aged Ibo man (approximately thirty-eight years old at the beginning of the story), has spent much of his adult lifetime attempting to eradicate the image of being weakly and effeminate, which he fears he has inherited because of his worthless father. While still quite young, Okonkwo gains recognition both as a wrestler and as a warrior, and in the ensuing years he demonstrates his worth as an industrious farmer. About to fulfill his final dreams by taking the highest titles his society can bestow upon him, he is brought down by the accidental murder of a young boy. Because of tribal law, he must flee with his family into exile to a near-by village for seven years. During the period of this exile, the white man arrives in the form of Christian missionaries and British government officials. Upon Okonkwo's return to Umuofia, he attempts to convince his fellow villagers that they must drive the white man from the area; but the village will not support him, and, after killing one of the white man's messengers, Okonkwo, realizing that he has lost the support of his clan, hangs himself. This synopsis is nothing more than a skeleton of Achebe's novel, and the impressive innovations and alterations the author has made in the Western novel form defy summary and can only be discovered by examining the text in a much more leisurely manner.

Things Fall Apart is divided into three sections. The first, comprising more than half the length of the novel, the first thirteen chapters, establishes a composite picture of traditional life in Iboland before the arrival of the white man. This part of the novel is heavily anthropological but contains the seeds of germination for the latter half of the book wherein the conflict (in relation to a well-made plot) is introduced. In essence, this tension is introduced in Part I of Achebe's novel because the old African way of life, as typified by Okonkwo, is unable to adapt to the new, to the West. Part II, chapters fourteen through nineteen, is devoted to telling the story of Okonkwo's exile from Umuofia and establishing his personal conflict as it is related to his desire to return to his village and rid the clan of the white man. Part III, chapters twenty through twenty-five, chronicles Okonkwo's return to Umuofia and his abortive attempt to lead his villagers in battle against the white man.

Achebe's concern in Book I is to present a composite picture of traditional Ibo life, sealed off from any influences of Western civilization. There is virtually no plot as such, in the sense of a developed narrative or a major conflict involving the protagonist—Okonkwo—although there are a number of immediate problems with which he is confronted. Instead, Achebe presents an overview of traditional Ibo customs, relating them wherever possible to Okonkwo and his extended family. Not until the last chapter in this first portion of the novel is any real attempt made to establish a major problem which Okonkwo must overcome (exile because of the accidental killing), and only when the reader completes the first part of the novel does he realize what the title of Achebe's work implies: it is the traditional life established in Part I which will fall apart when it is exposed to Western civilization—Christianity and British colonial rule—as seen in the later sections of the novel. This "plotless" nature of Part I has led in large part to several of the misinterpretations of Achebe's work, and, as we will see, the supposed looseness of the narrative is in part due to many digressions removing us from Okonkwo: anthropological background and explanations, substories, and various forms of traditional Ibo oral literature.

Chapter One begins with the following paragraph:

> Okonkwo was well known throughout the nine villages and even beyond. His fame rested on solid personal achievements. As a young man of eighteen he had brought honor to his village by throwing Amalinze the Cat. Amalinze was the great wrestler who for seven years was unbeaten, from Umuofia to Mbaino. He was called the Cat because his back would never touch the earth. It was this man that Okonkwo threw in a fight which the old men agreed was one of the fiercest since the founder of their town engaged a spirit of the wild for seven days and seven nights.[2]

Significantly enough, but also somewhat misleadingly, the first word of Achebe's novel is "Okonkwo." (The first three chapters begin with his name, as he is the center of focus at the beginning of the novel. After that, however, the emphasis shifts—usually to something concerned with the clan or the village of Umuofia.) Okonkwo is characterized in the first paragraph almost as completely as he ever will be in the novel. His fame, as we are told, rests on personal achievements. Ibo society unlike the majority of traditional African societies was not chiefly directed, but was acephalous, achievement oriented: a man could not inherit title and rank from his family, but, rather, had to achieve these by his own abilities. At eighteen, Okonkwo gained his first success—in the public arena of wrestling, a sport which today in Iboland is second perhaps only to boxing. Achebe shifts his emphasis to Amalinze in the fourth sentence, thus leaving Okonkwo almost immediately, and relying for his further characterization on contrast with others of his clan. Interestingly enough, initially we do not have the kind of description of Okonkwo that we might expect, that is, a description of his physical stature, which is so fitted, we may assume, for wrestling. Achebe has found other ways of conveying this, however. In the second paragraph he states, "Amalinze was a wily craftsman, but Okonkwo was as slippery as a fish in water" (p.7). And in the third paragraph: "He [Okonkwo] was tall and huge, and his bushy eyebrows and wide nose gave him a very severe look."

These few sentences of pictorial description are about as much as Achebe ever uses to describe Okonkwo, at least physically, and we are reminded of Liyong's comment that the "traditional African sense of respect . . . prohibits an author from 'staring another in the face like a river snake. . . .' " [3] There is not one place in the novel where authorial commentary extends beyond a few descriptive facts —nothing comparable, for example, to Joyce Cary's initial description (on the first page) of Mr. Johnson in his novel of that title:

Johnson is not only a stranger by accent, but by color. He is as black as a stove, almost a pure Negro, with short nose and full, soft lips. He is young, perhaps seventeen, and seems half-grown. His neck, legs and arms are much too long and thin for his small body, as narrow as a skinned rabbit's. He is loose-jointed like a boy, and sits with his knees up to his nose, grinning at Bamu over the stretched white cotton of his trousers. He smiles with the delighted expression of a child looking at a birthday table and says, "Oh, you are too pretty—a beautiful girl." [4]

It has been argued, however, that Cary's description of Mr. Johnson is a stereotyped picture of an African by a white man.

In Achebe's novel, moreover, there is no characterization of Okonkwo established by dialogue in the first chapter—Okonkwo says nothing until the last page of Chapter Two. Throughout the novel, it will also be seen that Achebe rarely uses dialogue to develop any of his characters. There is a brief section in Chapter One, however, sketching in the personality (it can hardly be called a complete characterization) of Okonkwo's father, Unoka. Of his physical presence we are told only this: "He was tall but very thin and had a slight stoop. He wore a haggard and mournful look except when he was drinking or playing on his flute" (p.8). Again, a number of Unoka's personality traits are briefly sketched. In Ibo terms, his life was a failure; during his life his only distinction was the accumulation of many debts; and in a brief dramatic scene we are shown an incident from Unoka's past where a man who had loaned him money attempted to get it back. Achebe tells us, "When Unoka died he had taken no title at all and he was heavily in debt" (p.11). In an anthropological explanation, however, Achebe informs us, perhaps a little too obviously, that his father's faults were not held against Okonkwo: "Fortunately, among these people a man was judged according to his worth and not according to the worth of his father" (p.11).

Chapter One of *Things Fall Apart* establishes a limited sense of Okonkwo's character as much by contrasting his successes with his father's failures as by recording Okonkwo's early accomplishments. It is in the last paragraph that we are told, ". . . although Okonkwo was still young, he was already one of the greatest men of his time. Age was respected among his people, but achievement was revered. As the elders said, if a child washed his hands he could eat with kings" (p.12). I have quoted this last sentence, specifically, because it is an example of one of the African unifying devices that Achebe relies on to give form and pattern to his novel: the proverb, a form of traditional African oral literature. It will be of value if we return to the beginning of the chapter and examine the other examples of oral literature in this initial section of *Things Fall Apart*.

The first occurs at the end of the opening paragraph, and if it is not strictly oral literary material, it is at least oral history, in this case the myth concerning the origin of the clan. The last sentence ends: ". . . the fiercest [fight] since the founder of their town engaged a spirit of the wild for seven days and seven nights" (p.7). Hardly a sentence in length, it symbolically encompasses the entire motif of the clan and the significance it will have in this book. Achebe skillfully introduces this reference to the origin of the clan at the very beginning of his novel, carefully balancing it with the fall of the clan in the last paragraph.

In the second paragraph of the first chapter, we can see another kind of reliance on unwritten literature, figures of speech. As one might expect, Achebe relies on African figures of speech to describe his characters and situations. We noted earlier his contrast of Amalinze and Okonkwo: "Amalinze was a wily craftsman, but Okonkwo was as slippery as a fish in water" (p.7). To be sure, there is nothing exclusively African in the simile, "as slippery as a fish in water." There is nothing traditionally African here any more than in Cary's reference to Johnson's "legs and arms . . . as narrow as a skinned rabbit's." However, in the third paragraph of this chapter, Achebe does introduce a simile which is distinctly African in origin: ". . . Okonkwo's fame had grown like a bush-fire in the harmattan" (p.7). The harmattan is the northern wind, from the Sahara Desert, which descends into the tropical zone of the continent each year during the dry season and rapidly dries everything out, altering the surface of the land, covering it with a thin dust. It is at this time of the year, of course, that fires spread most easily, for there are no rains.

Achebe's reference to fire in the time of the harmattan to illustrate Okonkwo's fame is indeed fitting and clearly African in origin, and it is just one of many, many similes throughout the novel which originate in the African background.

In the same chapter, when a villager comes to Okonkwo's father's hut to request some money he has lent him, in a ritual act a kola nut is brought out, broken, and given to the guest. The villager says, " 'He who brings kola brings life' " (p.9), and we are thus introduced to the first proverb of Achebe's novel. Almost immediately, Achebe gives an ethnological explanation for the use of kola, linking it with an ancestral prayer—"Unoka prayed to their ancestors for life and health, and for protection against their enemies" (p.10). This is followed by an explanation of the use of proverbs in Ibo society: "Having spoken plainly so far, Okoye said the next half a dozen sentences in proverbs. Among the Ibo the art of conversation is regarded very highly, and proverbs are the palm-oil with which words are eaten" (p.10). The explanation, of course, is also in the form of a proverb. In their book, *An Igbo Revision Course*, J. Carnochan and B. Iwuchuku describe the function of the proverb in traditional Ibo life, saying,

> In debate, victory is assured to the Igbo who is most skilful in handling proverbs. The Igbo people respect most those who are persuasive in their speech. As salt enhances the flavour of food, so the proverb gives point to the bare statement of fact.[5]

As we will shortly see, Achebe makes frequent use of proverbs in his novel to explain individual sections of his story, to illustrate anthropologically what he can assume the non-African reader needs to know, and, more importantly, to unify his novel as a whole. In the same chapter there is an example of a proverb applying directly to Okonkwo's father. When Unoka tells his guest that he cannot repay the loan, he says, ironically, and at the same time characterizing himself, " 'Our elders say that the sun will shine on those who stand before it shines on those who kneel under them. I shall pay my big debts first' " (p.11). The reader already knows that Unoka is not the kind of person upon whom the sun will shine; Unoka does not rise before the sun, and borrowing as he does from everyone, without respect to age or tradition, Unoka does not kneel under the elders. Achebe's proverb, then, is an apt rejoinder, almost the final word on Okonkwo's worthless father, ironically spoken by Unoka himself—an oral example which also acts as a termination of the incident —a frequent function of proverbs in Achebe's novels.

At the end of Unoka's speech, Achebe returns to exposition instead of the more dramatic rendering by dialogue, and this brings the chapter to a conclusion. Yet, in the final paragraph, there is another traditional oral expression given to explain the initial story of Okonkwo's intense drive to excel and thus destroy the image of his father which he fears his villagers associate with him. It reads:

> When Unoka died he had taken no title at all and he was heavily in debt. Any wonder then that his son Okonkwo was ashamed of him? Fortunately, among these people a man was judged according to his worth and not according to the worth of his father. Okonkwo was clearly cut out for great things. He was still young but he had won fame as the greatest wrestler in the nine villages. He was a wealthy farmer and had two barns full of yams, and had just married his third wife. To crown it all he had taken two titles and had shown incredible prowess in two inter-tribal wars. And so although Okonkwo was still young, he was already one of the greatest men of his time. Age was respected among his people, but achievement was revered. As the elders said, if a child washed his hands he could eat with kings. Okonkwo had clearly washed his hands and so he ate with kings and elders. And that was how he came to look after the doomed lad who was sacrificed to the village of Umuofia by their neighbors to avoid war and bloodshed. The ill-fated lad was called Ikemefuna. (pp.11–12)

The significant development here is Achebe's reliance on rhetorical devices, the devices of unwritten oral literature, to bring his initial chapter to a close and unify it into a separately-developed and tied-off incident. Achebe's first device is to ask a question, not as if he were writing a novel, but as if he were telling a story to a group of people: "Any wonder then that his son Okonkwo was ashamed of him?" The second device is the use of the two sentences which begin with the conjunction *and*, as if Achebe were concluding a short oral tale. The first of these could, indeed, end the story of Okonkwo's excessive drive: "And so although Okonkwo was still young, he was already one of the greatest men of his time." Had Achebe left it at that, he would have told, essentially, a self-contained tale, but since he is writing something longer, the chapter continues for four more sentences, giving us a connective to the next chapter. "And that was how he came to look after the doomed lad who was sacrificed to the village of Umuofia by their neighbors to avoid war and bloodshed. The ill-fated lad was called Ikemefuna."

What is significant here is that Achebe has introduced a pattern in his first chapter which he will follow throughout much of his novel, especially in the first thirteen chapters. Essentially, his first chapter is a self-contained story, a direct outgrowth of traditional oral literature, complete with a conclusion and a quasi-moral tag (hard work leads to success). There will be many more of these "sub-tales" throughout his novel, some relating to Okonkwo, as this first one does, others having no actual relation to him at all other than adding to the over-all accumulation of impressions of life and its patterns in a traditional African village. Finally, in Chapter One, besides the unifying device of using materials from his own traditional oral literature, Achebe has begun to weave a thread of action—albeit not structured as yet like the typical "plot"—relating to the main character of his novel, Okonkwo.

We know, first, that Okonkwo achieved great fame "throughout the nine villages and even beyond" from his early achievement throwing Amalinze, the Cat. Secondly, we learn the prime reason for this: Okonkwo's drive to destroy the image of his father's worthlessness; and, third, although we do not yet know its significance, we know that Okonkwo somehow became involved with the "ill-fated lad . . . called Ikemefuna."

Chapters Two, Three, and Four are focused for the most part on Okonkwo and his relationship with the rest of his immediate family, the adopted Ikemefuna, and the village. More often than not, Okonkwo's character is built up through action (by the use of expository summary) rather than by Achebe's describing him or rendering his character by scene and dialogue. To a certain extent, this method of characterization is the most logical, for the reader is not supposed to regard Okonkwo as a thinker or as an eccentric who would best be characterized by means of caricature. Achebe tells us at one point, "He was a man of action, a man of war. Unlike his father he could stand the look of blood" (p.14). Then he illustrates these traits by backtracking and showing Okonkwo in action. When a man from the neighboring village of Mbaino kills a young girl from Umuofia, it is Okonkwo who is sent as an "emissary of war." And when Mbaino decides it will not risk a war with Umuofia, it is Okonkwo who returns home with a young virgin girl and the young boy, Ikemefuna, in payment for the murder of the "daughter of Umuofia." Achebe has shown us the respect that Okonkwo has achieved, illustrated by his village's decision to send him to negotiate with Mbaino. Moreover, the incident itself introduces the motif of the village (Umuofia) which is so crucial to an understanding of the novel and which will slowly be developed until the last page. So important is this sense of village unity and cohesiveness that it is possible to say that

Umuofia, and not Okonkwo, will become the main character of *Things Fall Apart*. In his depiction of the village, Achebe is not unlike Thomas Hardy in his creation of Wessex in his own novels, yet Achebe more often than not uses the word "Umuofia" as a leitmotif.

The motif of the village is first introduced in Chapter Two. The girl's murder is referred to as an abomination against Umuofia as a whole and not as a crime against her own specific family. At a meeting of the villagers in the market place, Ogbuefi Ezeugo tells the entire village ("There must have been about ten thousand men there . . .") (p.14) of the murder: ". . . in a clear unemotional voice he told Umuofia how their daughter had gone to market at Mbaino and had been killed" (p.15). Achebe tells then of Umuofia's power: "Umuofia was feared by all its neighbors. It was powerful in war and in magic, and its priests and medicine men were feared in all the surrounding country" (p.15). In a period of two paragraphs, the village is mentioned five times, strengthening the image of village power and unity so that each time its name is repeated in later sections of the novel, its full force and weight are clearly recalled, thus bearing the power of a leitmotif. When Mbaino wisely decides not to go to war with Umuofia, Okonkwo is asked by the clan to look after Ikemefuna. "And so for three years Ikemefuna lived in Okonkwo's household" (p.16). The last sentence concludes the substory of the Umuofia/Mbaino dispute and, again, because of the conjunction gives the impression that Achebe has just told a traditional tale of Umuofia's glorious actions.

Achebe rapidly sketches in the three years of Ikemefuna's life with Okonkwo, but his emphasis is, for the most part, on creating a more detailed picture of Okonkwo. "Okonkwo ruled his household with a heavy hand," Achebe tells us, and Okonkwo's ". . . whole life was dominated by fear, the fear of failure and of weakness" (p.16). Later he adds, "It was the fear of himself, lest he should be found to resemble his father" (p.17). In addition to Okonkwo, several members of his family are also introduced, including Nwoye, Okonkwo's first son, who is twelve years old. We are also given a few additional facts about Okonkwo's father who "died of the swelling which was an abomination to the earth goddess" (p.21), a subtle use of irony which will be significant only when we learn that Okonkwo's own death is an abomination. Another flashback, which reads more like a story within a story because of its beginning and ending, relates how Okonkwo, many years earlier, struggled the first year on his farm. The flashback begins as follows: "There was a wealthy man in Okonkwo's village who had three huge barns, nine wives and thirty children (p.21). The opening is immediately reminiscent of the "Once upon a time" convention used at the beginning of many oral tales. It is from this rich man that Okonkwo borrows his first yam seedlings to begin his farm. In spite of insurmountable odds, Okonkwo survives a tragic farming season: "The year that Okonkwo took eight hundred seed-yams from Nwakibie was the worst year in living memory" (p.25). A drought continued for eight market weeks and much of the crop was burned out. So bad was the yam crop that "One man tied his cloth to a tree branch and hanged himself" (p.27). The hanging is significant because it foreshadows Okonkwo's own suicide. Besides the oral unifying devices Achebe has introduced into his novel, he relies heavily on the more usual fictional conventions such as this example of foreshadowing.

Achebe's dialogue in *Things Fall Apart* is extremely sparse. Okonkwo says very little at all; not of any one place in the novel may it be said that he has an extended speech or even a very lengthy conversation with another character. And as for authorial presentations of his thoughts, they are limited to two or three very brief passages. Indeed, Achebe relies for the development of his story usually on exposition rather than the dramatic rendering of scene, much as if he were telling

an extended oral tale or epic in conventional narrative fashion
—almost always making use of the preterit. Again and again
the reader is told something about Okonkwo, but he rarely
sees these events in action. In such a manner we are told that
Okonkwo became very fond of Ikemefuna, and that "Ikemefuna called him father" (p.30). Achebe tells us things like this,
but he rarely ever shows them. He tells the reader, for example, that "Okonkwo never showed any emotion openly,
unless it be the emotion of anger. To show affection was a
sign of weakness" (p.30). We are told of Okonkwo's affection for Ikemefuna, rather than shown it. Okonkwo's anger,
also, is usually illustrated not by dramatic narrative but by
summary, such as in his breaking of the Week of Peace:

> Okonkwo was provoked to justifiable anger by his youngest
> wife, who went to plait her hair at her friend's house and did
> not return early enough to cook the afternoon meal. . . .
>   In his anger he had forgotten that it was the Week of Peace.
> His first two wives ran out in great alarm pleading with him
> that it was the sacred week. But Okonkwo was not the man to
> stop beating somebody half-way through, not even for fear of a
> goddess. (pp.30–31)

The ramifications of this incident are more significant for
the clan than they are for illustrating Okonkwo's anger.
Ezeani, a priest of the earth goddess, tells Okonkwo, " 'The
evil you have done can ruin the whole clan. The earth goddess whom you have insulted may refuse to give us her in-
crease, and we shall all perish' " (p.32). The incident is important because it illustrates traditional social controls and
because of the shift once again from the individual to the
group. In his book, *The Igbo of Southeast Nigeria*, Victor C.
Uchendu states of Ibo unity,

> Igbo individualism is not "rugged" individualism; it is individu-
> alism rooted in group solidarity. The Igbo realized that "a river
> does not eat a blind calabash" (that is, a person with backers
> escapes dangers unhurt). There is a great emphasis on com-

munal cooperation and achievement. The "communal" character of the Igbo must be traced to the formative influence of
their traditional social patterns, the influence of their nucleated
residence pattern, and the ideological urge "to get up." The
idea of cooperation, illustrated in work groups, credit associations, and title-making societies, pervades all aspects of Igbo
culture.[6]

For the sake of the clan, Okonkwo is told to make a sacrifice
at the earth goddess' shrine, yet "people said he had no respect
for the gods of the clan" (p.32).

There is a further move away from Okonkwo in chapters
five through twelve of *Things Fall Apart*, for while it is true
that the reader is never at too far a distance from Okonkwo,
it is in these eight chapters that Achebe relies most heavily on
anthropological background for the establishment of his composite picture of traditional Ibo life before the coming of the
white man. In these chapters there is virtually no plot (no
central narrative) and almost nothing happens. There are no
obstacles that Okonkwo must overcome, though there are
two significant incidents which illustrate his somewhat hidden
affection for Ikemefuna and his daughter, Ezinma. More important, however, is Achebe's desire to give his non-African
reader (and even his African reader for that matter) a complete picture of the cycle of life in traditional Ibo society:
birth, marriage, death. Each one of these chapters illustrates
these and other facets of Ibo life.

Chapter Five, for example, is devoted in part to the Feast
of the New Yam Year, "an occasion for joy throughout
Umuofia" (p.38). Achebe relies heavily on anthropological
description and the feast is, of course, another example of a
communal experience. In Chapter Six, Achebe depicts the
entire village watching a wrestling match, complete with
drummers and dancers. The chapter adds nothing to the plot,
but we are reminded again that wrestling for the Ibo was not

so much an individual art as communal recreation. The ethnological sections of the seventh chapter are limited to depicting a season when the locusts return to Umuofia. There is a
fairly elaborate description of the coming of the locusts, their
harvesting by the villagers who roast, dry, and eat them as
delicacies. In Chapter Eight, Achebe records the ritual involved in arranging a traditional marriage: gifts, and the settling of the bride-price, for instance. The ninth chapter concerns Okonkwo's daughter, Ezinma, and the ethnological
material is related to the supernatural, the birth of *ogbanje*
children, (children who are born over and over again, always
dying in childhood) and the search for Ezinma's *iyi-uwa*, her
life spirit.

The tenth chapter is again concerned with specific communal ceremonies, this time with the presentation of a traditional trial. A young husband who has been beating his wife
is brought to trial by her family. The traditional law court, in
the form of the nine *egwugwu*, is described in some detail.
Chapter Eleven, which is devoted to a continuation of the
Ezinma story, is also ethnological in the picture it presents of
Chielo, "the priestess of Agbala, the Oracle of the Hills and
the Caves" (p.48). In the twelfth chapter Achebe continues
his presentation of traditional marriage arrangements, the
marriage itself; and in the first part of the thirteenth chapter,
this is followed by the presentation of a traditional funeral.
Thus the cycle of life has been presented in its three major
stages, with references to childbirth and the extremely high
infant mortality rate; marriage and the adjacent customs concerning brideprice and divorce; and, finally, the funerary rites
surrounding death. The emphasis is almost always on the
group instead of the individual.

I have already noted the strong aversion that many Western critics have toward the anthropological overtones present
in African fiction, except for the anthropologist, of course,
who is looking for this kind of thing. This aversion of the

literary critics, however, is no doubt due to their equation of the anthropological with the local colorists at the end of the last century and the beginning of this one. However, in a work such as *Things Fall Apart*, where we are not presented with a novel of character, the anthropological is indeed important. Without it there would be no story. The only way in which Achebe can depict a society's falling apart is first by creating an anthropological overview of that culture, and it should be clear that it is not going to be Okonkwo's story that Achebe is chronicling as much as the tragedy of a clan. It is the village of Umuofia, which has been sketched in so carefully, which he will now show as falling apart, crumbling from its exposure to Western civilization. But before we analyze this we need to examine one or two of the anthropological passages more carefully and illustrate how they often become for Achebe the equivalent of descriptive passages in Western literature.

The piling up of ethnological background, I suggest, is often the equivalent of atmospheric conditioning in Western fiction. Achebe's anthropological passages are what Hardy's descriptive passages are for him—equivalent to Hardy's evocation of atmosphere and mood. Indeed, it is extremely difficult to find a passage of pure description of a natural setting anywhere in Anglophone African writing of the first generation. There is very little that can be related to "landscape painting" in English fiction except for the anthropological passages. For example, in Chapter Seven of *Things Fall Apart*, when the oracle decides that Ikemefuna must be sacrificed, and when he is being led into the forest where a quasi-ritualistic sacrifice will take place, one might expect that Achebe would make use of landscape description to evoke a mood fitting for Ikemefuna's death. The description which the reader encounters, however, is as follows:

> The sun rose slowly to the center of the sky, and the dry, sandy footway began to throw up the heat that lay buried in

it. Some birds chirruped in the forests around. The men trod
dry leaves on the sand. All else was silent. Then from the distance came the faint beating of the *ekwe*. It rose and faded
with the wind—a peaceful dance from a distant clan.

"It is an *ozo* dance," the men said among themselves. But no
one was sure where it was coming from. Some said Ezimili,
others Abame or Aninta. They argued for a short while and
fell into silence again, and the elusive dance rose and fell with
the wind. Somewhere a man was taking one of the titles of his
clan, with music and dancing and a great feast.

The footway had now become a narrow line in the heart
of the forest. The short trees and sparse undergrowth which
surrounded the men's village began to give way to giant trees
and climbers which perhaps had stood from the beginning of
things, untouched by the ax and the bush-fire. The sun breaking through their leaves and branches threw a pattern of light
and shade in the sandy footway.   (p.57)

Achebe's description in this passage may seem hardly relevant
to the tragedy he is about to relate. Birds are chirruping and
although there is the beating of a drum, it is not, so far as
can be determined, in any sense intended as foreboding.
Rather, it is the drum and music for "dancing and a great
feast." Even the sun breaking through the leaves and branches
evokes no mood of imminent tragedy or despair, but, if anything, one of peacefulness and serenity. If one compares this
passage with that in Joseph Conrad's *Heart of Darkness* when
Marlow is going up the river in search of Kurtz, it is easy to
see how little Achebe uses description in a Western sense to
evoke mood and atmosphere. Rather, it is that his description,
when it is present, is used more directly for functional than
for aesthetic purposes. The forest is there—Ikemefuna cannot
be killed inside the village, so in order to place him in the
forest, Achebe relies on only the sparsest, most functional
description needed—simply enough to let the reader know
where he is.

Furthermore, in this passage depicting Ikemefuna's death,
what Achebe illustrates is another aspect of Okonkwo's

rigidity, and we might say that Ikemefuna's death has been put into the story primarily to show its relationship to Okonkwo. It is Okonkwo who actually delivers the death blow which cuts Ikemefuna down:

> As the man who had cleared his throat drew up and raised his machete, Okonkwo looked away. He heard the blow. The pot fell and broke in the sand. He heard Ikemefuna cry, "My father, they have killed me!" as he ran towards him. Dazed with fear, Okonkwo drew his machete and cut him down. He was afraid of being thought weak.   (p.59)

There is an alteration in Okonkwo, however, after Ikemefuna's death:

> Okonkwo did not taste any food for two days after the death of Ikemefuna. He drank palm-wine from morning till night, and his eyes were red and fierce like the eyes of a rat when it was caught by the tail and dashed against the floor. He called his son, Nwoye, to sit with him in his *obi*. But the boy was afraid of him and slipped out of the hut as soon as he noticed him dozing.   (p.61)

Ikemefuna's death begins to destroy the relationship between Okonkwo and Nwoye, father and son.

In the chapter following Ikemefuna's death, the reader encounters the second most important character in the novel, Okonkwo's friend, Obierika. It is significant that on his first appearance Obierika is immediately presented as a man of thought, rather than a man of action like Okonkwo. When Okonkwo asks Obierika why he did not take part in the killing of Ikemefuna, Obierika replies,

> "You know very well, Okonkwo, that I am not afraid of blood; and if anyone tells you that I am, he is telling a lie. And let me tell you one thing, my friend. If I were you I would have stayed at home. What you have done will not please the Earth. It is the kind of action for which the goddess wipes out whole families."   (p.64)

Obierika's comment is the first indication in the novel of the ultimate tragedy which Okonkwo's own life will become.

Balanced next to the substory of Ikemefuna and Nwoye is the story of Okonkwo's favorite child, Ezinma, who when the novel begins is ten years old. In the chapter after Ikemefuna's death, Chapter Eight, Achebe leads us more directly into Okonkwo's mind. It is one of the rare occasions where Okonkwo's thoughts are presented—in the form of a dialogue which he supposedly has with himself. There are a number of thoughts that are important here in contrasting the Ikemefuna/Nwoye/Ezinma substories. First, Okonkwo, still listless from his involvement in Ikemefuna's death, looks at Ezinma and says to himself, " 'She should have been a boy. . . .' " (p.61). The reflection is important because of Okonkwo's concern for masculinity and his fear that Nwoye will turn out like his grandfather, whom he has always equated with femininity. Secondly, Okonkwo questions his own show of emotions in the days after Ikemefuna's death, fearing that he is becoming a woman:

> "When did you become a shivering old woman," Okonkwo asked himself, "you, who are known in all the nine villages for your valor in war? How can a man who has killed five men in battle fall to pieces because he has added a boy to their number? Okonkwo, you have become a woman indeed." (pp.62–63)

The images of manhood and womanhood are extremely important here, as they are throughout the entire novel. The reader has already noted the images of femininity which Achebe used to characterize Okonkwo's father, and the linkage goes far beyond people to inanimate objects, such as the use of the word "yam" as a leitmotif and its equation with such qualities as masculinity, hard work, and success. Now the traditional male and female roles will be reversed with Nwoye and Ezinma, an obvious indication of the break-up of traditional Ibo roles.

Chapters Nine and Eleven bring to conclusion the subplot of Ezinma's struggle for life and the adjacent supernatural world Ezinma becomes involved in with the priestess, Chielo.

The chapters are largely anthropological, and I am in agreement with Eldred Jones that one major weakness of *Things Fall Apart* is Achebe's introducing the potentially fascinating Ezinma but failing to develop her characterization in the second and third parts of the novel.[7] The unities that are operative within the substory concerning Ezinma are of more concern for us here, however, than what happens to Ezinma herself. In Chapter Eleven, for example, Achebe has included a complete oral tale involving the tortoise and how his shell was broken. (Symbol hunters will no doubt argue that the tortoise is another symbol of Ibo traditional society.) The story, which extends uninterrupted for four pages, is told by Ezinma's mother, Ekwefi, to her daughter, and the tale is so structured that it could be removed from the novel and published by itself. When Ekwefi completes her tale—with the moral tag, " 'That is why Tortoise's shell is not smooth' " (p.94)—then Ezinma begins a tale of her own, but hers is interrupted by Chielo's chanting. The effect of the two chapters devoted to Ezinma is that we have a story ("Why Tortoise's Shell Is Not Smooth") within a substory (Ezinma and her struggle for life) within the wider framework of Okonkwo's love for Ezinma and his wish that she were a son instead of a daughter. Once again in the entire substory devoted to Chielo's leading Ezinma through the forest at night, mood and atmosphere are for the most part secondary to a much more functional depiction of the forest and the night itself, and the occasional use of anthropological explanations.

If we think of conflict as caused by something which thwarts a character's intentions or plans, or a situation which must be resolved before an objective can be achieved, then, for Okonkwo, at least, the conflict in which he is involved does not come about until the end of Chapter Thirteen of *Things Fall Apart*. To be sure, there are other sources of tension all along the way, but Achebe does not give them the magnitude of the accidental murder. The early desires to excel in his community (in wrestling, warfare, and farming) have already been accomplished by the time the novel begins. The momentary conflict within himself over Ikemefuna's death can be no more than that, because Okonkwo accepts the decree of the oracle for Ikemefuna's death. Even the fear that Nwoye is not showing enough manliness is something that Okonkwo, in his stoicism, pretty well ignores, since there is still a source of pride in Ezinma. Thus the "plotlessness" of *Things Fall Apart* is changed only in Chapter Thirteen, the last chapter of Part I.

The chapter begins with the sounds of the *ekwe* announcing the death of an important villager. We are reminded that in the previous chapter Achebe relied on anthropological explanation to present a picture of traditional marriage; in Chapter Thirteen he follows with a traditional funeral, thus, symbolically, at least, completing his cycle from birth to death in traditional Ibo life:

> The land of the living was not far removed from the domain of the ancestors. There was coming and going between them, especially at festivals and also when an old man died, because an old man was very close to the ancestors. A man's life from birth to death was a series of transition rites which brought him nearer and nearer to his ancestors.
>
> Ezeudu had been the oldest man in his village, and at his death there were only three men in the whole clan who were older, and four or five others in his own age group. Whenever one of these ancient men appeared in the crowd to dance unsteadily the funeral steps of the tribe, younger men gave way and the tumult subsided.
>
> It was a great funeral, such as befitted a noble warrior. As the evening drew near, the shouting and the firing of guns, the beating of drums and the brandishing and clanging of machetes increased. (p.115)

And, then, the tragedy intervenes:

> The drums and the dancing began again and reached fever-heat. Darkness was around the corner, and the burial was near. Guns fired the last salute and the cannon rent the sky.

And then from the center of the delirious fury came a cry of agony and shouts of horror. It was as if a spell had been cast. All was silent. In the center of the crowd a boy lay in a pool of blood. It was the dead man's sixteen-year-old son, who with his brothers and half-brothers had been dancing the traditional farewell to their father. Okonkwo's gun had exploded and a piece of iron had pierced the boy's heart.

The confusion that followed was without parallel in the tradition of Umuofia. Violent deaths were frequent but nothing like this had ever happened. (pp.116–117)

When the reader encounters this passage, he remembers that in an earlier chapter, Chapter Five, Achebe made reference to Okonkwo's gun and his inability to fire it properly: "He had an old rusty gun made by a clever blacksmith. . . . But although Okonkwo was a great man whose prowess was universally acknowledged, he was not a hunter" (p.39). Obierika's warning that the earth goddess will revenge Ikemefuna's death has been fulfilled.

The only course open to Okonkwo was to flee from the clan. It was a crime against the earth goddess to kill a clansman, and a man who committed it must flee from the land. The crime was of two kinds, male and female. Okonkwo had committed the female, because it had been inadvertent. He could return to the clan after seven years. (p.117)

Ironically, Okonkwo, whose greatest fear is that he will be called feminine, has committed a female crime; the accidental murder that acts as a harbinger of his own suicide has already struck at the heart of his obsession with manliness. The narrative continues:

That night he collected his most valuable belongings into head-loads. His wives wept bitterly and their children wept with them without knowing why. Obierika and half a dozen other friends came to help and to console him. They each made nine or ten trips carrying Okonkwo's yams to store in Obierika's barn. And before the cock crowed Okonkwo and his family were fleeing to his motherland. It was a little village called Mbanta, just beyond the borders of Mbaino.

As soon as the day broke, a large crowd of men from Ezeudu's quarter stormed Okonkwo's compound, dressed in garbs of war. They set fire to his houses, demolished his red walls, killed his animals and destroyed his barn. It was the justice of the earth goddess, and they were merely her messengers. They had no hatred in their hearts against Okonkwo. His greatest friend, Obierika, was among them. They were merely cleansing the land which Okonkwo had polluted with the blood of a clansman.   (p.117)

The passages just quoted are significant as an illustration of Achebe's terseness, his use of exposition to develop the narrative line of his story at an extremely rapid pace. In a matter of a handful of paragraphs we encounter as much action and resultant conflict as he has shown in the entire first half of his novel. All of the narrative is in summary rather than in scene, the most logical form for a rapid progression of events. The passage also illustrates village unity and a more modified form of Achebe's use of the anthropological. Westerners tend to believe that traditional African societies had no laws (since they were unwritten) to hold them together. The example given here is clearly to the contrary. Perhaps it has been years since there has been an accidental murder in Umuofia, but immediately when one occurs, everyone knows what to do. The village acts as a unit and purifies itself by sending Okonkwo away for seven years, cleansing itself with the ritual incineration of Okonkwo's house. It is the communal action which is again so significant—the situation which involves everyone and not just Okonkwo. The earth goddess has been offended and stability must be restored within the clan.

In what I consider one of the major philosophic achievements of his novel, Achebe, in the final paragraph of Chapter Thirteen, shifts his emphasis from the communal, back to the individual, in a symbolic probing of the future:

Obierika was a man who thought about things. When the will of the goddess had been done, he sat down in his *obi* and

mourned his friend's calamity. Why should a man suffer so
grievously for an offense he had committed inadvertently?
But although he thought for a long time he found no answer.
He was merely led into greater complexities. He remembered
his wife's twin children, whom he had thrown away. What
crime had they committed? The Earth had decreed that they
were an offense on the land and must be destroyed. And if the
clan did not exact punishment for an offense against the great
goddess, her wrath was loosed on all the land and not just on
the offender. As the elders said, if one finger brought oil it
soiled the others.   (pp.117–118)

Obierika, who is clearly a man ahead of his times, begins to
question the traditional values of his society, and, in showing
him doing so, Achebe has symbolically illustrated the adaptation which will eventually have to come about if Ibo society
is not to be totally destroyed by the West. The great chain
which has held the society together is beginning to weaken.
In Obierika's questions, Achebe has indicated that the man
of the future will not be a man of action, but a man of
thought. Fittingly, too, the proverb in the last sentence brings
the first part of *Things Fall Apart* to a conclusion and ties the
threads of the story together.

Part II of *Things Fall Apart*—Okonkwo's seven years of
exile in Mbanta—is composed of Chapters Fourteen through
Nineteen. These chapters are much more conventional, much
more Western, than those which make up Part I of the novel.
There is hardly any reliance on the anthropological, and there
is much more stress on plot and the development of a sus-
penseful narrative. Although ostensibly concerned with
Okonkwo's exile from Umuofia, Part II shows him increasingly kept in the background, for Achebe's intention in the
central section of his novel is to record the coming of the
white man into Eastern Nigeria, and the communal rather
than individual conflict. Achebe's portrayal of the clash is
not only historically accurate but undoubtedly the finest piece

of fictive writing portraying the African/Western clash in its initial stages. Earlier in the novel Achebe takes great pains to foreshadow the coming of the white man. In Chapter Eight, for example, at the marriage of one of Obierika's daughters, Obierika talks of white men who he has heard "are white like [a] piece of chalk" (p.71), and a joke is made about a leper whose white skin looks like the white man's.

Chapter Fourteen begins with several references to Okonkwo and the gradual alteration that comes over him now that his plans have been thwarted,

> Work no longer had for him the pleasure it used to have, and when there was no work to do he sat in a silent half-sleep.
> His life had been ruled by a great passion—to become one of the lords of the clan. That had been his life-spring. And he had all but achieved it. Then everything had been broken. He had been cast out of his clan like a fish onto a dry, sandy beach, panting. (p.121)

In the following chapter, a year later, Obierika visits Okonkwo in exile. He tells Okonkwo of the tragedy in Abame, a neighboring village that has been wiped out in a battle with the white man:

> "During the last planting season a white man had appeared in their clan . . . he was riding an iron horse. The first people who saw him ran away, but he stood beckoning to them. In the end the fearless ones went near and even touched him. The elders consulted their Oracle and it told them that the strange man would break their clan and spread destruction among them. . . . And so they killed the white man and tied his iron horse to their sacred tree because it looked as if it would run away to call the man's friends . . . the Oracle . . . said that other white men were on their way. They were locusts, it said, and that first man was their harbinger sent to explore the terrain. And so they killed him." (p.128)

Several months later, a band of white men and black men shot everyone in the Abame market. Okonkwo's reaction is that the people of Abame were fools, " 'They had been warned that danger was ahead. They should have armed themselves with their guns and their machetes even when they went to market'" (p.130). Obierika's reaction is "'Who knows what may happen tomorrow? Perhaps green men will come to our clan and shoot us'" (p.131).

Two years later when Obierika again visits Okonkwo in exile, the missionaries have arrived in Umuofia. Shortly thereafter, they advance to Mbanta, and Okonkwo's oldest son, Nwoye, becomes an early convert. Achebe's presentation of the missionaries and their work is done with objectivity and rare sensitivity. He does not condemn Christianity nor does he praise it—he only admits that in relation to the traditional animism, the differences are overpowering. The following paragraph illustrates, for example, Nwoye's reaction to the missionaries:

> But there was a young lad who had been captivated. His name was Nwoye, Okonkwo's first son. It was not the mad logic of the Trinity that captivated him. He did not understand it. It was the poetry of the new religion, something felt in the marrow. The hymn about brothers who sat in darkness and in fear seemed to answer a vague and persistent question that haunted his young soul—the question of the twins crying in the bush and the question of Ikemefuna who was killed. He felt a relief within as the hymn poured into his parched soul. The words of the hymn were like the drops of frozen rain melting on the dry palate of the panting earth. Nwoye's callow mind was greatly puzzled. (p.137)

When the missionaries ask for a plot of land upon which to build their church, the elders give them the Evil Forest, assuming that they will be dead in a matter of days. Yet, they prosper and slowly gain converts, and when Okonkwo learns of Nwoye's conversion, it is all he can do to control his rage: "A sudden fury rose within him and he felt a strong desire to take up his machete, go to the church and wipe out the entire vile and miscreant gang" (p.142). And soon it is learned "that the white man had not only brought a religion but also a gov-

ernment" (pp.144–145). Yet, Okonkwo is unsuccessful in convincing the people of Mbanta to kill the missionaries. "This
was a womanly clan, he thought" (p.148), as Achebe shows
us a rare moment of introspection. As always, Achebe makes
the conflict communal, equating it with a lack of masculinity.
When Okonkwo's seven years of exile are completed, one of
the elders of Mbanta tells him, " 'An abominable religion has
settled among you. A man [Nwoye] can now leave his father
and his brothers. He can curse the gods of his fathers and his
ancestors, like a hunter's dog that suddenly goes mad and
turns on his master. I fear for you; I fear for the clan' "
(pp.155–156). Okonkwo's exile runs parallel to the final destruction of the clan; Nwoye's conversion is an indication that
the only pathway for the future is cultural syncretism.

Part III of *Things Fall Apart* concentrates in the intensi-
fied conflict between Umuofia and the new dispensation—
Christianity. Okonkwo returns to his village after seven years
of exile. Achebe begins this section as follows:

> Seven years was a long time to be away from one's clan. A
> man's place was not always there, waiting for him. As soon as
> he left, someone else rose and filled it. The clan was like a
> lizard; if it lost its tail it soon grew another.   (p.157)

The lizard that Achebe uses to symbolize the clan has already
lost its tail. Okonkwo knows that the new religion has dras-
tically altered his village:

> Okonkwo knew these things. He knew that he had lost
> his place among the nine masked spirits who administered justice
> in the clan. He had lost the chance to lead his warlike clan
> against the new religion, which, he was told, had gained ground.
> He had lost the years in which he might have taken the highest
> titles in the clan.   (p.157)

Okonkwo's plans to return to Umuofia in pomp and splendor
are the first to be thwarted. The church has already divided
the village, and Obierika warns him that to fight the church

is to fight one's own clansmen, and the image of the village takes on an ironic twist. The white man's government is already involved in corruption in land disputes. When Okonkwo asks Obierika if the white man understands their customs about land, Obierika replies:

"How can he when he does not even speak our tongue? But he says that our customs are bad; and our own brothers who have taken up his religion also say that our customs are bad. How do you think we can fight when our own brothers have turned against us? The white man is very clever. He came quietly and peaceably with his religion. We were amused at his foolishness and allowed him to stay. Now he has won our brothers, and our clan can no longer act like one. He has put a knife on the things that held us together and we have fallen apart." (p.162)

Obierika realizes that fighting the white man is the same as committing suicide. The clan is rapidly disintegrating; the village is no longer what it was. Old traditions are losing their power.

Okonkwo's other plans are also thwarted. He returns the wrong year to initiate his elder sons into the *ozo* society. Achebe tells the reader: "the initiation rite was performed once in three years in Umuofia, and he had to wait for nearly two years for the next round of ceremonies" (pp.167–168). Okonkwo realizes the end has come:

Okonkwo was deeply grieved. And it was not just a personal grief. He mourned for the clan, which he saw breaking up and falling apart, and he mourned for the warlike men of Umuofia, who had so unaccountably become soft like women. (p.168)

The references to femininity are obvious, culminating in a crescendo of defeat.

When Enoch, a zealous convert, unmasks one of the village's sacred *egwugwu*, the stage is set for Okonkwo's final symbolic act. The villagers regard Enoch as having killed an ancestral spirit, and Achebe tells his reader, perhaps a little too obviously, "It seemed as if the very soul of the tribe wept for a great evil that was coming—its own death" (pp.171–172). The ensuing denouement is brought to an hysterical conclusion, with Okonkwo's determination to rid the clan of its curse. They burn down the white man's church and three days later Okonkwo and five other village leaders are humiliated by the District Commissioner and thrown into jail. The District Commissioner orders Umuofia to pay two hundred bags of cowries as reparation for the destroyed church. Once the fine is paid (inflated by the white man's messengers), the six leaders are released from prison. A village meeting is called to decide whether Umuofia should go to war against the white man, but before the meeting takes place, the white man's messenger arrives, ordering that the gathering be broken up. Achebe's twenty-fourth chapter ends with Okonkwo's abortive act:

> In a flash Okonkwo drew his machete. The messenger crouched to avoid the blow. It was useless. Okonkwo's machete descended twice and the man's head lay beside his uniformed body.
>
> The waiting backcloth jumped into tumultuous life and the meeting was stopped. Okonkwo stood looking at the dead man. He knew that Umuofia would not go to war. He knew because they had let the other messengers escape. They had broken into tumult instead of action. He discerned fright in that tumult. He heard voices asking: "Why did he do it?"
>
> He wiped his machete on the sand and went away. (p.188)

The concluding chapter of *Things Fall Apart* is one of the highlights of contemporary African fiction. In less than three pages, Achebe weaves together the various themes and patterns he has been working with throughout much of his novel. Technically, the most significant aspect of this final chapter is Achebe's sudden shifts in point of view. To be sure, the chapter is told in the third person, as is the rest of the book. But whereas the other twenty-four chapters are told strictly from the point of view of the objective African novelist, the twenty-fifth chapter shifts the viewpoint back and forth between Obierika and the white District Commissioner, for much of the action in this chapter is seen through the eyes of the latter. The chapter begins:

> When the District Commissioner arrived at Okonkwo's compound at the head of an armed band of soldiers and court messengers he found a small crowd of men sitting wearily in the *obi*. He commanded them to come outside, and they obeyed without a murmer.
>
> "Which among you is called Okonkwo?" he asked through his interpreter.
>
> "He is not here," replied Obierika.
>
> "Where is he?"
>
> "He is not here!"
>
> The Commissioner became angry and red in the face. He warned the men that unless they produced Okonkwo forthwith he would lock them all up. The men murmured among themselves, and Obierika spoke again.
>
> "We can take you where he is, and perhaps your men will help us."
>
> The Commissioner did not understand what Obierika meant when he said, "Perhaps your men will help us." One of the most infuriating habits of these people was their love of superfluous words, he thought. (p.189)

No longer is an African narrating Okonkwo's story. In the last sentence quoted above, Achebe has put us within the mind of the white District Commissioner, and even Obierika's function is little more than giving out bits and pieces of information. Obierika leads the District Commissioner behind Okonkwo's compound where Okonkwo has hanged himself and asks the District Commissioner if his men can help cut Okonkwo down.

> The District Commissioner changed instantaneously. The resolute administrator in him gave way to the student of primitive customs.
>
> "Why can't you take him down yourselves?" he asked.

"It is against our custom," said one of the men. "It is an abomination for a man to take his own life. It is an offense against the Earth, and a man who commits it will not be buried by his clansmen. His body is evil, and only strangers may touch it. That is why we ask your people to bring him down, because you are strangers." (p.190)

Okonkwo, who would save the clan, has committed a grave offense against the earth goddess by committing suicide, and therefore, by extension, directly against the clan itself. Obierika tells the District Commissioner, " 'That man was one of the greatest men in Umuofia. You drove him to kill himself; and now he will be buried like a dog. . . .' " (p.191). The concluding paragraph is as follows:

The Commissioner went away, taking three or four of the soldiers with him. In the many years in which he had toiled to bring civilization to different parts of Africa he had learned a number of things. One of them was that a District Commissioner must never attend to such undignified details as cutting a hanged man from the tree. Such attention would give the natives a poor opinion of him. In the book which he planned to write he would stress that point. As he walked back to the court he thought about that book. Every day brought him some new material. The story of this man who had killed a messenger and hanged himself would make interesting reading. One could almost write a whole chapter on him. Perhaps not a whole chapter but a reasonable paragraph, at any rate. There was so much else to include, and one must be firm in cutting out details. He had already chosen the title of the book, after much thought: *The Pacification of the Primitive Tribes of the Lower Niger.* (p.191)

The shifting point of view back and forth between an African and a Western viewpoint symbolizes the final breakup of the clan, for *Things Fall Apart,* in spite of the subtitle on the first American edition, *The Story of a Strong Man,* is only in part Okonkwo's story, and, as we have noted, as the book progresses, the story becomes increasingly that of a village, a clan. Achebe clearly indicates this in the final paragraph of his novel where he reduces Okonkwo's story to nothing more than a paragraph in a history book, for history is facts and not individuals, and the history of the coming of the white man to Africa is not the story of the pacification of individuals but of entire tribes of people and even beyond that. The title of the District Commissioner's book tells us essentially this. Achebe has moved throughout his book away from the individual (Okonkwo) to the communal (Umuofia) and beyond that to the clan. And in the last paragraph, the extension is even further beyond the Ibo of Southeast Nigeria to that of the *Primitive Tribes of the Lower Niger*, ergo, the entire African continent.

The conclusion to *Things Fall Apart* has often been considered over-written, anti-climactic, unnecessarily didactic. My students on occasion have argued that the novel should close with the end of Chapter Twenty-four or when the District Commissioner encounters Okonkwo's dangling body. Certainly it can be argued that Achebe takes pains to make his message clear, but I feel that the shift to the District Commissioner's point of view strengthens rather than weakens the conclusion. It seems impossible for any one to read Achebe's last chapter without being noticeably moved, and if it is didactic in the sense of tying things up a little too nicely, then I would have to insist that this was Achebe's intention from the beginning and not merely an accident because of his background of oral tradition. In an article in *The New Statesman* called "The Novelist as Teacher," Achebe has written about the functional value of literature in a young nation —young in written literature. Achebe states, "The writer cannot expect to be excused from the task of re-education and regeneration that must be done. In fact he should march right in front. . . . Art is important but so is education of the kind I have in mind. And I don't see that the two need be mutually exclusive." [8] In short, the novelist in an emergent nation cannot afford to pass up a chance to educate his fellow

countrymen, and as we will see, contemporary African literature and others forms of African art have inherited a cultural
inclination toward the didactic which in regard to African
tradition may be called functionalism.

The ending of *Things Fall Apart* also illustrates the di-
chotomy of interpretations which cultural backgrounds im-
pose upon a reader. Most Western readers of Achebe's novel
seem to interpret the story of Okonkwo's fall as tragic if not
close to pure tragedy in classical terms. They cite Okonkwo's
pride, his going against the will of the gods (for instance,
breaking the Week of Peace, and killing Ikemefuna), and interpret the ending as tragic and inevitable, citing, usually, a
parallel to Oedipus. Achebe's own feelings about Okonkwo
and the conclusion to the novel, however, would tend to indicate a rather different interpretation. The most obvious clue
is Achebe' title, *Things Fall Apart*, taken from William Butler
Yeats's poem, "The Second Coming." Although Yeats's title
may be applied ironically to Achebe's story, the indications
are that Achebe views the new dispensation as something inevitable, perhaps even desirable. His criticism is clearly of the
old way of life which is unsatisfactory now that the West
has arrived. This interpretation is supported by several comments Achebe has made about his novel. In a filmed interview for National Educational Television, when asked about
the weaknesses of traditional Ibo society, Achebe replied,
"The weakness of this particular society is its lack of adaptation, not being able to bend. But I can't say that this represents
the Ibo people today. I think in this time, the strong men
were those who did not bend and I think this was a fault in
the culture itself." [9] Lack of adaptability, then, is what
Achebe implies led to the collapse of traditional Ibo society.*
Achebe adds, ". . . this particular society has believed too

---

* In a later interview which appeared in *Cultural Events in Africa*,
No. 28 (March 1967), Achebe said, ". . . my sympathies were not
entirely with Okonkwo. . . . Life just has to go on and if you refuse
to accept changes, then tragic though it may be, you are swept aside."

much in manliness. Perhaps this is part of the reason it crashed in the end. . . .[10] As a further example of the non-Aristotelian interpretation of the novel's ending, it is interesting to notice that Ibo students today reading *Things Fall Apart* tend to lose all respect for Okonkwo when they learn that he has committed suicide. It must be pointed out, too, that the new Iboman is clearly foreseen in several passages within Achebe's novel. Obierika is the most obvious example, and at the beginning of Chapter Twenty-one, Achebe says,

> There were many men and women in Umofia who did not feel as strongly as Okonkwo about the new dispensation. The white man had indeed brought a lunatic religion, but he had also built a trading store and for the first time palm-oil and kernel became things of great price, and much money flowed into Umofia. (p.163)

An even more obvious example is the voices Okonkwo hears immediately after he has killed the District Commissioner's messenger: " 'Why did he do it?' " (p.188). One is led to believe that within the past eighty years, Ibo society has shifted radically from one extreme to the other, from the active Okonkwo's to thinking Obierika's. The Ibos today are often regarded as the most adaptable (read "most Westernized") of all the major tribes of West Africa.

We have examined at length the structure of Achebe's novel and his main character, Okonkwo, but the two should actually be examined together. The narrative situation of the novel, we have seen, does not actually develop from a major source of conflict for Okonkwo until the end of Part I, until more than half of the novel has passed. Of the three major divisions of the book, only the trajectory of Parts II and III resembles the traditional Western well-made novel with conflict—obstacles to be overcome by the protagonist. Part I is especially loose, incorporating as it does section after section of anthropological background. The effect is, of course, to re-create the entire world of day-to-day existence in tradi-tional Ibo society, and Achebe takes pains to make certain that the major stages of life are included: birth, marriage, and death. In the symbiosis which results, Umuofia, rather than Okonkwo, becomes the main character of *Things Fall Apart*, and the transformation it undergoes is archetypal of the entire breakdown of traditional African cultures under exposure to the West.

The novel itself, as I stated at the beginning, must also be regarded as archetypical for the form and patterns Achebe has given it. If we compare the novel very briefly with Joyce Cary's *Mister Johnson* it is readily evident that *Things Fall Apart* is not a story about a character as is Cary's novel and as I feel we tend to regard Western novels as being. For example, Achebe could never have called his novel *Okonkwo*,* though it could have been given the name of Okonkwo's village if Achebe had thought that the situation did not extend beyond that one locale within Nigeria. Okonkwo himself does not alter at all throughout the novel. He is the same at the end-ing as he is at the beginning of the story. Thus, *Things Fall Apart*, because of its emphasis on community rather than in-dividuality, is a novel of situation rather than of character, and this is undoubtedly its major difference from the traditional Western genre, which in the twentieth century, at least, has emphasized the psychological depiction of character.

In Chapter Five we will examine more carefully the situ-ational African novel in relation to the works by James Ngugi. Let it simply be noted here that the situational plot is indeed the most typical narrative form one encounters in contem-porary African fiction. The reason for this is that by and

---

* I am aware, however, that the title of the German edition is *Okon-kwo oder das Alte sturzt* and of the Slovene edition, *Okonkvo*. No doubt these choices resulted because of the difficulty in translating the fragment from Yeats' poem, "The Second Coming," that Achebe chose for his title.

large the major theme of African writing to date has been the conflict of Africa with the West, whether this is shown in its initial stages, as in Achebe's *Things Fall Apart*, or at any one of several different later stages. All four of Achebe's novels are examples of the situational plot, for what happens is ultimately more significant for the group than for the individual whom Achebe uses to focus the situation. The significance, then, is felt by the village, the clan, the tribe, or the nation. In *No Longer at Ease*, a sequel to *Things Fall Apart*, Okonkwo's grandson, who has acquired a university education and works in the Civil Service in Lagos, takes a bribe and thereby brings humiliation on the Umuofia Progressive Union which has paid for his overseas education. In *Arrow of God*, the chief Priest, Ezeulu, because of his humiliation at the hands of the white man, refuses to announce the New Yam Feast; and, in order to prevent their crops from going to ruin, the villagers sacrifice to the Christian God rather than to their traditional god. Christianity wins the village over in one fell swoop, and the faith in the old religion is lost almost overnight. In Achebe's fourth novel, *A Man of the People*, we again encounter a situational plot, since the story involves a military coup which affects the livelihood of an entire nation.

In conclusion, it should be noted that *Things Fall Apart* does not necessarily give the impression that the story is "plotless" in spite of the fragmentary nature of many of the substories or tales incorporated into Part I of the novel. We have already noted how Achebe's use of the proverb can act as a serious counterpart for the more continuous surface progression of the story. Although I have not taken pains to point out all of them here, Achebe continues to use these proverbs throughout Parts II and III of his novel. The other unities which he relies on to give form and pattern to the story are the traditional oral tale or tale within a tale—a device no longer in favor with contemporary Western novelists, yet a convention at least as old as the "Man in the Hill" episode in Fielding's *Tom Jones*. The use of the leitmotif and its associations with stagnancy in Umuofia, masculinity, land, and yam also act as connective links throughout the narrative. It is because of these unities and others, which are vestiges of his own traditional culture, that Achebe's *Things Fall Apart* deserves its position in the forefront of contemporary African writing. Achebe has widened our perspective of the novel and illustrated how a typically Western genre may be given a healthy injection of new blood once it is reshaped and formed by the artist whose vision of life and art is different from our own.

3

Pamela in Africa:

Onitsha Market Literature

IN SPITE OF THE BRIEF PERIOD SINCE ITS INCEPTION
the flood of African writing during the past twenty-five years
has made the term "African literature" obsolete. Such a term
is already thoroughly inadequate for use in discussing the
many different contemporary literatures of modern Africa,
and even in limiting the area to fiction alone, one immediately
runs into almost as many generalizations as have been made
about the term "African literature" itself. Africa is simply
too large and there are too many different cultures producing
too many distinctly different literatures for such a term to
have any real function other than that of simple geographical
classification.

The African novel itself almost defies categorization in
spite of attempts to identify similarities and dissimilarities with
the Western genre to which it can trace its inspirations. Missing from this particular study are any references to the vast
amount of North African fiction from such countries as
Algeria, Tunisia, Morocco, and Egypt. The traditions of the

novel in these areas are decidedly different from the kind we have already noted in the African novel south of the Sahara. Nevertheless, these areas are considered "African" by virtue of their geographical location. In South Africa, it is possible to speak of a whole group of white novelists whose works, for the most part, have not deviated from English literary traditions and yet who often prefer to think of themselves as "African novelists" instead of European novelists: Alan Paton, Doris Lessing, Nadine Gordimer, Harry Bloom, and further back, Olive Schreiner. The novel in Afrikaans has also firmly established its prominence over the past fifty years, resulting in the recent crescendo of the *Sestigers,* and the international reputation of the most talented of these novelists: Etienne Leroux. To be truly comprehensive, an analysis of the African novel would have to include all of these writers.

Even in tropical Africa itself, generalizations of a critical nature on literary matters can be at best tentative, for actually there is no such thing as a "typical" African fictional form. The novel here varies as greatly from one ethnic group to another (that is perhaps a better distinction at this stage than by nationality) as does, say, the nineteenth-century German novel from its counterpart in England or France. Thus it is as impossible, on the one hand, to talk of a typical form and pattern for African fiction, as, on the other, unavoidable that we do so. It is not simply a matter, either, of cutting down the field of African fiction into French and English, although as I have already indicated, the major innovations in African fiction have been made by the African who has written in English rather than French. The reason is rather obvious, dependent mostly on the French cultural policy of assimilation which, in its attempt to sever the African's ties with his past, brought him closer to Western literary tradition except, perhaps, in the movement of French African poetry known as "*négritude.*" As we will later see with Camara Laye's *Le regard du roi* (*The Radiance of the King*), the African novel written in French is in technical matters usually closer to the Western novel than the African novel written in English. This does not mean, of course, that other aspects of the Francophone African novel are not similar to the Anglophone African novel: the attitude toward time, the treatment of the individual in regard to his society, for instance. Here the parallels between the two are often much closer.

To talk of a typical form or pattern for African fiction, therefore, is almost an impossibility. There are simply too many varieties—Africa is very large. Differing cultural needs have imposed differing influences, though there are some tendencies which appear to be widespread. Certainly it may be said that many African novelists, over the entire continent, have made use of oral literary conventions, yet it would be erroneous to conclude, for example, that the use of the proverb —in the way in which Chinua Achebe uses it—is typical of most African novelists or even a large proportion of them. It simply is not so, and one is led to conclude that proverbs have had an especially important function in Ibo society (as Carnochan and Iwuchuku have illustrated), more so than in many other African societies. And it seems to be thus with practically all of the various differences we have already noted in regard to African fiction. In many writers description may be almost completely missing; in many other African novelists, description may be more or less the same as it is in the West. In a large group of African novels, conflict and its determination of the plot are of little or no importance in regard to the individual character—what is important instead is the ultimate effect an event may have for a larger group of people. With other African writers, particularly with the younger novelists who have begun writing in the past few years, the individual has a status similar to, if not the same as, that of the individual in the West, and therefore characterization is often of equal significance. Ultimately, a study such as this must be in relation to the individual African novelist and the often unique contribution his works have made to the total complex of what we think of as African fiction.

If there is any group of African writers who may be said to cluster into a norm, however, that statement surely applies to the group of aspiring "novelists" who compose what to-day, in retrospect, must be called the "Onitsha Market Writers." Here at least is one group of writers numbering in the dozens whose works constitute an almost unselfconscious movement. It should be added that the movement may have been conscious in some aspects, for on one occasion a number of these writers formed a society or organization for their writing; and it is obvious, too, that many of these writers were familiar with each other and illustrated a knowledge of each other's works—often to the degree of imitation or even parody.

The antecedents of Onitsha market literature may be traced back, roughly, some twenty-five years, to the end of World War II. At that time, Onitsha, which is situated on the banks of the Niger River in Eastern Nigeria, was just beginning to experience the growing pangs of urbanization which eventually led to its becoming the unofficial capital of Iboland and the site of the largest market in all of West Africa. Schoolboys and schoolgirls flocked to Onitsha in search of Civil Service and white collar jobs, and traders from all over the country and beyond hawked and traded their wares. Before the market's destruction in the Nigerian Civil War (the place was leveled), it was said that anything could be purchased in the maze of Onitsha markets—as long as one was willing to pay the price: foodstuffs from all over the world, household goods, clothing, books and other imported educational supplies, automobile parts, imported medicines sold without prescription, love potions manufactured by local herbalists, marijuana and other illegal drugs, machine guns and other armaments, and the latest potboiler by an Onitsha writer.

The Onitsha printers—who operated also as general stationery and educational suppliers—discovered shortly after the war that the time was ripe for indigenously written material. Students especially, or young people who had completed a limited amount of formal education and were working in Onitsha, were eager to read works by Nigerian writers— works written for Nigerians. And printers who were willing to try a hand at publishing local material discovered that the sophisticated, newly-literate, urban Nigerian was interested in reading stories about his fellow countrymen, instead of the Victorian novels taught in the British-controlled educational system. Furthermore, it was soon evident that this newly-created reading audience was interested in devouring short booklets (rarely over a hundred pages, more frequently averaging about thirty), which could be purchased for a shilling or less, instead of imported books selling for considerably more, treating a foreign world, and running into hundreds of pages.

Thus was born Onitsha market literature, the product of a unique series of cultural upheavals: urbanization, economic need, the approach to independence coupled with the need for pride in local artists, and a rapidly increasing "literate" audience in search of topical and racy material—local color which could easily be identified and understood. The situation was not very different from the flowering and eventual fading of the dime novel in our country at the turn of the last century. The United States, too, was undergoing similar alterations in education, economics, and urbanization, the frustrations of a society constantly in flux.

In an article in *Transition*, Donatus I. Nwoga, who is Ibo, has stated that by 1963 there were at least two hundred Onitsha titles in existence (and this may be a conservative estimate).[1] My own estimate is that another two hundred titles were printed between 1963 and the outbreak of the Nigerian Civil War in 1967. Of these several hundred titles, about a third fall into the category of "Onitsha novels." These "fictions" probably had most of their popularity among school students, but, increasingly, the Onitsha printers also catered to other members of the emerging middle class: Civil Servants, traders and lorry drivers, even market women and farmers, who, if they could not read English themselves, could probably get someone to read aloud to them. To these latter groups, especially, two other types of Onitsha publications were particularly appealing: the self-help book and the political or topical pamphlet concerned with current events in Africa or biographies of important world leaders.

There were, for example, in the self-help category itself, dozens of popular titles, all aimed at teaching the ever socially conscious Ibo how to keep one step ahead of the Joneses. (Or the Okonkwos, as it would probably have been in this case.) Books such as *The Way to Success in Life* or *The Game of Love and How to Play It* enjoyed particularly successful sales. Some titles seemed to run away from their authors, as, for example, the following: *How to Avoid Misatkes and Live a Good Life: A Moral Instructions On Don'ts in Public Meetings, Social Gatherings and Functions for Boys & Girls, Workers and Traders* [sic]; or, another, called *How to Write Love Letters and Win Girls' Love: 95 Love Letters and How to Compose Them*—an especially popular title among schoolboys. And there were other "etiquette" books perhaps a little more suggestive in the implications of their titles: *How to Make Friends With Girls; How to Make Love;* and *The Nigerian Bachelor's Guide*, which Nancy Schmidt has said sold 40,000 copies.[2]

Among the political and topical pamphlets—the second major grouping—the following were especially popular during the mid-1960's: *How Lumumba Suffered in Life and Died in Katanga; The Struggles and Trials of Jomo Kenyatta;* and

Zik in the Battle for Freedom, an account of Nnamdi Azikiwe, the former President of Nigeria, and his work leading to the country's independence in 1960. Shortly after the assassination of John F. Kennedy, a series of "fictionalized" biographies of the greatly-admired American president sold by the thousands. In one book, *The Life History and Last Journey of President John Kennedy,* by Wilfred Onwuku, written partly in the form of a drama, Kennedy, just after he has been shot, stands up in his automobile and delivers a three-page oration on the American black man's struggle for social equality and the need for political unity among African nations.[3]

The fictional category rightfully includes both novels and dramas, although it is the Onitsha novel with which we are most directly concerned here. The following titles enjoyed their own notoriety: *The Disappointed Lover; The Sorrows of Love; Miss Rosy in the Romance of True Love; Rosemary and the Taxi Driver;* and an especially intriguing title, *How to Get a Lady in Love.* The title of this last work suggests the kind of writing frequently encountered in Onitsha literature: bad grammar heightened by texts replete with typographical errors,* racy literature undoubtedly influenced by the cinema and patterned to a certain extent after Western models imported from overseas (*Maria Monk* is one title which seems to have had a considerable influence), and of a level of sophistication limited only by the writer's unworldliness and naivete when examined from a non-African point of view.

The self-help books are obvious examples of a literature for the masses, written primarily to educate and improve the mind; but also, in the Onitsha novellas the attempt to be educative, moral, or edifying is equally important. A random sampling from the cover blurbs, author's prefaces and fore-

---

* Donatus I. Nwoga has further noted: "many of these printing firms are staffed with compositors so poorly educated that they produce spellings so extraordinary that a reader has to work to extract the writer's words." ("Onitsha Market Literature," *Transition,* No. 19 (1965), 26–27.)

words clearly indicates that much of this fictional writing is designed to serve a specific function, that is, as a lesson on life. Indeed, one may go so far as to say that the tendency toward the didactic is one of the most marked traits of Onitsha fiction. The antecedents of this tendency should probably be traced not solely to the Victorian novel (standard fare for students in Nigerian schools until a few years ago) and the differing moral system introduced by the West, but no doubt also back to oral literature and its basic educative values. In traditional Ibo society, and I dare say in most traditional African societies, since there was no written codification of laws, written history of the clan, or written forms of etiquette, it was logical that the lesson or moral of the oral tale would be functional. We have already noted Ekwefi's tale to her daughter, Ezinma, in Achebe's *Things Fall Apart* and the moral tag with which it ends.[4] As Robert Scholes and Robert Kellog have written in *The Nature of Narrative,* "When an oral tradition is driven 'underground' by a dominant written literature, it will naturally reflect the intellectual, esthetic, and social experience of those among whom it flourishes."[5] The functional tendency of a great amount of African oral literature (folklore and mythology in a larger sense) appears, then, to be an obvious antecedent of the didacticism encountered in the Onitsha writers and in the more sophisticated novelists we have already been referring to. Especially with the Onitsha writers catering to the Nigerian who has left the traditional familial ties, it is logical that the new written literature would continue to fulfill some of the same functions as the older unwritten form, namely this tendency to be educative.

Because of their excessive didacticism in fiction dealing with every-day situations in contemporary Africa the Onitsha writers often give the impression of creating eighteenth- or nineteenth-century stories with twentieth-century settings. The result is often a hybrid literature which reads as if it were a retelling of Samuel Richardson's *Pamela* in Africa, or in some cases—when the heroine bends to the wishes of her pursuers—of Moll Flanders in West Africa. Yet the moral is almost always there, frequently reiterated throughout the entire novel, for as Nwoga has written, ". . . these authors are trying to teach people to live a more moral life" (p.27). I cannot stress too strongly that this "moral life" is often one imported from the West, often contradictory to African tradition, yet understandable because of the great flux in this type of African society. The result is that the writer of an Onitsha potboiler almost always spells out his moral for his reader in one way or another, but it is a moral which often seems inconsistent with African life. The introduction to *The Sorrows of Love*, by Thomas Iguh, states, for example, "This Novel . . . is designed to serve as a lesson to some of our young boys and girls who feel that there is another heaven in the game of love." [6] And, then, just in case the reader has missed all the clues along the way, Iguh informs his reader on the last page of his novel:

> Dear readers just immagine what the feeling of Mr. Okolo and his wife would be. They laboured for more than twenty-years before God gave them Christopher as their only son and then see for your selves how Christopher dissappointed them. If he had heeded his father's advice, he could not have died from the hands of girls. (p.40)

J. U. Tagbo Nzeako ends his novella, *Rose Darling in the Garden of Love*, in a similar manner. The last chapter reads as follows:

> Rose's life was a marvellous example of a lost life, characteristic of a meretrix. Her jealous, amorous and unsteady character, coalesced to epitomize the character inherent in the generation that produced her. This is proved by the fact that her toothless mother, as old as she was, the winds of summer still stirred in her romantic soul; and she fell romantically in love with a young man of slender build, whose age was her grandson's.
> Rose, whom scores and hundreds of different lovers danced in the ballroom of her hungry, romantic heart, died alone in

complete desolation; no one to kiss her drying lips, none to embrace her for the last and the worst of it all, none to do her that last honour usual to the departing.

Her inevitable doom, on the other hand, was typical of Heaven's final punishment to those in the shoes of Rose Darling, as the deceiver must never go undeceived.[7]

The central concern of this novel, as in so many others of the Onitsha school, is based on a new attitude toward marriage —love, instead of marriage-by-arrangement for procreation of the race. The "new" African rebels against the older, traditional attitudes toward marriage and bases his courtship now on love which at the same time often leads to isolation of one kind or another. It is impossible, however, to illustrate the Onitsha school of writing without examining one or two of these works in greater detail. Our first example is a work called *Mabel the Sweet Honey*, a best-seller among secondary school students in the mid-1960's.

Mabel the Sweet Honey (a seventy-page novella by a writer who uses the pen name, Speedy Eric), is subtitled *That Poured Away* and the cover blurb, under the picture of a curvaceous Caucasian girl in a low-cut dress,* reads as follows: "Her Skin would make your blood flow in the wrong direction. She was so sweet and sexy, knew how to romance. She married at sixteen. But she wanted more fun. Yet it ended at seventeen. And what an-end? So thrilling."

The setting of the novel is Onitsha—the setting for so many of the writings by the Onitsha authors. (Anthropologists

---

* It has been argued that the characters and situations in Onitsha fiction are not African at all but the writer's attempt to conceptualize Western life. This belief was expressed during a panel on African writing at the African Studies Association Convention in Los Angeles in 1967, the specific argument being that Caucasians are often pictured on the covers of Onitsha publications. The explanation is a little less complex. A close examination of these pictures will reveal that many of the "Europeans" are wearing elaborately knitted sweaters. Somehow the printing mats for a sweater catalog reached an Onitsha printer, and this accounts for their frequency.

and sociologists have had a field day studying the Onitsha writers; and the local color in the novels makes them especially appealing to the Nigerian reader who is already familiar with the locale described in the works.) Chapter One, entitled, "A look at a girl's skin," begins as follows:

> Have you ever looked at a girls' skin and felt that if you pinched her she would shed blood. A skin as smooth as glass and also round and plumpy. No trace of nerves or bones on the skin.
>
> Add to these an underformed and elegant structure, hips that would raise temperature of every full-blooded young man, an oval face, full lips, high cheek bones a pointed nose; black eye lashes under pencilled eye-brows within which you have two sparkling eyes, set a bit deep in the eye sockets.
>
> And when the sugary lips open there are two rows of equal and well-sized teeth. Can your imagination travel and gather all these qualities and then combine them at one place? Then you have a picture of Mabel. The picture of seventeen years-old Mabel. The daughter of Mrs. Helen Ojina from Orlu town. Mr. Ojina unfortunately had died in a car crash when Mabel was eleven. The family then were living at Onitsha in a two-storey plot of Mr. Ojina. After the death of Mr. Ojina, Helen and her daughter gave up the whole rooms to tenants and took up a bungalow at Moore Street. Helen being a very good cook decided to convert the whole bungalow into an eating house with Mabel to help her.[8]

After this brief introduction, the "novel" jumps back several years to the opening of the eating establishment when Mabel is eleven, waiting on tables. The reader is also introduced to Margie, a somewhat older and more sophisticated girl who waits on tables in Mrs. Helen's hotel/restaurant. It is Margie who introduces Mabel to the wages of sin. In a number of voyeuristic scenes, Mabel (also the reader) watches Margie and her boyfriends romping in an upstairs bedroom. Of the two, our author tells us in a tone which is evident throughout the entire novel, "One may say that Margie was corrupting her [Mabel] but one thing is certain—she is predisposed for corruption. She had an unhealthy desire for sexual matters" (p.23). Ergo, sex has become something other than procreation—enjoyment—and enjoyment, under the newly imposed Puritan morality, is, of course, bad. In scene after scene, Margie sneaks off with her lovers to the upstairs bedroom. And Mabel watches.

Repeatedly, our author tells us that Mabel is being exposed to a world of degradation and inevitable doom. There are frequent asides to the reader, such as, "We Shall See What Mabel Did In Her Own Case. Read On, Dear" (p.20). And shortly thereafter, "Dear reader you watch for yourself how the only daughter of Mrs. Helen (or even the only child) is drifting slowly to her ruin" (p.23). And the plot thickens —again because of Margie's bad company. When Mabel asks Margie why she does not get pregnant, Margie tells her about contraceptives, and later, in a scene where she is about to run upstairs to one of her boyfriends, Margie says, swallowing the pills, " 'For two hours from now . . . I am entirely free from pregnancy. I can even be taking the thing for twenty times' " (p.31). Onitsha fiction is always long on action and short on character development; though there is rarely a lessening of tension, the characters tend to remain pretty much the same throughout the narratives.

For a time, Mabel remains true to Richardsonian virtue. Yet the pressures become overpowering. She is frequently tempted to alter her way of life. In one such garbled incident, the author tells us, "The man gave her no time to think but caught her by the waist and placed her on his laps" (p.36). But in the nick of time—rather reminiscent of heroines in Gothic novels—Mabel escapes her tormentor's evil designs. Needless to say, Mabel is becoming more and more attractive.

She was just fourteen and half years. But she was real sweet honey. The mere looking at her would hold up the flow of your blood for sixty seconds. Mabel had become aware of her power over men. And when ever somebody looked steadily

at her she would blink and make such soft eyes that your tem-
perature would speed up to hundred degrees farenhiet.
(pp.37–38)

And then another attempted seduction.

Finally, Mabel's resistance becomes considerably lowered.
She is attracted to a young man named Gilbert, who almost
succeeds in seducing her—but Margie walks in the room and
interrupts the two young lovers. Later the same day, however,
Gilbert sends Mabel a love letter:

> MY SWEET HONEY,
> No tongue can speak What I have suffered this afternoon.
> Despite the fact that we were disturbed, the way you de-
> layed and teased me, while I suffered and burned like a flame
> inside me, it was so painful. Oh! I don't think I can forgive you.
> Look, I promise you everything you can choose to ask of
> me. Even I will give my life willingly, provided you first let
> me in before I die. What are you afraid of? I have sworn that
> you won't have any trouble.
> Please my honey, I am coming down there by seven this
> evening and as your mother is away we can go out and see a
> picture or go to another hotel or even walk about and back.
> *Please reply this letter through the bearer.*
> *I am longing terribly for you,*
> GILBERT.   (p.43)

The use of letters in Onitsha fiction is extemely common, with
some narratives structured almost entirely on the events revealed therein. The epistolary form is, no doubt, again instruc-
tional and related to the great number of Onitsha chapbooks
which are nothing but letter-writing guides. This technique is
also reminiscent of the eighteenth-century novel.

The same night that Mabel's mother is away from Onitsha,
Mabel and Gilbert go out on the town. First to a movie, *Rock
Pretty Baby,* and then Gilbert takes Mabel to his room where
there will be no interruptions (except the moralizing of the
author), and Mabel is unable to fight him off:

> But he carried her, fighting, into his bed, and there too he
> had more trouble. The real trouble in breaking a virgin.

Look dear reader, for the sake of my mother and father who may come across this book, I am ashamed to tell you the rest of how Gil overcame the second part of this trouble. Imagine it for yourself. But I must tell you this, He did overcome it, but his body was covered with sweat and he was breathing as if he had done a cross-country run. But Mabel too, how she screamed at one point! (pp.48–49)

From here on until the end of the novel (twenty more pages) Mabel's life—our author would have us believe—is one downhill slide. Mabel, prodded by her mother, marries Gilbert but "the romance did not last long on Mabel's side. After the first month the insatiable taste for man in her was beginning to show" (p.58). Mabel goes to visit her mother for a few days, and Speedy Eric tells us, "This was the begining of the END. Mabel came home not just to see her mother. She wanted her liberty. Liberty to live and enjoy herself to the full. She wanted a change of man" (p.59). Her life becomes one of promiscuity: "there were a handful of other men who she had made romance with. Her purse was increasing day by day. She had more clothes than she could ever wear. She got to know many of the best hotels in the township. She had learnt how to dance very well and was a regular picture-goer" (p.63). A remark that Ulli Beier has made about Onitsha writing is particularly apt here: "The subject matter of these novels and plays can best be described with the West African term 'Highlife'. Highlife is a reaction against the austerity of traditional African life." [9] Again and again in Onitsha fiction, youth rebels against traditional values.

One night, when Gil returns to Mrs. Helen's hotel, he catches Mabel sleeping with another man. This is, of course, the end of their marriage. Shortly thereafter, Mabel leaves Onitsha for Port Harcourt, on the southern coast of Eastern Nigeria, where she continues her carefree life:

She lasted only three months at Palace Hotel. But within that three months many young men had left the town unable to continue their business, having been sucked to the bare-bone by

Mabel. Others were owing so much money which would take them more than a whole year to pay.

How did the sweet honey pour away? Within two months of her arrival in Port Harcourt Mabel found out that she was to expect a baby in the next six months. (p.69)

By now, of course, the reader realizes that Mabel has to pay the price for her life of degradation. She decides to kill the child, and, in an ending which should be a warning to all young Nigerian girls, Speedy Eric quickly brings Mabel's life to a gruesome conclusion:

She took her contraceptives and in overdose too. The next day the result came. In the middle of the day the arbotion took place, but a hell of blood followed.

There was no mother or sister to help. No friend like Margie to come and carry her to the hospital. No one even took notice of her agony. She was in the lavatory. From eleven a.m. she began to have the colie aches and went into the lavatory.

There she wriggled and moaned in pain. The rest of the outside world went on moving without ever feeling that something had missed. At the Palace Hotel music was going on merrily in the bar up at the third floor.

Inside the lavatory our seveen years old sweet honey was pouring away. The agony lasted from that eleven a.m. till four thirty p.m. Mabel prayed and moaned. For the first time in the life she asked for forgiveness of her sin from God. She knew she had a patron saint, she prayed and prayed.

The blood flowed freely unchecked. by about four thirty to last drop that held her together flowed away. And she colapsed and died. END. (pp.69–70)

So how are we to interpret Onitsha fiction? Perhaps by looking at a work from a totally different culture, we can arrive at a comparative understanding of the significance and defining characteristics of Speedy Eric's novella:

The subject matter is supplied by scenes of love and family life in which now the erotic, now the sentimental is more strongly emphasized, but in which neither element is rarely completely absent. When the occasion permits, clothes, utensils, furnishings are described or evoked with . . . meticulousness and great delight in movement and color. . . . Secondary characters from all classes, commercial transactions, and a variety of pictures of contemporary culture in general are woven into the action . . . for we hear a great deal about money . . . there is realism everywhere. On the other hand the author wants us to take his story seriously; he endeavors to make it in the highest degree moral and tragic. As for its moral aspcts, we hear a great deal about honor and virtue. [The heroine's] nature is such that she loves pleasure above everything.[10]

With scarcely any modification these comments about a Western novel from Erich Auerbach's *Mimesis* apply to the social and erotic situations developed in *Mabel the Sweet Honey*. Auerbach is writing specifically about the Abbé Prévost's novel, *Manon Lescaut*, which was published in 1731, yet with few exceptions his comments are applicable to the subject matter of a vast amount of Onitsha fiction. The sentimental and the erotic are both highly important in *Mabel the Sweet Honey* with many scenes in the story bordering on pure titillation. The comment that Auerbach makes about Manon and the Chevalier could easily be applied to the initial scenes between Mabel and Gilbert:

The pleasure which the author endeavors to evoke in his readers by his representation of his lover's childishly playful and un-principled corruption, is in the last analysis a sexual titillation, which is constantly interpreted in sentimental and ethical terms while the warmth it evokes is abused to produce a sentimental ethics. (p.401)

Mabel's concern with money and new clothes becomes increasingly important as she begins to realize the benefits of complete economic independence—obviously something new in African life where women have traditionally been dependent on men. And how does Mabel achieve this independence? Just like Manon, by being good in bed. As our author tells us, "Others were owing so much money which would take them more than a whole year to pay" (p.69). And there is realism and local color—Onitsha and Port Harcourt—everywhere. Again, a quotation from *Mimesis* on *Manon* illuminates Speedy Eric's novel:

> The increasingly bourgeois cast of society, the stability of po-
> litical and economic conditions, the settled security of life in
> the intermediate and well-to-do strata of society, the conse-
> quent absence of professional and political worry for the young-
> er generation in those strata—all this contributed to the devel-
> opment of the moral and aesthetic forms which can be gathered
> from our text and from many similar ones. . . . The realistic
> representation is colorful, varied, lively, and graphic, there is no
> lack of portrayals of the basest vice. . . . The social milieu is
> an established frame of reference, which is accepted as it hap-
> pens to be. (p.401)

The career of at least one writer who started publishing in Onitsha has expanded beyond that publishing locale. The writer is Cyprian Ekwensi, who many people feel—in spite of his later publications—has not "developed" beyond the rather sensational and melodramatic tendencies which typify so many of the Onitsha novelists. Undoubtedly, Ekwensi's popu-larity within his own country is due in large part to his Onitsha origins, and it is probably a safe generalization that many of Ekwensi's earliest readers have followed his rather precarious literary career as, in turn, their own reading tastes and skills have carried them to the more lengthy narrative, yet one still rooted in the action-packed Onitsha formula. Ekwensi is probably the most widely-read novelist in Nigeria —perhaps even in West Africa—by readers whose literary tastes have not been exposed to the more complex writings of Chinua Achebe and other more skilled African novelists.

Ekwensi's first published work, *When Love Whispers*, ap-peared in Onitsha in 1947. On the second page of the Amer-ican edition of *Jagua Nana* (originally published in England in 1961, but in the United States not until 1969), Ekwensi has listed his complete works, beginning with *When Love*

Whispers. The nineteen titles on this page easily make him the most prolific writer living in tropical Africa today, although seven of these works, including *When Love Whispers*, are called "novellas," four are referred to as "folklore," two are collections of short stories, leaving only six as full-length works. However, the sheer quantity of Ekwensi's work can in no way be equated to, say, the consistent level of achievement of another Nigerian writer, Wole Soyinka, whose literary career not only extends over the genres of drama, fiction, and poetry, but illustrates an excellence unattained by any other living African writer.

Ekwensi's early *When Love Whispers* is, in retrospect, a significant document because of the light it sheds on almost all of his later work, for Ekwensi has never really stepped beyond the pulp fiction level that thousands of his African readers yearn for. Ekwensi's popular success is, in this essence, comparable to the successes of a number of contemporary American writers—Irving Wallace, Harold Robbins, even Frank Yerby—who produce formula fiction for a large indiscriminate reading audience desiring a little variety in their lives. Sex, violence and brutality, mystery and intrigue, and a glorification of African women are dominant themes in almost all of Ekwensi's books—all present in *When Love Whispers.* Of these various themes, it is undoubtedly the first and the last that distinguish Ekwensi from most of his fellow African novelists, for, except for the Onitsha writers, the erotic or even the theme of masculine/feminine love is generally missing from African fiction. Most of the time African writers, because of the different concept of love and marriage in African societies, have not written stories whose plots depend on these matters. Of the first generation African novelists, Ekwensi is the only consistent exception, and his concept of the novel is that of the true romance or quasi-confessional.

One distinction which marks Ekwensi from his fellow Onitsha writers is his usual avoidance of the tragic ending, in spite of the fact that his novels are generally concerned with women of questionable character. Ekwensi simply cannot work himself up to killing off his heroines or punishing them as in the manner, say, of a Speedy Eric. He is too fascinated by his heroines to do this, and thus not only do Ekwensi's Pamelas quickly fall into the Moll Flanders category, but they keep to the Moll Flanders pattern: although they may have sinned, usually they do not get hurt too much because they reform before it is too late. Ashoka in *When Love Whispers* is exactly this kind of character: Pamela to Moll Flanders to quasi-happy ending.

When Love Whispers begins *in medias res.* Ashoka is already in love with John Ike and it is her father (as in so much Onitsha writing) who attempts to thwart her desires by marrying her off to the security and prestige of an older man, in this case (again, consistent with the Onitsha pattern), the local chief, a representative, of course, of the older generation. Ashoka's father tells her when he learns of her growing predilection for John Ike,

> "You can not marry him. He has no wealth, no position. He is merely deceiving you. You'll soon forget him. Look here my daughter, you must be careful about these young men and their tongues. It isn't everybody who tells you he's going to marry you that will actually marry you." [11]

The story begins with the love of Ashoka and John already established, and the additional conflict developing from John's departure for England for further studies.

At this early stage of Ekwensi's story, the reader is led to believe that Ashoka, who teaches at a Catholic girls' school in Lagos, is pure and virtuous—the innocent Pamela. Hardly has John Ike left, however, before Ashoka is pursued in much the same manner as her eighteenth-century English counterpart. First, Ashoka is told to move out of the household of her sister and brother-in-law because of the latter's claim that Ashoka is a corrupting influence on their marriage. Then because of a misunderstanding, Ashoka is chastised by a Priest for going to a night club, resulting in her quitting her teaching position at the "convent." From here on to the end, much like *Mabel the Sweet Honey*, Ashoka's story is another progression downward.

First, she is abducted by the villain, Mr. Williams, who in spite of his name is African. (All the evil-intending men in the novella have Western names whether they are Africans or Europeans.) Williams intends to sell Ashoka to a white slaver named Steiner (who is European), but in the nick of time, after a frantic pursuit, Ashoka escapes her pursuers. Ekwensi, like the other Onitsha writers, injects frequent moralisms into his narrative. Of Williams' apartment, for example, he says:

> Rare works of art hung from the walls. But they were of such a vulgar type, that it was easy to assess the mentality of the owner. Women bathing by the pools, women looking at the reflections of their nude forms in mirrors: all the pictures showed nude women doing quite ordinary things. (p.21)

Thought of in terms of traditional African life—where there was no taboo against nudity—this passage seems completely out of place, and we are again led to believe that didacticism in Onitsha writing is a combination of both Christian qua Victorian morality, totally incongruous to African life, and the traditions of oral literature and their characteristic pattern toward the educative.

The setting of Ekwensi's novella, up until the time of Ashoka's escape from Williams and Steiner, has been Lagos, as the corruptions of urban life have always intrigued Ekwensi and his fellow pamphleteers. Yet, once Ashoka realizes she is living in a city of sin where no good can possibly come to her, she flees back to her father's village, where the theme of the younger generation in conflict with traditional authority again rises to the surface. The Oba (the chief) renews his offers of marriage. Ashoka's father asks her,

"Have you changed your mind about the Oba yet?"

"I haven't," she said. "I don't want to marry him."

"He still wants you as his wife. You'll be happy with him. There'll be little to do, you'll have a big name; your mother will be very proud of you: the Oba's wife." (p.31)

Love is more important to Ashoka than the traditional means of security. Additional conflict—there is rarely a lack of conflict in Onitsha fiction—soon develops when a third man, Olu Tayo, also expresses his affections for Ashoka. Nevertheless, Ashoka asserts her desire to remain faithful to John Ike. Or so the reader believes until Ekwensi reveals that Ashoka, as the result of a weak moment, is expecting a child by Olu Tayo. But then in an unpredictable twist, Tayo, out of respect for his best friend (John Ike), tells Ashoka that he cannot marry her.

Ashoka, like Mabel, attempts to abort the child she is carrying, but at this juncture Ekwensi breaks away from the typical pattern and tells us that she is not successful. The medicine makes her ill, but she does not lose the child. In an ending which thus unites the older generation with the younger, Ekwensi marries her off to the Oba, who says, " 'Does that matter? I'm a modern Oba. And the daughter: who will ever argue about her? Women do not rule in this country' " (p.41). Ashoka replies, " 'Please give me time to recover . . . I have suffered much' " (p.41). Yet, her suffering is not so severe: "On her wedding day, she was in velvet and gold trinkets, and the Oba made a great show of her. For Ashoka was beginning to bloom again, though there was always a sadness in her eyes now, and she was often silent" (pp.41–42).

Ashoka's daughter is followed eventually by a son—an heir for the Oba—"a successor to his chieftaincy" (p.42), and one fine day, when John Ike returns from his studies in England and visits Ashoka, she tells him—in an ending rather reminiscent of Rousseau's *La Nouvelle Héloïse*—" 'John, please go. Go before you wake up my love for you: it is dead

now. Love has no part in my life now. Only duty'" (p.43).
Ekwensi further spells out his moral on the last page of his
novel—duty to one's elders, trust in God.

> She took her daughter's hand, and together they went into
> the bedroom. After all, she thought, it is all over. John has kept
> his word; he still loves me. But God knows how he arranges
> His things. In many ways I am happy. (p.44)

For Ekwensi, at least, the new Pamela may lose her virtue,
but the traditional attitudes toward the value of children are
still strong enough to win in the long run; and the Oba—who
says he is modern—is, more accurately, traditional.

The pattern of Ekwensi's later novel, *Jagua Nana,** is
much the same, and, if anything, more unbelievable, more
fantastic because, by the time Ekwensi wrote this notorious
work, he was able to punish his heroine even less than Ashoka
in *When Love Whispers*. The setting of *Jagua Nana* is, again,
mostly limited to Lagos—that Nigerian capital of sin, or so
Ekwensi would have us believe. The throb of the city is
apparent through most of the book—the reader is constantly being bombarded by sensations of the city's pulse:
prostitution, night clubs, politics, the Lagos underworld—all
contribute their effect so strongly that the end result is a
book which has more often delighted sociologists and anthropologists than literary critics. Nevertheless, the total effect
is a vivid picture of West African realism, circa 1960.

The plot of *Jagua Nana* is almost the same as that of *When
Love Whispers*, except that Ekwensi's heroine, Jagua Nana, is
already a fallen woman by the time the narrative begins. Fallen
may be an understatement, for Jagua is a forty-five-year-old
prostitute, and it is probably her age which stretches the
credibility of the non-African reader more than anything else.
(Not so the African reader, however.) Jagua's nightly haunt

---

* Ekwensi's intention was not to allude to Zola's *Nana* but rather to the
expensive British automobile.

is the Tropicana, and with almost predictable regularity, Ekwensi brings his story back to this throbbing night club. An early description of the women who ply their trade at the Tropicana sets the tone for his story:

> All the women wore dresses which were definitely undersize, so that buttocks and breasts jutted grotesquely above the general contours of the bodies. At the same time the midriffs shrunk to suffocation. A dress succeeded if it made men's eyes ogle hungrily in this modern super sex-market. The dancers occupied a tiny floor, unlighted, so that they became silhouetted bodies without faces and the most unathletic man could be drawn out to attempt the improvisation which went by the name *High-life*.[12]

Ekwenski's obsession with bodies, and especially breasts, becomes apparent to the reader in almost every chapter of the novel. Again and again, I dare say at least fifty times, Ekwensi describes Jagua's remarkably preserved body, dwelling on her breasts. Indeed, Jagua spends much of her time sitting in front of a mirror, adoring herself.

The conflict—what little there is, since, for the most part *Jagua Nana* is a picaresque tale—revolves around Jagua's many affairs, the most important being her on-again, off-again affair with Freddie Namme, a young man twenty years her junior. Like John Ike in *When Love Whispers*, Freddie Namme goes to England to further his education, not without, however, falling under Jagua's magic spell: "He was sinking into the soft abyss of this erotic woman" (p.51). Ekwensi's prose, at its best, is grade *B* true-confessions style. When Freddie falls for the much younger Nancy Oll, Ekwensi informs his reader: "They had been good friends but now, with this new taste of Nancy on his lips, Freddie felt fortified to face Jagua's possessive love for him" (p.22).

During the eighteen months when Freddie is in England studying law—without the separation of lovers there would probably be no Onitsha fiction—Jagua has a number of affairs with a series of other men, including an idyllic relationship with Chief Ofubara, which results in the improbable substory of Jagua's settling a royalty dispute between the two villages which have split from Freddie Namme's extended family. The scene temporarily takes us away from Lagos, as does an even briefer incident which follows and shows us Jagua's failure to become a "Merchant Priestess" in the Onitsha market, failure because of the lack of money. When Jagua returns to Lagos, however, the pace rapidly quickens to such an extent that *Jagua Nana* reminds the reader a little too much of serialized fiction: there is always another temporary problem to be overcome, always something new for the reader and Jagua to be exposed to.

In a brief encounter with Dennis Odoma, Jagua and the reader are given a glimpse of Lagos underground life: gangsters and thieves. Ekwensi follows this subplot with Jagua's affair with Uncle Taiwo, Secretary of O. P. #2, and the topic of the novel for a time is politics. Specifically, corrupt politics, for by this time Freddie has returned to Lagos—married to Nancy Oll—and become Uncle Taiwo's opponent for a seat on the Lagos Council from the Obanta constituency. Freddie gets roughed up by Uncle Taiwo's henchmen, however, and dies shortly thereafter. As a result, Uncle Taiwo loses the election.

At this stage, Ekwensi appears to run out of steam. Even Jagua—whose thoughts up to now have mostly been concerned with the genital urge—realizes that life in Lagos has not been quite as fulfilling as she expected. What to do? Ekwensi drags his heroine back to the village of her birth, Ogabu, for her father's funeral, and in an explanation to the reader, just as in *When Love Whispers*, Ekwensi brings up the problem of duty:

> She had become housekeeper to the family, and more important still, custodian of her mother's will to go on living. Her duty was to look after the property, to avoid marriage, for that would

take her away from home and mother. If any children came to her through casual love affairs she must bear them and they would simply become part of the household. She was still free, but in a new and penitent way. So her brothers had decided at the family meeting before they all dispersed and so it must be. She must suffer in silence. (pp.193–194)

However, Ekwensi cannot bear to see his heroine waste away in Ogabu, and once she has suffered enough for her sins, he alters Jagua's life of boredom to one of stability and implied success. First, however, Jagua gets pregnant—in spite of her near fifty years—but the satisfaction from her casual affair and the birth of a son is short-lived. The child dies within a matter of days. But Ekwensi still has one trick in his bag, or, more specifically, in Uncle Taiwo's bag, for the evening that Uncle Taiwo lost the election, he had entrusted a suitcase to Jagua, a suitcase she has believed is filled with party documents. When she opens it, months after her return to Ogabu, Jagua discovers that it is filled with money— £5000—and the novel ends with Jagua on the brink of a new career: " 'I wan' to become proper Merchant Priestess. I goin' to buy me own shop, and lorry, and employ me own driver. I goin' to face dis business serious. I sure dat God above goin' to bless me' " (p.207).

If the ending of *Jagua Nana* is a little less didactic than Ekwensi's earlier novella, *When Love Whispers*, or other Onitsha novels, one only has to remember that Ekwensi has balanced Jagua's carefree life with a center of morality throughout his heroine's adventures. For Jagua knows all along that she is doing wrong, that her life is more or less lived in a vacuum, and it does not take very long for the reader to realize that Jagua's eventual reform is inevitable. Time and again she is thwarted in her plans; all of her affairs in Lagos—with Freddie, Dennis, and Uncle Taiwo—end tragically with their deaths. And Ekwensi's moralizing breaks through in almost every episode of his story. When Freddie catches Jagua procuring, he tells her,

"What you wan' from de worl', Jagua? You jealous, but you no fit to keep one man. You no fit take your eye see money in a man hand. You mus' follow any man who give you money. Whedder he get disease or not. So far as he got money. You mus' go to Tropicana every night. You must feel man body in your belly every night. Any day you don' see anodder man private you sick dat day. If dat be de kin' of life you choose, why you wan' me den?" (p.57)

In another place, Jagua, after she has returned to Ogabu, realizes that Lagos has been only a cul-de-sac out of which it was nearly impossible to escape:

. . . in Lagos MAN was always grappling to master an ENVIRONMENT he had created. It was money, money, yet more money. She did not find the same rush here, the desire to outstrip the other fellow. No time, sorry, too busy, time is short. Time, time. I must go now! . . . None of that here. She was resting. (p.194)

Environment is undoubtedly the key for understanding Ekwensi's work and that of the Onitsha school of pamphleteers, for all of these writers are directly concerned with the lives of characters who have hitherto not experienced urban situations. Local color is their forte, whether it be Ekwensi's city of chaos, Lagos, or Onitsha which is the setting of so many of the "Onitsha" novels; and the Nigerian reader is placed for the first time in a perspective which has been previously unexplored in African fiction. Onitsha writing is clearly popular literature for the masses, and the publications by these authors are literally devoured by an audience starved for material mirroring their own social conditions or personal dreams and fantasies. It is not untypical to see an Onitsha pamphlet literally falling to shreds, having been read by so many readers.

One of the prime reasons for the popularity of the Onitsha

writers has undoubtedly been their depiction of everyday occurrences (real or imagined) in an identifiable contemporary social situation, and their writings are among the best depictions of realism that the African novel has seen to date. As such, in spite of their weaknesses, the Onitsha writings deserve to be considered seriously as examples of literature growing out of a series of parallel social needs and situations: urbanization, increased literacy, economic stability, the liberated African female, the new bourgeoisie world with its new value system—part African, part Western. Perhaps the true value of these works can be explained only by an African literary critic. Summing up the function of Onitsha market writing, Donatus I. Nwoga states,

> . . . these books are significant both as literary efforts and in their revelation of the popular attitudes to socio-cultural phenomena. We have a new life and a new language. In the unassuming simplicity and directness of Onitsha Market Literature we find authentic evidence of what these new elements mean to the common man and what are his reactions to them. (p.33)

4

Time, Space, and Description:

The Tutuolan World

AMOS TUTUOLA'S UNIVERSE IS ALMOST TOTALLY
different from that of the Onitsha pamphleteers. While theirs
is a world of urbanization and neo-realism, Tutuola's is one
of jungle and bush—fantasy, supernaturalism, and surrealism.
Whereas the Onitsha writers as a group regularly break almost every grammatical rule in the English language,
Tutuola's private idiom is almost uniquely his own—sometimes heard in West African English but rarely duplicated by
any other African writers. We have already examined the
initial reactions to this idiom, noting Gerald Moore's comment
that Tutuola's style is a kind of quasi-cultural cul-de-sac. It
is easy to conclude that Tutuola's novels would be impossible
to translate into other languages, yet Tutuola's works have
been successfully translated into French, Italian, German, and
many other languages; [1] and Tutuola's writings have led to
a score of scholarly articles and at least one book-length
study.[2] One doubts that his Onitsha counterparts will ever
share a similar kind of attention. Whereas the Onitsha school

of writers lean most clearly toward the West, Tutuola in the eyes of many students of African writing remains a "pure" example of contemporary African writing—the African writer par excellence—the only original African talent, almost totally uninfluenced by the West. No doubt these admirers of his work have come to this conclusion because of his clear relation to the oral tradition, myth, and archetype.

The oral tradition is an integral part of every work by Amos Tutuola, and it is exactly this reliance on the traditional tale which is anathema to many of Tutuola's readers, for he is not the kind of writer one is likely to have mixed opinions about. One either likes him or one does not. One either reads *The Palm-Wine Drinkard* totally enraptured by Tutuola's inventive genius or, as too many people have told me, one quickly places the book aside after reading a few brief pages. Nor is Tutuola the type of writer that the average reader returns to again and again, and I doubt if more than a handful of people have read through his collected works. In any case, it must be admitted that Tutuola is first and foremost a storyteller—the major similarity he shares with his Onitsha contemporaries, for both are a link between traditional and modern African literature. In Tutuola's case, however, the story is not formula fiction but a highly skilled weaving of material from Yoruba culture—filtered through Tutuola's neverflagging imagination and reshaped in a narrative form often more closely related to the medieval quest or voyage narrative, *Gulliver's Travels*, *Pilgrim's Progress*, or, more recently, Nathanael West's *The Dream World of Balso Snell*, Céline's *Journey to the End of the Night*, or Kafka's *The Castle*. As with these later works, it is the psychological implications of Tutuola's world that many readers find so enthralling, his personal groping toward an understanding of man's relationship to the external world and the spirit world—the ontological gap. As Margaret Laurence has written in her book on Nigerian literature, Tutuola writes best when most intuitively and most intensely inward. His forests are certainly and in detail the outer ones but they are, as well, the forests of the mind, where the individual meets and grapples with the creatures of his own imagination. These creatures are aspects of himself, aspects of his response to the world into which he was born, the world to which he must continue to return if he is to live as a man.[3]

In Tutuola, West African "experimentation" in prose fiction reaches its zenith, for the oral tradition which he uses is more specifically a private mythology where daring tricks and innovations in time, space, and description—no doubt at times unintentionally—attain a level which makes them almost pure examples of surrealism. This surrealism is indigenous or even spontaneous—not based on Tutuola's knowledge of the French surrealist movement. However, Tutuola's remarks about the brief amount of time he spends writing a novel suggest something akin to André Breton's theory of automatic writing: ". . . an attempt . . . to express, either verbally, in writing or in any other manner, the true functioning of thought. The dictation of thought, in the absence of all control by the reason, excluding any aesthetic or moral preoccupation." [4] Except for the last comment about the "moral preoccupation," this definition characterizes Tutuola's writing quite patly.

Outwardly, like parts of Achebe's *Things Fall Apart,* Tutuola's *Palm-Wine Drinkard* is fragmented and shaped by many short and often apparently unrelated tales and incidents. Like Ekwensi's *Jagua Nana,* Tutuola takes his main character through a series of picaresque-like incidents and events. Thematically, there is the outer quest of the Drinkard in search of his lost palm-wine Tapster; inwardly this is paralleled by the voyage toward an understanding of the ontological gap—the relationship of man to his surrounding, his environment, the universe in which he lives. It is this essence of the voyage or inner journey of the Drinkard which makes it tempting to relate Tutuola's narrative to the symbolist and surrealistic writing of the early part of this century, and a case could be made for Tutuola's writing as an almost ideal marriage of the symbolist archetype of the dream, the subconscious, the super-ego. It must be acknowledged, too, that the non-African reader is often at a disadvantage in understanding many of the subtle nuances, private referents, and ethnic myths in Tutuola's writing. But also the reactions of his fellow Nigerians—including Yorubas—indicate that even being a Yoruba might not automatically lead to a full understanding of Tutuola's private world, in spite of the fact that a Yoruba student once told me that he had heard many of the tales and separate events in *The Palm-Wine Drinkard* as a child. Like all good storytellers, Tutuola makes up many of the incidents or substories in his novels, especially when he cannot find something suitable from his reserve of Yoruba folklore.

The basic narrative of the *Drinkard* is simple enough: the Drinkard's search for his dead palm-wine Tapster. The story is told in the first person, yet by a first person narrator endowed with certain omniscient powers rarely encountered in Western fiction. In almost every episode, the Drinkard is faced with a test of one sort or another, often a trick which he must identify and then overcome if he is to survive the macabre intentions of the many creatures he encounters. There are roughly a dozen such events or substories within the narrative, and dozens of briefer incidents, told in a page or two or even less, wherein the Drinkard must overcome some opponent or obstacle. A brief analysis of the first two or three of these will be helpful for an understanding of our later analysis of Tutuola's indigenous experimentation.

The opening paragraphs, which develop the initial conflict, have already been quoted: the Drinkard's loss of his Tapster who had tapped palm-wine for him for fifteen years.

Shortly thereafter, the Drinkard tells us, "I took all my native juju [supernatural powers] and also my father's juju with me and I left my father's hometown to find out whereabouts was my tapster who had died." [5] Seven months later, the Drinkard encounters an old man ("this old man was not a really man, he was a god") (p.10) who puts the Drinkard (who was also "a god and juju-man") (p.10) to a test. The old man asks the Drinkard to bring back an unnamed object from a blacksmith in another town. After turning himself into a bird, with the aid of his juju, the Drinkard learns that the object is a bell, which he brings to the old man, but as in so many occasions in the story, the antagonist does not fulfill his promise; he does not tell the Drinkard where he can find his dead Tapster. Instead, he puts the Drinkard to a second test: "He told me to go and bring 'Death' from his house with [a] net" (p.11). Again, the Drinkard succeeds, though the old man's intentions are that the Drinkard will be killed, and as a result the old man becomes a partial victim of his own evil intentions. The end unit, which concludes this episode in the narration—without the Drinkard's learning the whereabouts of his Tapster —is similar to the type we have already noted in many of the substories in Achebe's *Things Fall Apart:* "So that since the day that I had brought Death out from his house, he has no permanent place to dwell or stay, and we are hearing his name about in the world" (p.16). Like Achebe, Tutuola has included in his narrative a complete oral tale, and his transition to the next incident takes us back again to the quest nature of his story: "Then I left the town without knowing where my tapster was, and I started another fresh journey" (p.16).

The second major episode in the Drinkard's search for his dead Tapster is more fruitful. The incident—which is frequently referred to as the "Complete Gentleman" story—is also one of the most widely known passages in Tutuola's writings, and variants of the tale in other African ethnic groups attest to the permeation of folktales from culture to culture.* This time, however, the tale more directly involves someone other than the Drinkard himself—the young woman who will later be his wife. In his peregrinations, the Drinkard meets another man who informs him that he will tell him where he can find his dead Tapster. But first the Drinkard must prove his worth and rescue the man's daughter, a young woman who refused to marry the man her father desired that she wed. Instead, the young woman (unnamed) followed a "beautiful 'complete' gentleman" from the market into an endless forest.

It is at this juncture in the narrative that Tutuola gives the Drinkard total omniscience about the young woman's fate, and the woman's story is related from several different time periods. As the Complete Gentleman made his way toward his home, he returned each part of his body (feet, belly, ribs, chest, arms, and neck) to the various people from whom he had rented them. At last he was reduced to a skull, and the young woman became his prisoner. The Drinkard, with the aid of his magic juju, later rescues the woman from her captor, and after he returns her to her father, the old man bestows his daughter on the Drinkard for his accomplishments. "So, I saved the lady from the complete gentleman in the market who afterwards reduced to a 'Skull' and the lady became my wife since that day. This was how I got a wife" (p.31). The conclusion contains the implied moral that the lady would have avoided all her difficulties had she married her father's choice of a suitor in the first place.**

---

* For two other variants see Melville J. and Frances S. Herskovits, *Dahomean Narrative* (Evanston, Illinois: Northwestern University Press, 1958), pp. 243–245. The Herskovitses have titled their version, "The Chosen Suitor." Timothy M. Aluko, who is Yoruba, like Tutuola, has recorded the same basic story in his novel, *One Man, One Matchet* (London: Heinemann Educational Books, 1964), pp. 20–24.

** The moralizing is more overt in both the Herskovits and the Aluko versions. The Herskovitses state, "That is why from that day to this

What is of particular importance in the Complete Gentleman episode is Tutuola's employment of the omniscient first person narrator, for the Drinkard is constantly jumbling up the chronological events in his narration and telling us facts which he as a first person involved narrator could not possibly know. Past, present, and future merge into one time, and the telling of the young woman's plight with the Complete Gentleman defies all normal rules of first person limited narration. The Drinkard tells us at one point,

> After I looked at him for so many hours, then I ran to a corner of the market and I cried for a few minutes because I thought within myself why was I not created with beauty as this gentleman, but when I remembered that he was only a Skull, then I thanked God that He had created me without beauty, so I went back to him in the market, but I was still attracted by his beauty. (p.25)

It would have been impossible for the Drinkard to know at that moment that the Complete Gentleman was only a Skull, because the Drinkard had not yet followed the Complete Gentleman into the forest. Later, after he has followed the Complete Gentleman to his home, the Drinkard discovers that the old man's daughter has a cowrie shell tied around her neck which prohibits her from talking or eating. Two pages later, however, the Drinkard gives her a leaf to eat, and in spite of the fact that she supposedly cannot swallow anything, she does, and is soon able to talk. I do not attribute these two incidents to errors in Tutuola's thinking or inconsistencies in the text (the average reader probably would not even notice their existence). Rather, it seems to me that they typify the protean nature of Tutuola's work, reminiscent of Strindberg's *Dream Play;* for in Tutuola, too, characters

day, one listens to the advice of one's father and mother. It is because of this that a woman takes the husband her father chooses for her." The Aluko version concludes, "Since that day every girl must marry whichever man her parents ask her to marry." Tutuola's version is a little more subtle, working by implications rather than by direct moral comment.

merge into one another, change sex, the dead return to life, time is frequently ignored, slowed down, or speeded up, and only the dream or nightmare pervades.*

In the remaining episodes of *The Palm-Wine Drinkard*, the hero is no longer alone but accompanied by his wife, and many of the incidents directly involve the two of them. After they have been married three years, the Drinkard's wife gives birth to a child—but the child does not come from her womb, but from her thumb, because, as the Drinkard tells us, "she did not conceive in the right part of her body as other women do" (p.32). After they have escaped the tribulations of the Thumb Child, the two of them lead a peaceful existence as farmers on the "Wraith-Island," but their happiness is short-lived and they are almost killed by the evil creatures in the "Unreturnable-Heaven's town." This incident is followed by another period of peace and prosperity under the care of "The Faithful Mother in the White Tree" and three more episodes of strife and turmoil involving the "Red People," a hired laborer called "Give and Take," and a "Wise King in the Wrong Town with the Prince Killer."

Finally, almost four-fifths of the way through the narrative, the Drinkard reaches the "Deads' Town" where he meets his dead Tapster who recounts his version of what happened to him after his fall from the palm tree. In one of the few social comments in the novel, the Drinkard states that his Tapster "told us that both white and black deads were living in the Deads' Town, not a single alive was there at all. Because everything that they were doing there was incorrect to alives and everything that all alives were doing was incorrect to deads too" (p.100). Before the Drinkard returns to the world of the alives, his Tapster gives him a magical egg.

The return trip from the Deads' Town to the Drinkard's

---

* The Drinkard himself, with the aid of his juju, is capable of changing into a lizard, a bird, a canoe, fire and air.

own town is considerably shorter than the original quest, yet it comprises several incidents including an encounter with a "Hungry Creature." When the Drinkard finally arrives home with his wife, they encounter a famine which has been going on for six years. The magical egg feeds all of the Drinkard's townspeople until it is accidentally broken, at which time a sacrifice is made to heaven, and the rain comes and ends the famine: "But when for three months the rain had been falling regularly, there was no famine again" (p.125). With this sentence Tutuola ends his narrative.

It is important to realize that each of the incidents alluded to forms a complete tale, each with its own conflict and solution, testing the ingenuity of the Drinkard and leading him closer to his destination or teaching him something about the people and strange creatures he encounters. Virtually any one of these tales could be extracted from the narrative itself and published as an individual oral tale as an example of traditional Yoruba (albeit Tutuolan) mythology. Some of these tales, as already noted, have appeared in separate collections of African folklore in slightly different versions,[6] and since other people have already interpreted many of these stories,[7] my analysis here is limited to Tutuola's literary techniques alone. It should be noted, first, of the basic narration itself that Tutuola often uses rhetorical questions (like an oral story-teller) to advance his narrative situation and build up tension for a specific event, such as, during the encounter with a half-bodied child, when the Drinkard asks the reader, "Ah! how could we escape from this half-bodied baby?" (p.37). Narrative development also frequently reverts to Tutuola's private mythology, his own private world, as in the following incident:

Then I told my wife to jump on my back with our loads, at the same time, I commanded my juju which was given me by

"Water Spirit woman" in the "Bush of the Ghosts" (the full
story of the "Spirit woman" appeared in the story book of the
Wild Hunter in the Bush of the Ghosts).   (p.40)

The reference in parentheses is to an earlier Tutuola work,
My Life in the Bush of Ghosts (1954), written, but unpublished at the time *The Palm-Wine Drinkard* was published,
nevertheless indicating the wider framework of Tutuola's
world, encompassing all of his works, all of his private dreams.

It is in his use of time that Tutuola differs so widely from
the Western writers with whom he has often been compared
and even from some of his African contemporaries. In *The
Palm-Wine Drinkard*, the reader is always conscious of time,
because Tutuola constantly makes references to hours, days,
weeks and months, even years; * still there is the impression that
many of the events that the Drinkard encounters are beyond
the control of the normal dictates of time. One is reminded that
many years ago Spengler maintained that interest in time is
peculiar to Western civilization. If lack of interest in time
may often be more typical of non-Western cultures, Tutuola
is in many ways a perfect example.

The narrated time of *The Palm-Wine Drinkard* is a little
more than eleven years. The Drinkard himself is approximately
twenty-five years old at the beginning of the story (after being
a palm-wine drinkard for fifteen years.) Although Tutuola's
references to specific periods of time are somewhat inconsistent, he does inform his reader that ten years have passed from
the time the Drinkard begins his search for his Tapster until
the time when he locates him; and the references to blocks of
time add up to a little more than a year for the return journey.
Here alone there appears to be an inconsistency; if the trip to

---

* Numbers tend to be whole units instead of fractions. Time is usually
referred to in complete hours (such as eight o'clock p.m.) rather than
by minutes or portions of hours, as if Tutuola is not quite used to
having to pinpoint exact periods of time.

the Deads' Town takes ten years, why is barely more than a year involved for the return? The answer, however, has nothing to do with space or the actual distance between the Drinkard's own village and the Deads' Town. Rather, time is related to the incidents involved in the Drinkard's going and coming from the Deads' Town and in the relative value of these incidents; and the return, even though it involves only a few pages of the text, seems overdrawn simply because the quest has been for the most part fulfilled.

It may be easier to understand Tutuola's presentation of time by considering his references to temporal factors and their relationship to a more traditional value system. Such an interpretation gives us "evil time" and "good time" and in both categories time may be speeded up or slowed down. Many of the terrible creatures in the *The Palm-Wine Drinkard* exist in a time that is proportional to their function in the novel. Their evil doings are successful because they may be accomplished almost instantaneously. The "Skull" who keeps the Drinkard's future wife as prisoner, for example, "could jump a mile to the second before coming down. He caught the lady in this way: so when the lady was running away for her life, he hastily ran to her front and stopped her as a log of wood" (p.22). Clearly, the Skull catches his victims because he operates in a time different from theirs. The evil child born from the Drinkard's wife's thumb is also at an advantage because of a differing time system. Tutuola tells us,

> . . . the thumb bust out suddenly and there we saw a male child came out of it and at the same time that the child came out from the thumb, he began to talk to us as if he was ten years of age.
> Within the hour that he came down from the thumb he grew up to the height of about three feet and some inches and his voice by that time was as plain as if somebody strikes an anvil with a steel hammer. (pp.31–32)

The Thumb Child's obnoxiousness is indeed related to his rather abrupt growth. Another evil creature encountered in the story is capable of destroying a freshly cleared field in a few minutes: "but before 30 minutes that he was watching the field, he saw a very tiny creature who was just a baby of one day of age and he commanded the weeds to rise up as he was commanding before" (p.50). Tutuola also describes a flock of evil birds whose havoc is due in large part to their suddenness:

> When these birds started to eat the flesh of those animals, within a second there we saw about 50 holes on the bodies of those animals and within a second the animals fell down and died, but when they began to eat the dead bodies it did not last them more than 2 minutes before they finished them (bodies) and as soon as they had eaten that, they would start to chase others about. (p.53)

Closely related to the terrible birds is a creature called "Spirit of Prey" who is capable of eating "off the dead body of [a] buffalo within four minutes . . ." (p.55). In all of these cases, the havoc or evil these creatures are capable of causing is directly proportional to the speed with which they are able to carry out their deeds.

On occasion—and it depends where the Drinkard and his wife are—speeded-up time operates to the advantage of the Drinkard too. In both of the substories of the novel where the Drinkard and his wife encounter no harmful creatures, good time operates quickly to their advantage. During the "Wraith-Island" incident where the Drinkard and his wife become farmers, time is definitely on their side. After the Drinkard plants his crops he tells us,

> to my surprise, these grains and the seeds germinated at once, before 5 minutes they became full grown crops and before 10 minutes again, they had produced fruits and ripened at the same moment too, so I plucked them and went back to the town (the Wraith-Island). (p.48)

Good time also operates in the Faithful Mother's kingdom in the white tree: "within a week that we were living with this mother, we had forgotten all our past torments. . . ." (p.69). The hair on their heads, which had been so brutally scraped off in the Unreturnable-Heaven's town so that their heads were bleeding, returns within a week from the treatment in the Faithful-Mother's hospital. And the magical egg that the Drinkard takes back to his village "produced food and drinks for each of these people, so that everyone of them who had not eaten for a year, ate and drank to his or her satisfaction" (p.121), within a matter of a few brief moments.

It is easy to argue that in many literary works which are outside the bounds of realism—that in all tales and stories, and especially in folklore and mythology—time operates in no logical manner. Tutuola's world is not that simple, however, as his occasional references to time in his own life clearly indicate. In the five-page autobiographical account appended to *The Palm-Wine Drinkard*, Tutuola describes a youthful experience, by informing the reader:

> I was trekking this distance of 23¾ miles instead of joining a lorry, because I had no money to pay for transport which was then only 2d. If I left home at 6 o'clock in the morning, I would reach the village at about 8 o'clock in the same morning or when my people were just preparing to go to farm, and this was a great surprise to them, because they did not believe that I trekked the distance but joined a lorry. (p.128)

Twenty-three and three-fourths miles in two hours through African bush would indeed make Tutuola one of the fastest runners in the world! * When asked during an interview for National Educational Television how long it took him to write *The Palm-Wine Drinkard*, Tutuola replied "three days,"

---

* The distance from the school where I taught in Eastern Nigeria and the Onitsha market was thirteen miles, yet I was rarely able to cover this distance (only in part over bush roads) on my motor scooter in less than an hour.

later stating that most of his works take no more than two or three weeks.[8] If this is true, one wonders why Tutuola has published only six works during his eighteen-year literary career.

The implication is certainly that Tutuola views time in some other way than we do in the West, as related to some definite system involving good (accomplishment) and evil (hindrance or stagnation); and, by extension, that time in an African sense has little to do with actual blocks of time as measured in a Western sense but rather with human values and human achievements. Certainly this is true of a number of other African novels far removed from the folkloristic domain. Yambo Ouologuem's *Le devoir de violence*, I have already noted, begins in the year 1202 and ends in the year 1947. Ouologuem's novel is a bloody chronicle of violence and brutality which he implies are basic factors in African tradition, and it is a fact that these atrocities perpetuate themselves down through the ages that Ouologuem records so sadistically in his novel. Even in a work such as Chinua Achebe's *Things Fall Apart*, time definitely appears to be related to human accomplishments rather than to clocks and Western measurements, for it is only during Okonkwo's seven years of exile that time plays any significance in the development of the story. For Okonkwo, time exists (in a Western sense) only when the conventional value system has been thrown out of balance. Much the same may be said for Chief Priest Ezeulu in Achebe's later novel, *Arrow of God*.

As a corollary, space and its treatment in *The Palm-Wine Drinkard* is also something frequently quite removed from the Western concept as shown in much Western fiction. Tutuola makes constant references to vast distances (to miles and miles and miles) that his hero and other characters are capable of covering in very limited periods of time in spite of the fact that in many cases there are no roads or pathways from one place to another, as for example on the way to the Deads' Town where "there was no road or path which to

travel, because nobody was going there from that town at all"
(p.41). At a later stage in their advance toward the Deads'
Town, the Drinkard and his wife illustrate that space, like
time, is often regarded in a manner different from that of the
West:

> Then we continued our journey as usual to the Deads' Town
> and when we had travelled for 10 days we were looking at the
> Deads' Town about 40 miles away and we were not delayed by
> anything on the way again. But as we were looking at the town
> from a long distance, we thought that we could reach there the
> same day, but not at all, we travelled for 6 more days, because
> as we nearly reached there, it would seem still to be very far
> away to us or as if it was running away from us. We did not
> know that anybody who had not died could not enter into that
> town by day time, but when my wife knew the secret, then she
> told me that we should stop and rest till night. When it was
> night, then she told me to get up and start our journey again.
> But soon after we started to go, we found that we need not
> travel more than one hour before we reached there. Of course
> we did not enter into it until the dawn, because it was an un-
> known town to us.   (p.95)

The Drinkard's advance here is much like K's attempt to
reach the castle in Kafka's novel, *The Castle;* time and space
frequently repel one another. However, whereas K is unsuccessful, the Drinkard reaches his destination.

Also like Kafka, Tutuola's merging of time and space
frequently leads to surrealistic passages, as the physical aspects
of the environment divide, alter, and coalesce into new forms.
On one occasion a termites' house changes into a market while
the Drinkard and his wife are sleeping. Again:

> As we were going on in this bush, we saw a pond and we
> branched there, then we started to drink the water from it, but
> as the water dried away at our presence and also as we were
> thirsty all the time, and there we saw that there was not a single
> living creature.   (p.52)

The most heightened example of the surreal, however, occurs
when the Drinkard and his wife enter into the Faithful-

Mother's tree. The tree itself, before they enter it, is described as being "about one thousand and fifty feet in length and about two hundred feet in diameter" (p.65). As soon as they enter it, they discover that it is large enough to contain a whole Alice-in-Wonderland-like world: "When we entered inside the white tree, there we found ourselves inside a big house which was in the centre of a big and beautiful town . . ." (p.67). Later, the Faithful-Mother takes them "to the largest dancing hall which was in the centre of that house, and there we saw that over 300 people were dancing all together. . . . This beautiful hall was full of all kinds of food and drinks, over twenty stages were in that hall with uncountable orchestras, musicians, dancers and tappers" (p.68). The exposition continues to describe the dining hall, the kitchen "in which we met about three hundred and forty cooks" (p.69) and the Faithful-Mother's hospital. The Drinkard and his wife remain with the Faithful-Mother for one year and two weeks; upon leaving, the Drinkard states that "what made us very surprised was that we saw the tree opened as a large door, and we simply found ourselves inside the bush unexpectedly, and the door closed at once and the tree seemed as an ordinary tree which could not open like that" (p.71).

As in Achebe's *Things Fall Apart* and in the works of the Onitsha writers, description in *The Palm-Wine Drinkard* tends to be functional, very rarely related to mood and atmosphere or landscaping in spite of the fact that landscape description would seem likely to occur in the many sections of the *Drinkard* that deal with the bush. Undoubtedly the most detailed descriptions are limited to the curious creatures themselves, such as Tutuola's picture of the Complete Gentleman:

> He was a beautiful "complete" gentleman, he dressed with the finest and most costly clothes, all the parts of his body were completed, he was a tall man but stout. As this gentleman came

to the market on that day, if he had been an article or animal for sale, he would be sold at least for £2000 (two thousand pounds). (p.18)

The functional is obvious here: the Complete Gentleman would have to be described in rather complete detail.

On the "Wraith-Island," the Drinkard encounters the following creature:

> . . . I saw a terrible animal coming to the farm and eating the crops, but one morning I met him there, so I started to drive him away from the farm, of course I could not approach him as he was as big as an elephant. His fingernails were long to about two feet, his head was bigger than his body ten times. He had a large mouth which was full of long teeth, these teeth were about one foot long and as thick as a cow's horns, his body was almost covered with black long hair like a horse's tail hair. He was very dirty. There were five horns on his head and curved and levelled to the head, his four feet were as big as a log of wood. (p.47)

Still later, one of the terrible red creatures is described in this manner:

> At the same time that the red fish appeared out, its head was just like a tortoise's head, but it was as big as an elephant's head and it had over 30 horns and large eyes which surrounded the head. All these horns were spread out as an umbrella. It could not walk but was only gliding on the ground like a snake and its body was just like a bat's body and covered with long red hair like strings. It could only fly to a short distance, and if it shouted a person who was four miles away would hear. All the eyes which surrounded its head were closing and opening at the same time as if a man was pressing a switch on and off. (pp.79–80)

The eyes which switch on and off are an excellent example of the many Westernizations which creep into Tutuola's narrative.

Much more typical, for describing a person or creature, is the Tutuolan comparison, illustrating a power or a trait by relating it to another. The Drinkard's Thumb Child is characterized in this manner: "This was a wonderful child, because if a hundred men were to fight with him, he would flog them until they would run away" (p.33). At other times, Tutuola will use a series of comparisons to illustrate the consummate powers of a character. In such a way, the Drinkard describes the Complete Gentleman's beauty:

> I could not blame the lady for following the Skull as a complete gentleman to his house at all. Because if I were a lady, no doubt I would follow him to wherever he would go, and still as I was a man I would jealous him more than that, because if this gentleman went to the battle field, surely, enemy would not kill him or capture him and if bombers saw him in a town which was to be bombed, they would not throw bombs on his presence, and if they did throw it, the bomb itself would not explode until this gentleman would leave that town, because of his beauty.   (p.25)

It should be noted also that Tutuola makes extensive use of sounds and noises throughout his narrative to further illustrate character and quasi-superhuman powers, such as the Thumb Child who "was whistling as if he was forty persons" (p.36), or two red fish "making a noise as if it was a thousand persons. . . ." (p.79).

In spite of being established primarily by these types of comparison or limited physical description, characterization in *The Palm-Wine Drinkard* tends to be utilitarian. Characters are for the most part named because of their specific function or purpose. The Drinkard and his wife, of course, are the best examples of this. Only the Tapster and the Thumb-Child have actual names, and the Tapster's name (Baity) is not given until the Drinkard reaches the Deads' Town. Other characters Tutuola realizes are designated best by their actions and deeds, often again implying a value system comparable to that of Tutuola's conception of time and space: Faithful-Mother, Give and Take, the Wise King, the Hungry Creature. In the case of the Drinkard's wife, except for her tendency to speak in parables, we know little about her other than her early attempt to try to avoid an arranged marriage.

The Drinkard himself is, of course, best characterized by the many heroic challenges he accepts and overcomes. In spite of the fact that he narrates the entire novel, there are very few passages which could actually be referred to as introspection. The following is perhaps the closest example: "then I *thought within myself* how could we get money for our food etc." (p.39. Italics mine). Nor does Tutuola use extended dialogue to develop the Drinkard's or any other character's personality. Instead, dialogue in *The Palm-Wine Drinkard*, too, appears to play a completely utilitarian purpose. The following passage is typical of Tutuola's sparse use of it:

> The questions that their king asked us went thus:—From where were you coming? I replied that we were coming from the earth. He asked again how did we manage to reach their town, I replied that it was their road brought us to the town and we did not want to come there at all. After that he asked us where were we going to? Then I replied that we were going to my palm-wine tapster's town who had died in my town sometime ago. As I had said already that these unknown creatures were very cruel to anybody that mistakenly entered their town, as I answered all the questions, he repeated the name of their town for us again—"Unreturnable-Heaven's town." He said:—a town in which are only enemies of God living, only cruel, greedy and merciless creatures. (pp.59–60)

It should also be noted that the Tutuolan world is replete with humor—often in the form of puns and curious anachronisms. There is a tendency, also, toward the didactic at the end of many of the incidents in the narrative and at many of the transitions from story to story. This didactic tendency, as we have already noted with other African writers, is in part a carry-over from traditional literary materials—in Tutuola's case the Yoruba oral tradition.

Storytelling is clearly at the heart of Tutuola's art, and Tutuola himself has said that even as a child he was admired by his playmates as a teller of tales. If this storytelling borders on the dreamlike, the surreal, the fantastic and the archetypal, we have only to note that Tutuola's tales are rooted in an oral tradition which is still very much alive in Yoruba society today—and the African reader often responds to these tales in a manner different from the non-African. In spite of the reshaping he often gives to his tales, Tutuola is for the African reader clearly a man whose work is grounded in the real world in which the African lives. When reading his work I am constantly reminded of the many essays I corrected when teaching English in Nigeria. Time and again, students related what to me appeared fantastic accounts of spirits and wild animals they had supposedly encountered in the bush. Tutuola's writing does just about the same thing. If Tutuola's imagination is frequently a bridge between the internal and the external world (the ontological gap), between the real and the surreal, between the realistic and the supernatural, we must at least point out in conclusion that passages of Tutuola's novels are rooted in a reality comparable to that of the more realistic works of his African contemporaries. The following is only one of dozens of possible examples:

> Then we left that town with gladness, we started our journey again, but after we had travelled about eighty miles away to that town, then we began to meet gangs of the "highway-men" on the road, and they were troubling us too much. But when I thought over that the danger of the road might result to the loss of our money or both money and our lives, then we entered into bush, but to travel in this bush was very dangerous too, because of the wild animals, and the boa constrictors were uncountable as sand.   (p.40)

Yet how can we be certain that this passage may not be fantasy, and that all of the curious creatures may not represent reality to a mind that could create the writings of an Amos Tutuola?

The "Situational" Novel:

The Novels of James Ngugi

IN THE NOVELS BY THE ONITSHA WRITERS AND BY Amos Tutuola, a theme exists which is not typical in African fiction: the isolated individual. Again, and again, the Drinkard must prove his heroism in the face of ubiquitously hostile creatures and forces. In the Onitsha novellas, there is a definite pattern of estrangement between the older and the more youthful characters, in large part due to these writers' concern with the problems of urbanization and the generation gap. This theme of isolation is for the most part missing from African fiction of the first generation. There are exceptions, of course, and as we will later see, alienation is becoming of increasing concern to second generation African novelists—such as Ayi Kwei Armah. The more typical pattern, however, is that of the group-felt experience which has already been illustrated in Chinua Achebe's *Things Fall Apart*. But before we analyze additional examples, it will be to our advantage to briefly examine and categorize the major subject concerns of the African novel to this date.

Exposure to the West, with the results of this exposure, has been the great theme of almost all African fiction with the exception of those few novels which have been set in the past, prior to the white man's penetration of Africa, or a handful of novels which have concentrated on village life relatively unaffected by Western ideas.* Although it is rare that a novel has only one aspect of this confrontation as its subject, it seems logical to say that the five subject areas of African fiction reflect a related series of cultural upheavals that all African societies have had to undergo at one time or another. These concerns are reflected in the following categories: (1) novels portraying the initial exposure to the West, such as Chinua Achebe's *Things Fall Apart*, or James Ngugi's *The River Between*, commonly concerned with the African's confrontation with Western religion and/or the initial stages of colonial government; (2) novels concerned with the problems of adaptation to Western education such as Cheikh Hamidou Kane's *L'aventure ambiguë* (*Ambiguous Adventure*), and Bernard Dadié's *Climbié*; (3) novels of urbanization best typified by Cyprian Ekwensi's Lagos novels and the novellas by the Onitsha writers; (4) novels concerned with the problems of politics or nation-building, either prior to independence (as in Peter Abrahams' *A Wreath for Udomo*) or in a post-independent situation (such as Chinua Achebe's *A Man of the People*); and (5) novels concerned with a more individualized life style, with a growing emphasis on the individual and his relationship toward a group from which he has become estranged (such as Armah's *Fragments*, or Ezekiel Mphahlele's *The Wanderers* which treats the problem of exile on the African continent itself, and extends this category to a Pan-

---

* Novels such as Khadambi Asalache's *A Calabash of Life*, E. C. C. Uzodinma's *Our Dead Speak*, and to a lesser extent, S. A. Konadu's *A Woman in Her Prime* and Flora Nwapa's *Efuru*. Tutuola's novels also belong here because of their relative lack of concern with the contemporary African situation.

African or Third World perspective, including all oppressed peoples everywhere.)

The fiction of African writers has not necessarily evolved in this order but, rather, when looked at as a whole, tends to cluster around these five general areas. Nor should we think that a given African novel has as its concern only one of these topics. Most frequently, African novels have been concerned with two or more of these aspects of the shift in cultural values, promulgated in one way or another by exposure to the West. For example, James Ngugi's first novel, *Weep Not, Child,* has as its concern both education and politics.

It should be emphasized that these five fictional subjects when examined in the order in which I have placed them appear to be evolutionary stages mirroring anthropological and sociological situations created by the frustrations of Western life. It is obvious, for example, that the first exposure to the West for thousands and thousands of Africans was Christianity; thus, the first category has been concerned with the clash between traditional religion and Christianity, which has been portrayed in many novels in one way or another. For many Africans "conversion" led to attendance at Mission schools, and, as a consequence, education was the second stage in their exposure to the West. Since so many Africans were educated in the rural areas, education and its promise of a new job (based on a money economy) often could be fulfilled only by leaving these rural areas. Thus, urbanization became the next stage of the African's indoctrination into a Western style of life. It follows, quite consistently, that these first three experiences prepared the way for the fourth concern of African fiction—which is in part a revolt against the West—politics, whether, as I said, this be with the struggle leading to independence or the problems of political stability in post-independent Africa. The fifth concern—the individual life-style—has no doubt been slow to evolve because of the more pressing problems of the first four. In this last category, I would place the novels by Ayi Kwei Armah (*The Beautyful Ones Are Not Yet Born,* and *Fragments*), Ezekiel Mphahlele's *The Wanderers,* Wole Soyinka's *The Interpreters,* and Camara Laye's *Le regard du roi,* though the educational theme is apparent here in a reverse manner.

The first four subjects or topics commonly explored by African writers were group-felt experiences, because they were stages in the continual chain of events to which the African was forced to submit as his culture felt the blows from the West. And from these confrontations—lasting in some cases over as many as a hundred years, in others as few, perhaps, as twenty or thirty—the African situational novel evolved. A village, a clan, a tribe, a nation, as we have already noted with Chinua Achebe's *Things Fall Apart,* bore the brunt of these changes, which affected the individual mostly as he was a member of a group. A glance at John Mbiti's *African Religion and Philosophy* illuminates the problem of our concern here. Of the individual and the relationship to his village, Mbiti states,

> In traditional life, the individual does not and cannot exist alone except corporately. He owes his existence to other people, including those of past generations. . . . He is simply part of the whole. . . . Whatever happens to the individual happens to the whole group, and whatever happens to the whole group happens to the individual.[1]

A similar statement is made in an essay by Mohamadou Kane, entitled "The African Writer and His Public":

> . . . our literature avoids anything that will exalt the individual who remains in harmonious union with the group: neither selfishness nor self-centredness are conceivable. The theme of loneliness is unknown; only a common fate prevails.[2]

The group-felt experience is so important that it might be more appropriate to call the African novel "communal" rather than "situational." In either case, let us use the following working description of this kind of novel: (1) unlike the novel that has evolved, according to Virginia Woolf's belief,

as an instrument to delineate character,* the situational novel
exists to present an experience or situation, and as a result of
this, often, to develop an idea or thesis; moreover (2) this
situation is a group-felt experience, though the story itself
may be focused on only one or two characters, implying, at
least, that in the cases where there is a definite emphasis on one
or two individuals, the final result is felt by *all* the people
involved in the story itself—the community, the "collective
consciousness" of the novel. Thus, in *Things Fall Apart*, although Achebe focuses on Okonkwo much of the frustration
that the typical Ibo felt, at the end of the story itself (at the
end of the situation) it is the entire community that has experienced the debasement rather than one separate individual. The
same statement may be made regarding James Ngugi's novel of
traditional life, *The River Between*, even though Ngugi's
characters are usually more fully realized than Achebe's, or, as
a character says in Ngugi's later novel, *A Grain of Wheat*,
" '. . . it is not easy for any man in a community to be left
alone.' " [3]

As would be expected, the very nature of the unique
African communal experience affects the structure of the
novel. We have already noted this in Part One of *Things
Fall Apart* where Achebe develops his composite picture of
traditional Ibo life. The plot is, of course, the direct result
of the author's manipulation of his characters, and it follows
that in the communal novel when characterization is de-em-
phasized the structure will be affected in one way or another.
A further breakdown of the situational plot concerns those
novels which simply have no main character at all (such as
Wole Soyinka's *The Interpreters*, James Ngugi's *A Grain of
Wheat* or Sembene Ousmane's *Les Bouts de bois de Dieu*),
or those novels where the individual is a mirror of the group
(*Things Fall Apart; Weep Not, Child*, among others).

From these statements it should be clear that the situational

* See Virginia Woolf's "Mr. Bennett and Mrs. Brown" and my comments on characterization in Chapter Six.

novel is not limited to African fiction alone but is a form which has long existed in the West. I tend to think of some of Henry James' works as belonging in this pattern—*The American*, for instance. André Malraux's *Man's Fate* seems to me to fit perfectly in the first group—since the emphasis is clearly on any number of characters rather than on one single person—characters experiencing the same basic situation. Other more recent examples, perhaps less commonly known, include David Caute's *Decline of the West*, which happens to be a novel with an African setting, and Peter Matthiessen's powerful story portraying the clash of religious ideologies in South America, *At Play in the Fields of the Lord*. All of these novels are concerned with expatriates from widely different cultures confronting a common problem with the indigenous population, and further suggest a category for the most part unexplored in African fiction: the "international" novel, presenting people from disparate cultural groups confronting the same situation. Although prediction is an unhealthy activity, it appears that in the future the African novelist will deal more commonly with multi-racial situations than he has in the past. Ngugi's *A Grain of Wheat* and Ezekiel Mphahlele's *The Wanderers* may be harbingers of this trend because of the multi-racial societies they depict.

Traditional ties in African cultures are altering so quickly that the group-felt experience is rapidly becoming a thing of the past, for the ties that once bound an individual to his community have been loosened by Westernization. Respect for the elders, for example, so common in the past, has been rapidly disappearing, and with it a respect for the traditions represented by the older generation. No longer does the African youth feel that he must have the permission of the chief or the elders before he marries—his bride today is one of his own choosing. There is a touching scene in Legson Kayira's *The Looming Shadow* (which I would call a situational novel) where the village headman is interrupted several times as he narrates a tale from the past to a group of his villagers. The children who are present are simply bored with his story, and their disrespect for the chief is readily apparent. Group solidarity held together by chieftaincy, respect for the traditions, the elders, or the ancestors, Kayira says—respect for the basic traditions themselves—is dying. In other areas, however, the situational aspect may be developed by the rights that a community (or a family) feels it has over the individual himself. This is so in any number of recent African novels— even one as far removed from the norm as Ayi Kwei Armah's *Fragments.* Sometimes the result is tragic, as is shown in the ending of James Ngugi's *The River Between,* where, as we will see, the community takes action against those it feels have transgressed the sacred oaths of the clan. We have already noted that in Chinua Achebe's second novel, *No Longer at Ease,* Obi Okonkwo's financial difficulties result in large part because of the pressures from the Umuofia Progressive Society —the rights the villagers feel they have over Obi since they paid for his education abroad. In Legson Kayira's second novel, *Jingala,* which concerns the conflict a young man has with his father (Jingala) and his community because he wishes to become a priest, the communal rights are clearly represented by his father who says,

"His Principal—he's a stubborn fellow—thinks I am the devil himself. Do you realize that man had the impertinence to tell me that I was destroying my son's happiness by taking him away from his studies? Just fancy it! He was more concerned about my son's so called happiness than by my happiness, your happiness, and this village's happiness." [4]

The idea that the community has an important part to play in the future of its youth is further illustrated in *Jingala* in this conversation between the Chief and Jingala:

"I will put it this way," the chief said. "Why do you think we have become so angry at you for wishing to become a priest?"

"Because you are forsaking our gods, that's why," Jingala

informed his son. "You are abandoning our gods for foreign ones."

"Your father is right," the chief said with great emphasis. "I will make this statement clearer as we go on. The most important thing we want you to know is that we are one people and have always been like that. I am not implying by this that we, as a people, are better than the people in this or that village. Not at all. Like all other villages, we too have our share of thieves and witches and all that lot and in this sense it would be untrue to claim that we are better than others. What I am saying is this, and mark me well: it is our oneness, our comradeship, our feeling of responsibility to one another that has kept us together through the ages and has made us what we are today." (p.97)

In *The Great Ponds,* by Elechi Amadi, the rights of the group are so important that the entire story is built around the rivalry of two communities for the fishing rights to the great ponds of Wagaba. The tension in the story is centered on an agreement between the two villages: if Olumba lives for six months, the pond will belong to his village, but if he dies, the pond will become the property of the other. Amadi illustrates an almost parental concern on the part of Olumba's fellow villagers in their attempt to shelter his actions and thus save the ponds for their village. Slowly Olumba realizes that he has no private life of his own at all—every move he makes must be considered for the village's welfare.

Other novels which seem to me to be particularly strong examples of the situational African novel are Timothy Aluko's *One Man, One Matchet;* Mongo Beti's *Le roi miraculé (King Lazarus),* and to a lesser extent *Le pauvre Christ de Bomba* and *Mission terminée (Mission to Kala);* Cyprian Ekwensi's *People of the City,* though it can be argued that the city is the antagonist and hence the situation in almost all of Ekwensi's novels; Camara Laye's *Dramouss (A Dream of Africa)* and in some ways, *Le regard du roi (The Radiance of the King);* Gabriel Okara's *The Voice;* Sembene Ousmane's *Les bouts de bois de*

Dieu (*God's Bits of Wood*); Yambo Ouologuem's *Le devoir de violence;* Stanlake Samkange's *On Trial for My Country,* and David Rubadiri's *No Bride Price.* The works by other novelists, such as Ferdinand Oyono and Onuora Nzekwu, also belong in this pattern, though to a lesser extent.

With the publication of *Weep Not, Child* in 1964, James Ngugi appeared on the African literary scene, becoming the first important novelist from East Africa. Ngugi's appearance marked the belated beginnings of the novel in East Africa at a time when the West African novel was already well established. Achebe published his third novel the same year; Ekwensi had published four full length books; Amos Tutuola and Camara Laye had already written their most significant works. But the novel in East Africa, mostly as a result of more limited educational opportunities than those that were available in West Africa, was just making its initial appearance. The result was clearly worth waiting for. James Ngugi's second and third novels have placed him in the forefront of all the East and Central African writers who have appeared since 1964. Furthermore, Ngugi and other East African novelists, although still fewer in number than their brothers across the continent, have benefited by their exposure to the West African novel. The heavy reliance on anthropological background which has marked and in some cases hindered a number of West African writers' work (Onuora Nzekwu, Clement Agunwa, S. A. Konadu, John Munonye, and Flora Nwapa, for example) has not been similarly overdone by the East African novelist. It is safe to say, I feel, that the West African writers pioneered the novel in Africa, and as a consequence their works are generally more readily distinguished by cultural influences. Unlike his West African counterpart, the East African novelist has had a decade-long tradition to study and, in some ways, improve upon.

In form and pattern, James Ngugi's first novel, *Weep Not,*

Child, bears a remarkable similarity to Chinua Achebe's *Things Fall Apart*. Like Achebe, Ngugi also relates the story of a community that crumbles because of exposure to the West. Unlike Achebe, however, Ngugi has chosen a more recent period of time—the 1950's and the rise of the Mau Mau in Kenya—in essence writing a novel based on an historical event still very much alive in the memory of the average African reader. In large part the success of his novel—its beauty and its horror—consists in exactly this presentation of an historical event so recent that hardly an adult Kenyan reading the book will fail to remember the Mau Mau rebellion which involved everyone: Africans who took the oath, and those who did not, white settlers who were sympathetic toward the African situation and those who were not, the evil and the innocent. Ngugi's supreme achievement is in illustrating how individual families came to be pulled in several different directions as various members formed new loyalties and rejected older ones within the traditional power structure. The result is a powerful picture of Kenya undergoing a war of liberation, a violent time of chaos and destruction in which it became impossible for every adult and child not to become involved, to remain neutral to the events purging the land. Ngugi's concentration is upon one specific family, and is situational in the sense that this family becomes a microcosm of the entire nation.

The title is taken from Walt Whitman's poem, "On the Beach at Night,"

> Weep not, child
> Weep not, my darling
> With these kisses let me remove your tears,
> The ravening clouds shall not be long victorious,
> They shall not long possess the sky . . .

The title establishes a lyrical tone for the novel, for Ngugi's prose at its best is never far removed from poetry. There is the presence, too, of a lyrical center (the collective consciousness) throughout all three of Ngugi's novels, an unseen eye which observes much of what takes place. The weeping child motif is reiterated at several crucial times in Ngugi's narrative—the "ravening clouds" are ubiquitous.

Part One is called "The Waning Light" and in form and pattern, as I suggested above, is reminiscent of Part One of Achebe's *Things Fall Apart*. Ngugi establishes a composite overview of Kikuyu society in the first half of his novel—based upon dozens of short staccato-like scenes depicting Kenya under colonial domination prior to the Mau Mau revolt. The first chapter introduces the family upon whom Ngugi focuses his story, and the two dominant motifs of his novel—education and land:

> Nyokabi called him. She was a small, black woman, with a bold but grave face. One could tell by her small eyes full of life and warmth that she had once been beautiful. All the same, Nyokabi had retained her full smile—a smile that lit up her dark face.
>
> "Would you like to go to school?"
>
> "Oh, Mother!" Njoroge gasped. He half feared that the woman might withdraw her words.
>
> There was a little silence till she said, "We are poor. You know that."
>
> "Yes, Mother." His heart pounded against his ribs slightly. His voice was shaky.
>
> "So you won't be getting a mid-day meal like other children."
>
> "I understand."
>
> "You won't bring shame to me by one day refusing to attend school?" [5]

The educational theme is introduced first and will later be linked with the land motif. Almost at once, Ngugi uses a technique Achebe never really explored in *Things Fall Apart*: character introspection. As the opening scene continues, we are thrust immediately into Njoroge's mind, into his thoughts: *"Oh, Mother, I'll never bring shame to you. Just let me get there, just let me"* (p. 21). Njoroge thinks shortly thereafter,

Oh, Mother, you are an angel of God, you are, you are.
Then he wondered. Had she been to a magic worker? Or else how could she have divined his child's unspoken wish, his undivulged dream? *And here I am, with nothing but a piece of calico on my body and soon I shall have a shirt and shorts for the first time.* (p.22)

The concentration here at the beginning, as in much of the book, will be on Njoroge and his changing attitudes toward the situation around him. The characterization (which we will analyze more fully in the next chapter) is impressionistic and vivid, full of sounds and colors and emotional tones rarely expressed in the African novel. Almost immediately, Ngugi emphasizes the important role Western education will play in this story. (Almost as if it were planned by the colonial government to alienate the youth from his family and his culture.) Njoroge's older brother is undergoing his apprenticeship as a carpenter. As Martin Tucker has written, "One child will be responsible for the mental and intellectual duties of the family; the other child will specialize in the affairs of trade" (p.11).

Hardly more than two pages later Ngugi introduces his reader to the lyrical presence (the collective consciousness) of the novel. This stylistic convention is identified by the use of the second person pronoun *you*, injecting the reader into the heart of the story:

There was only one road that ran right across the land. It was long and broad and shone with black tar, and when you traveled along it on hot days you saw little lakes ahead of you. But when you went near, the lakes vanished, to appear again a little farther ahead. Some people called them the devil's waters because they deceived you and made you more thirsty if your throat was already dry. And the road which ran across the land and was long and broad had no beginning and no end. At least, few people knew of its origin. Only if you followed it it would take you to the big city and leave you there while it went beyond to the unknown, perhaps joining the sea. (p.23)

It is an effective device, a technique Ngugi perfects in his later novels, for, in essence, the second person is the communal element entering into the situation, the unseen witness who understands everything, records everything, the communal center of balance. Shortly thereafter, for example, the lyrical presence introduces the motif of land—its control and exploitation by the white settlers—for unlike the writings from West Africa, which was never a settler area, Kenyan fiction has reflected the dominant conflict of Kenyan life, life in a multi-racial society:

> You could tell the land of Black People because it was red, rough and sickly, while the land of the white settlers was green and was not lacerated into small strips.
>
> Kipanga town was built in this field. It was not a big town like the big city. However, there was one shoe factory and many black people earned their living there. The Indian shops were many. The Indian traders were said to be very rich. They too employed some black boys whom they treated as nothing. You could never like the Indians because their customs were strange and funny in a bad way. . . .
>
> . . . Black people too bought things from the Indians. But they also bought in the African shops, which stood alone on one side of the town near the post office. The Africans had not many things in their store and they generally charged higher prices so that although the Indians were not liked and they abused women, using dirty words they had learned in Swahili, people found it wiser and more convenient to buy from them. Some people said that black people should stick together and take trade only to their black brethren. (pp.26–27)

The communal element is also present in the recurrent motif of black solidarity, reflected frequently in the African child's inability to understand the other ethnic groups: "You did not know what to call the Indian. Was he also a white man?" (p.27).

The scene shifts abruptly from the confusions of multi-racialism to one of the centers of community life—the barber shop—and Ngugi tellingly records the noises and impressions in a dramatic set piece: "The barber lets his clippers go flick . . . lick . . . lick . . . lick. Everyone stands expectantly by waiting to hear about the Big War. The barber takes his time" (p.28). Ngugi's picture of the barber's shop is that of a meeting place for the men of the community. Directly thereafter, the first chapter shifts to what is going on in the mind of Njoroge's father, Ngotho:

> . . . Ngotho made his way through the crowd into the open. He always loved to listen to the barber. Somehow the talk reminded him of his own travels and troubles in the First World War. As a boy he had been conscripted and made to carry things for the fighting white men. He also had to clear dark bush and make roads. Then, he and the others were not allowed to use guns. But in the barber's war! Ah! that was something. His own two sons had also gone to this one. Only one had returned. And the one who had returned never talked much about the actual war, except to say that it had been a terrible waste of life.
>   Ngotho bought four pounds of meat. But they were bound into two bundles each of two pounds. One bundle was for his first wife, Njeri, and the other for Nyokabi, his second wife. A husband had to be wise in these affairs otherwise a small flaw or apparent bias could easily generate a civil war in the family. Not that Ngotho feared this very much. He knew that his two wives liked each other and were good companions and friends. But you could not quite trust women. They were fickle and very jealous. When a woman was angry no amount of beating would pacify her. Ngotho did not beat his wives much. On the contrary, his home was well known for being a place of peace. All the same, one had to be careful. (pp.29–30)

The image of peace that Ngugi instills within Ngotho's family is central to his novel. As Ngotho's family begins to crumble, so does British colonial influence in Kenya. Time and again Ngugi will return to this picture of Ngotho's family and the external forces which will slowly lead to its collapse. The end

of the first chapter returns us to the educational theme again
—Ngotho and Nyokabi talking about Njoroge's schooling.

The remaining chapters in Part One carefully balance
Ngugi's two primary motifs—education and land—education
for the youth, restoration of the usurped land for the elders.
In Chapter Two, Njoroge goes to school with Mwihaki, "a
daughter of Jacobo. Jacobo owned the land on which Ngotho
lived" (p.33). A strong friendship grows between the two
of them, a brotherly-sisterly love which must always remain
that because of the strained relationship which develops between their parents. The estrangement that Njoroge is later
to feel because of his exposure to Western education is briefly
foreseen in an incident between Njoroge and Mwihaki—
Njoroge's embarrassment at being seen without his school
clothes:

> Before Njoroge went very far, he saw her now coming
> along the same path but from the opposite direction. If he went
> on he would meet her. Suddenly he realized that he did not
> want to meet her while he had on that piece of calico, which,
> when blown by the wind, left the lower part of his body with-
> out covering. For a time, he was irresolute and hated himself
> for feeling as he did about the clothes he had on. Before he had
> started school, in fact even while he made that covenant with
> his mother, he would never have thought that he would ever be
> ashamed of the calico, the only dress he had ever known since
> birth. (p.40)

After the shortest of times, Njoroge is already becoming a
victim of Western ideas, Western morality and values. The
scene is a subtle indication of things to come—the new clothing
Njoroge wears will soon cover up his old life.

Ngugi also develops the sense of family unity early in his
novel because, like the nation it reflects, Ngotho's family is
shortly to be destroyed by the uprising. "Boro, Kori, and
Kamau were all sons of Njeri, Ngotho's eldest wife. Njoroge's
only true brother was Mwangi, who had died in the war"

(pp.43–44). When the family is all together, Ngotho tells the Kikuyu creation myth to his sons; thus Ngugi, like Achebe, makes use of a complete oral tale within his narrative. Ngugi connects his story to the present time, and the land which Ngotho relates as belonging to the first man (Gikuyu) and the first woman (Mumbi) is related to Ngotho's exile from his ancestral lands now controlled by the white land owner, Mr. Howlands. Ngotho works for Howlands and lives on property owned by Jacobo, one of the few Africans in the area who possesses any land. The white man confiscated most of it during World War I; Ngotho's tale ends with his dream of the return of the land. "For Njoroge, it was a surprising revelation, this knowledge that the land occupied by Mr. Howlands originally belonged to them" (p.49). Shortly thereafter, the usurpation is linked to Ngotho's son, Boro: "There was no land on which he could settle, even if he had been able to do so" (p.49). The exile from his farm land serves as the initial cause for agitation between father and son. Boro asks his father, " 'How can you continue working for a man who has taken your land? How can you go on serving him?' " (p.50).

Throughout his novel, Ngugi consistently balances character with character. Ngotho, for example, is contrasted with his white employer, Howlands, who also lost a son in the First World War. Later, Howlands' other son will be paired off with Njoroge, and the land/education motif is also eventually connected through the two sons. The first connection between the two motifs, however, occurs in the fourth chapter where Ngotho says the following to Njoroge:

"Education is everything," Ngotho said. Yet he doubted this because he knew deep inside his heart that land was everything. Education was good only because it would lead to the recovery of the lost lands.

"You must learn to escape the conditions under which we live. It is a hard way. It is not much that a man can do without a piece of land." (p.64)

The almost mystical reverence that Ngotho has for the land is brought out in another parallel that Ngugi draws between Ngotho and Jacobo, on whose land Ngotho lives. The contrast between their two households is of particular importance as the story develops, and Ngugi states of Ngotho's: "The feeling of oneness was a thing that most distinguished Ngotho's household from many other polygamous families" (p.67). It is the closeness of Ngotho's family which results in their feeling the eventual turmoil of the Mau Mau revolt more deeply than other families. Yet, with so many sons with their differing backgrounds, it is logical that there will soon be more to pull Ngotho's family apart than there will be in other families. Njoroge, for example, "came to place faith in the Bible and with his vision of an educated life in the future was blended a belief in the righteousness of God" (p.77). Later Ngugi states,

> Whenever he was with Mwihaki, he longed to impart some of these things to her. Yet when he tried to define them in words, he failed. So he kept them all to himself, walking alone in the fields and sometimes finding companionship with the nights. (p.78)

Education slowly alienates Njoroge from the active political lives of his older brothers.

Part One comes to an abrupt end as the tone of the novel suddenly shifts from peacefulness and serenity to fear and imminent violence. In a particularly touching scene, Ngugi effectively connects the educational theme once again with the problem of the restoration of the land, the black man's dignity. Both Njoroge and Mwihaki pass from primary to intermediate school, but even as they run home to convey the results of the examinations to their families, their dreams of the future are diminished. Mwihaki rushes in to tell her mother her news only to be informed that an attempt has been made on her father's (Jacobo's) life. Njoroge, with the childhood enthusiasm and pride that can only be fulfilled by breaking the good news to his mother, is informed that a strike has taken place—his father will now be jobless. Only later do we learn that it was Ngotho who attacked Jacobo, the stooge of the white government. Shortly thereafter Jacobo orders Ngotho off his land—the exile motif is continued. The first part of Ngugi's novel ends with an interlude—a State of Emergency has been declared by the government. No one will escape the falling darkness. Land and education ultimately affect everyone in the country.

Part Two—"Darkness Falls"—destroys the idyllic life described in Part One and presents in extremely objective terms what, at times, appears to be an historical account of the Mau Mau revolt against British colonial rule. It is one of the marks of Ngugi's skill that he can present his white characters almost as realistically and as sympathetically as his African characters, and this seems to be exactly his intention, for the Mau Mau uprising involved the best and the worst people on both sides. As the second half opens, Ngotho is no longer living on Jacobo's land, but on land belonging to another African; Jacobo has been made the local chief; Howlands is the new District Officer. Boro has gone into the forest, and the tension between Ngotho and Boro is once again related to the problems of the generations; Ngotho refuses to take the oath from his son—from someone younger than he, telling him what to do:

> he felt the loss of the land even more keenly than Boro, for to him it was a spiritual loss. When a man was severed from the land of his ancestors where would he sacrifice to the Creator? How could he come into contact with the founders of the tribe, Gikuyu and Mumbi? What did Boro know of oaths, of ancient rites, of the spirits of the ancestors? Still the estrangement cut deeper and deeper into Ngotho's life, emaciating him daily. (p.110)

In Ngugi's most overt comment on the land, he states of Ngotho ". . . he had now lost every contact with his ancestral land. The communion with the spirits who had gone before him had given him vitality" (p.109). Boro articulates the younger generation's passions, not realizing that his father feels much the same way,

". . . All white people stick together. But we black people are very divided. And because they stick together, they've imprisoned Jomo, the only hope we had. Now they'll make us slaves. They took us to their wars and they killed all that was of value to us. . . ." (p.111)

Ngugi describes the various factions which are slowly coalescing; it is not simply a matter of Africans against the white landowners. Ngugi says,

Mr. Howlands despised Jacobo because he was a savage. But he would use him. The very ability to set these people fighting among themselves instead of fighting with the white men gave him an amused satisfaction. (p.115)

Jacobo, desirous of revenging Ngotho's earlier attack on him, tells Howlands that Ngotho " 'may be the real leader of Mau Mau' " (p.117), and after this Ngotho's life completely falls apart. Howlands has his land; Jacobo gets his revenge over him; Boro believes his father is too weak to take the oath. The final straw that breaks him comes when Boro humiliates him in front of his family. The family, once so closely knit, has lost all of its former oneness.

As the darkness falls on the country, Njoroge withdraws increasingly into himself, using his education—which has miraculously continued—as an escape from the everyday realities. If there is a flaw in Njoroge as he is portrayed by Ngugi it is that he becomes almost totally inactive—removed from the events around him. In all fairness to Ngugi, it should be stated, however, that Njoroge is still a young schoolboy, probably too young for initiation into the Mau Mau. Then, too, a Kenyan student of mine once told me that Njoroge typified the impotence he had felt as a schoolboy during the Mau Mau uprising. Njoroge's friendship for Mwihaki continues, in spite of their fathers, and in a particularly moving scene with the two of them high on the top of a hill, Njoroge asks, " 'Is it possible for a whole nation to sin?' " (p.136). As the scene ends, Ngugi's sense of futility bursts into lyricism:

> They moved together, so as not to be caught by the darkness. A bird cried. And then another. And these two, a boy and a girl, went forward each lost in his world, for a time oblivious of the bigger darkness over the whole land. (p.138)

Ngugi's skillful orchestration continues to juxtapose themes relating to Njoroge's education (peaceful, withdrawn, undemanding) with those of the increasing violence in the strife-torn land.

> In spite of the troubled time, people still retained a genuine interest in education. Whatever their differences, interest in knowledge and book learning was the one meeting point between people such as Boro, Jacobo and Ngotho. Somehow the Gikuyu people always saw their deliverance as embodied in education. When the time for Njoroge to leave came near, many people contributed money so that he could go. He was no longer the son of Ngotho but the son of the land. (p.148)

Ngugi's pattern of balancing opposites leads to a particularly prophetic scene between Njoroge and Stephen Howlands, son of the white landowners. In the middle of all of the turmoil, the two youths meet at an interschool football game:

> "I used to hide near the road. I wanted to speak with some of you." Stephen was losing his shyness.
> "Why didn't you?"
> "I was afraid."
> "Afraid?"
> "Yes. I was afraid that you might not speak to me or you might not need my company."
> "Was it all that bad?"
> "Not so much." He did not want sympathy.
> "I am sorry I ran away from you. I too was afraid."
> "Afraid?" It was Stephen's turn to wonder.
> "Yes. I too was afraid of you." (p.153)

The scene is reminiscent of the fear that separates the races in Alan Paton's *Cry, the Beloved Country*, a novel which may have had some influence on the shaping of Ngugi's own story. As the two schoolboys part, Ngugi states, "The two moved back to the field, again shy with each other. They moved into two different directions as if they were afraid of another contact" (p.155).

It is inevitable, of course, that Njoroge, too, becomes involved in the nation's chaos. Called from school by the authorities, he is brought back to his village and interrogated by Howlands. In this scene, he and the reader learn that Jacobo has been murdered and that Ngotho has confessed to having killed him. The tension of the novel increases almost unbearably. To gain back the respect he has lost from his sons—especially Boro—Ngotho confesses to a murder he did not commit. Howlands has him castrated, although he eventually realizes that Ngotho did not kill Jacobo. Njoroge watches his father die, feeling the futility to which he now realizes his education has led him. "His family was about to break and he was powerless to arrest the fall" (p.164). Ngugi adds, "For the first time Njoroge was face to face with a problem to which 'tomorrow' was no answer" (p.167).

Boro is reconciled with his dying father, and when he learns what Howlands has done to Ngotho, he enters Howlands' house and kills him. As the novel draws to a conclusion, Boro and Kamau, another brother, are both facing murder charges; Njoroge is working in an Indian's shop, still trying to escape the reality of the moment. When he learns that Mwihaki will not flee to Uganda with him, he decides to commit suicide:

She had conquered. She knew now that she would not submit. But it was hard for her and as she left him she went on weeping, tearing and wringing her heart. The sun was sinking down. Njoroge's last hope had vanished. For the first time he knew that he was in the world all alone without a soul on whom he could lean. (p.182)

The final scene in *Weep Not, Child*—Njoroge's attempted suicide—has disturbed a number of readers. At dusk, Njoroge leaves home and goes out to hang himself. But he is followed by both of his mothers and prevented from completing the first truly willed act of his life. The novel concludes with the following scene:

> Nyokabi clung to him. She did not ask anything.
>
> "Let's go home," she commanded weakly.
>
> He followed her, saying nothing. He was only conscious that he had failed her and the last word of his father, when he had told him to look after the women. He had failed the voice of Mwihaki that had asked him to wait for a new day. They met Njeri who too had followed Nyokabi in search of a son in spite of the curfew laws. Again Njoroge did not speak to Njeri but felt only guilt, the guilt of a man who had avoided his responsibility for which he had prepared himself since child-hood.
>
> But as they came near home and what had happened to him came to mind, the voice again came and spoke accusing him: *You are a coward. You have always been a coward. Why didn't you do it?*
>
> And loudly he said: *Because you are a coward.*
>
> "Yes," he whispered to himself. "I am a coward."
>
> And he ran home and opened the door for his two mothers.
> (p.184)

There are two aspects of the ending that are of symbolic importance. First, the attempted suicide itself and the admission that he is a coward, which I feel represents a major change in Njoroge from a passive observer to an active participant, one who from now on will not remain uninvolved. And, second, and of more importance, are the repeated references that Ngugi makes in the last few pages—and in the last words of his novel—to Njoroge's "two mothers." For it is out of the syncretism of the future—which will incorporate the best from the past, the best from the two worlds—that peace will once again return to the troubled land. The peacefulness of Ngotho's family, the lack of rivalry between his two wives, has been presented throughout the novel as an indication of the oneness which lies at the roots of African society—the basic family unit, and the adjacent communal life which nourishes it and can only be the foundation of the collective consciousness. Out of a regeneration of the basic values of traditional life, and especially the extended family, the new society will once again be purified.

Weep Not, Child gives the overall impression that there has been no possible escape, no path a person could follow during the Mau Mau uprisings which could lead to release from the turmoil of the land. At its very base, the novel probes the nature of loyalty to one's clan, one's nation—the rise of nationalism which is so important a theme in Ngugi's third novel, *A Grain of Wheat*. In between the publication of these two works, however, Ngugi published a book removed from the more contemporary problems of the Mau Mau resurgence, yet a novel which still questions the very nature of the individual's obligations toward his clan, his society. *The River Between* appeared in 1965 although it was written before *Weep Not, Child*. Ngugi's basic story is once again communal, and the situation he has created repeats the conclusions of *Weep Not, Child*—there is no escape from the clan, once it has asserted its rights, even for the man of good intentions.

The River Between can be called Ngugi's East African counterpart to Achebe's *Things Fall Apart*. Here again is a picture of a traditional African society undergoing the initial frustrations of Westernization. The opening paragraphs of his story distill the basic situation: the villages of Kameno and Makuyu, separated by the river between them, have co-existed peacefully for centuries:

> The two ridges lay side by side. One was Kameno, the other was Makuyu. Between them was a valley. It was called the valley of life. Behind Kameno and Makuyu were many more valleys and ridges, lying without any discernible plan. They

were like many sleeping lions which never woke. They just slept, the big deep sleep of their Creator.

A river flowed through the valley of life. If there had been no bush and no forest trees covering the slopes, you could have seen the river when you stood on top of either Kameno or Makuyu. Now you had to come down. Even then you could not see the whole extent of the river as it gracefully, and without any apparent haste, wound its way down the valley, like a snake. The river was called Honia, which meant cure, or bring-back-to-life. Honia river never dried: it seemed to possess a strong will to live, scorning droughts and weather changes. And it went on in the same way, never hurrying, never hesitating. People saw this and were happy.[6]

Westernization, however, in the form of Christianity, will soon tear the peacefulness of the two ridges asunder, much in the manner it destroyed Achebe's beloved Umuofia. In the early sections of his novel, Ngugi relies heavily on oral history to complete our view of traditional life in the two villages. Chege tells his son, Waiyaki, as they are standing together in the hills,

"That is a blessed and sacred place. There, where Mumbi's feet stood, grew up that tree. So you see, it is Kameno that supported the father and mother of the tribe. From here, Murungu took them and put them under Mukuruwe wa Gathanga in Murang'a. There our father and mother had nine daughters who bore more children. The children spread all over the country. Some came to the ridges to keep and guard the ancient rites. . . ."

". . . Mugo was born and grew up in Kameno before he went to tell people what he saw. For he saw many butterflies, of many colours, flying about over the land, disrupting the peace and the ordered life of the country. Then he cried aloud and said: 'There shall come a people with clothes like butterflies. . . .'" (pp.21–22)

The butterflies are, of course, the white men who have already established a mission in the nearby village of Siriana. Chege tells his son, " 'Go to the Mission place. Learn all the wisdom and all the secrets of the white man. But do not follow his vices. Be true to your people and the ancient rites' " (p.24). Waiyaki follows his father's advice, and spends a number of years attending the Mission school, but when he returns to the ridges, he rejects Christianity itself but not the education he has acquired at the mission. He establishes his own school when he returns to the ridges. The theme here—the revolt against Western education—is based on an historical event. Ngugi has stated of the Gikuyu Independent School Movement of the 1920's and 1930's: " 'These were schools which belonged to people who had rebelled against missionary schools [because] they wanted the kind of education that belonged to the people.' " [7] (Ngugi attended one such school himself.)

While Waiyaki attends the Mission school, Christianity is introduced to the people of the ridges by the zealous convert, Joshua, and shortly thereafter the new religion splits Kameno and Makuyu apart. "Joshua's centre was Makuyu, while Kameno was seen as the centre of the tribe" (p.125). Waiyaki establishes additional schools free from Christian indoctrination. After his father dies, however, an elder named Kabonyi becomes jealous of Waiyaki's popularity, in part because he feels his own son (Kaman) is more deserving.

The climax of the novel occurs when Waiyaki falls in love with Joshua's uncircumcised daughter, Nyambura. Waiyaki is accused by the clan of having secret dealings with the Christians (Joshua and the Siriana Mission); of planning to marry an uncircumcised Christian (Nyambura); and of breaking an oath and revealing the secrets of the Kiama society. The charges are in large part trumped up by Kabonyi and his followers. At the end of the story, Waiyaki and Nyambura await their fate at the judgment of the Kiama.

The communal aspect of *The River Between* is every bit as significant as in Achebe's *Things Fall Apart*. The ridges on the Honia river are trapped in a moment of history—just before the final penetration of the white man. Ngugi states, ". . . the missionaries had not as yet penetrated into the hills, though they sent a number of disciples to work there. The people remained conservative, loyal to the ways of the land" (pp.32–33). Waiyaki, who in some ways reminds one of a younger Okonkwo, is similarly trapped by the villagers who will not rally behind him. His prime intention is to unite the villagers—both the Christians and the non-Christians—against the white man. This he believes can be done only by an educational system which incorporates the best from the traditional African culture and from the West. Thus, Ngugi again works with the theme of education and what its role will be in the new Africa. It is also this theme that hinders his story, which at times—in its depiction of village strife—is unrealistic, unconvincing. *The River Between* is a minor work by James Ngugi, squeezed in between his two major novels. It lacks conviction, a sense of fulfillment.

Ngugi's third novel, *A Grain of Wheat* (1967), is his most impressive work and one of the most complicated novels written by an African novelist during the last twenty-five years. Like *Weep Not, Child*, it returns to recent Kenyan history—the State of Emergency during the Mau Mau revolt, thus again making use of an historical event still vivid in his compatriots' eyes. This time, however, the period of the Emergency is over and it is looked back at through the eyes of a handful of men and women from one village whose lives have become irrevocably intertwined. The total impression is of something akin to the obsession of German novelists with World War II in the past twenty-five years, and the reader often wonders how long it will be before Kenyans will be able to look each other in the face without wondering who was a traitor during the Emergency, which lasted from 1952 to 1960.

Structurally, *A Grain of Wheat* is much more involved than Ngugi's two earlier novels. Ngugi in flashbacks constantly shifts his point of view and his use of the temporal. The result is a mirror of the chaos of the Emergency itself. Besides telling the story from the point of view of several of his participants, the author again uses the lyrical collective consciousness—which has played an important technical part in all of his novels—often combined with a quasi-documentary technique which is effectively utilized at strategic points throughout his narrative. The result is a novel which has all of the passions of human drama coupled with an historical objectivity rarely found except in nonfiction. The novel itself has been broken into four distinct, though unnumbered portions—fourteen untitled chapters which then give way to four titled sections.

A Grain of Wheat is also one of the best examples of the African situational novel. Unlike Ngugi's two earlier books which mirrored the turmoil through one or two characters, *A Grain of Wheat* has no central character. Instead, there are six characters who play almost equally important parts in the checkerboard development of the story itself, and at least another six whose parts are indispensible to the action and narrative thread of the story. If there is any main character in the novel, it is the village of Thabai itself—the communal consciousness. Ngugi has abolished the second person he used so effectively in his two earlier novels and uses the communal "we" instead. Most of the important scenes are told from the point of view of the entire community, and Ngugi utilizes the possessive plural *our*: ". . . most people from *our* village came to the meeting. This was Kihika's day; it was Mugo's day; it was *our* day" (p.244. Italics mine).

It is almost impossible to summarize the elaborately entangled stories of the main characters in Ngugi's novel. When the novel begins, it is four days prior to Uhuru Day (Independence) for Kenya—December 12, 1963—and the village of Thabai is involved in the final preparations for the Independence celebrations. The story begins with Mugo, a farmer, alone in his hut:

Mugo felt nervous. He was lying on his back and looking at the roof. Sooty locks hung from the fern and grass thatch and all pointed at his heart. A clear drop of water was delicately suspended above him. The drop fattened and grew dirtier as it absorbed grains of soot. Then it started drawing towards him. He tried to shut his eyes. They would not close. He tried to move his head: it was firmly chained to the bed-frame. The drop grew larger and larger as it drew closer and closer to his eyes. He wanted to cover his eyes with his palms; but his hands, his feet, everything refused to obey his will. In despair, Mugo gathered himself for a final heave and woke up. (p.3)

Although it is in a dream, the suspended element of the drop of water is clearly intended as a symbol of Mugo's own predicament. Christlike, saintly, respected by his fellow villagers as the most heroic example of resistance to the white man during the Emergency, Mugo is inwardly a bundle of raw nerves. It is not until nearly a third of Ngugi's story has unfolded that the reader is let into all of Mugo's past life and learns that he is not the village hero, but the biggest traitor of them all. His guilt has become his obsession. Like the drop of water about to fall, Mugo's own life is about to be pommeled into extinction.

The opening pages of the novel relate in crisscross fashion some of the early years of Mugo's life; his lonely childhood; his upbringing by an alcoholic aunt. The communal aspect of the story is introduced at the beginning of the second chapter; Ngugi's technique here employs a combination of documentary and oral history materials:

Nearly everybody was a member of the Party, but nobody could say with any accuracy when the Party was born: to most people, especially those in the younger generation, the Party had always been there, a rallying centre for action. It changed names, leaders came and went, but the Party remained, opening new visions, gathering greater and greater strength, till on the eve of Uhuru, its influence stretched from one horizon touching the sea to the other resting on the great Lake.

Its origins can, so the people say, be traced to the day the whiteman came to the country, clutching the book of God in both hands, a magic witness that the whiteman was a messenger from the Lord. His tongue was coated with sugar; his humility was touching. For a time, people ignored the voice of the Gikuyu seer who once said: there shall come a people with clothes like the butterflies. They gave him, the stranger with a scalded skin, a place to erect a temporary shelter. Hut complete, the stranger put up another building yards away. This he called the House of God where people could go for worship and sacrifice. (p.13)

The passage continues, articulated by one of the minor characters in the novel, repeating a motif from Ngugi's earlier writing: when the Africans closed their eyes in church, their land was taken from them.

The village elders meet with Mugo and try to persuade him that he, as their most important hero, should give a speech at the Independence celebrations. Mugo declines and Gikonyo, a carpenter and respected member of the village, introduces an idea central to the development of Ngugi's story: " 'I know how you feel. . . . You want to be left alone. Remember this, however: it is not easy for any man in a community to be left alone . . .' " (p.29). The villagers believe that Mugo helped Kihika, one of the most promising of Thabai's youths who was later hanged by the colonial government. As we will later find out, it was Mugo who turned him in to the white District Officer. The elders believe that it is Karanja who is the traitor, and it is their intention to revenge Kihika's death by causing Karanja's at the Independence Day festivities, and thus, symbolically at least, purify their village.

The second part of *A Grain of Wheat* begins with Chapter Four and concentrates on the European expatriates and their remaining days in Kenya before Independence. The most important of the group is John Thompson, now working in the local Forestry Research Station, but the local District Officer during the Emergency. Karanja, whom the villagers believe is the traitor, is introduced here, too, employed as an assistant in the Research Center's library. The stories of these characters unfold in Ngugi's multiple use of flashbacks, and it is in this second part of the novel that Ngugi also begins to sketch in the story of Gikonyo's past life: his courting and winning of his wife, Mumbi, his years in the detention camps, his success in business after the Emergency. The point of view is altered several times as both Gikonyo and Mumbi begin to relate the story of their lives to the silent Mugo, during which time it is revealed that Mumbi had a child by Karanja, the suspected traitor, during the six years that Gikonyo spent in detention. At the beginning of the Emergency, Karanja turned to the white man's side so he could remain in the village close to Mumbi, whom he has always loved. He was appointed the local chief. As a result of their liaison, when Gikonyo returns to Thabai after his years in detention and sees the child he refuses to sleep with his wife and plans his revenge over both Karanja and Mumbi. Ngugi's picture of the jealousy and hatred these characters have for each other is totally human, filled with passion. The estrangement theme here—so infrequent in African fiction—reminds one of the lonely, isolated figures in Sherwood Anderson's *Winesburg, Ohio*. It is communication above all which is lacking among the villagers of Thabai. Gikonyo thinks, "One lived alone . . . went into the grave alone. . . . To live and die alone was the ultimate truth" (p.135). Coupled with this sense of isolation is the ubiquitous use of Christian religious imagery, especially surrounding Mugo:

> Yes. He would speak at the Uhuru celebrations. He would lead the people and bury his past in their gratitude. Nobody need ever know about Kihika. To the few, elect of God, the past was forgiven, was made clean by great deeds that saved many. It was so in the time of Jacob and Esau; it was so in the time of Moses. (p.146)

The third section of *A Grain of Wheat* begins with Chapter Nine and extends through Chapter Thirteen. The communal voice is present at the beginning: "Learned men will, no doubt, dig into the troubled times which we in Kenya underwent, and maybe sum up the lesson of history in a phrase. Why, let us ask them, did the incident in Rira Camp capture the imagination of the world?" (p.149). Some of the worst atrocities of the war were at Rira Camp, under John Thompson's orders. "What occurred next is known to the world. The men were rounded up and locked in their cells. The now famous beating went on day and night. Eleven men died" (p.152). Ngugi's tone is terse, almost journalistic. In an extended flashback the reader now hears the rest of Mumbi's story of her six-year separation from Gikonyo. Thabai village was destroyed as "a warning to other villages never to give food or any help to those fighting in the Forest" (p.164). The emphasis is always on the group experience during the Emergency. When Karanja was made a warrant chief by the colonial government, he became the terror of the village. The time is constantly shifted back and forth between the Emergency and the days prior to Uhuru.

> Karanja was the man who had betrayed Kihika. That Karanja should die on Independence Day seemed just: that he should be humiliated in front of a huge crowd, if he gave himself up, or else be made uncomfortable, was only a necessary preparation for the ritual. (p.175)

This section ends with the focus once again returning to Mugo, as he is seen from the village point of view: "Mugo, our village hero, was no ordinary man" (p.204). The Independence celebrations will be a memorial to the martyred Kihika.

> Wambui put it in this way: Independence Day without him [Mugo] would be stale; he is Kihika born again. She went around the market-place determined to put her secret resolve into practice. Women had to act. Women had to force the issue. "And, after all, he is our son," she told women at the market-place at an impromptu gathering after the rain. (p.204)

In a particularly touching scene, Mugo confesses to Mumbi that he was the one who turned in Kihika (her brother) to the authorities. The image of Mugo's pathetic loneliness is repeated once again. Mugo tells her, " 'I wanted to live my life. I never wanted to be involved in anything. Then he came into my life, here, a night like this, and pulled me into the stream. So I killed him' " (p.210). Ngugi adds to this:

> Mugo was deeply afflicted and confused, because all his life he had avoided conflicts: at home, or at school, he rarely joined the company of other boys for fear of being involved in brawls that might ruin his chances of a better future. . . .

> Jealously, he decided, unable to find another answer to his own question. The reflection revived his old hatred of Kihika now so strong it almost choked him. Kihika who had a mother and a father, and a brother, and a sister, could play with death. He had people who would mourn his end, who would name their children after him, so that Kihika's name would never die from men's lips. Kihika had everything; Mugo had nothing. (p.221)

For the person who tries to stray from the clan, the end can only be tragic.

All of the tensions of the story are brought together in the final portion of Ngugi's novel. In Chapter Fourteen, specifically, the inner hatreds, jealousies, and passions of the African characters are reflected in the foot race that takes place during the Independence Day celebrations. Mumbi, who has now left Gikonyo, watches as Gikonyo and Karanja race around the track, competing for her attention. Neither wins, however, because Gikonyo stumbles and Karanja falls over him, permitting another runner to attain the first place. A tree is planted where Kihika was hanged; the elders are ready to expose Karanja as the turncoat, but Mugo instead confesses to the crime.

The remaining four chapters—named instead of numbered —symbolically purify the village (ritually significant because of the rebirth at Independence) and return the community to normality. Karanja leaves the village, knowing that he will never win Mumbi and that the villagers will never forget his years as the white man's stooge.

> He was scared of black power: he feared those men who had ousted the Thompsons and had threatened him. He thought of standing up and publicly denying any guilt in Kihika's capture. But fear nailed him to the ground. Then that man, Mugo, had appeared with a confession which relieved Karanja. Mwaura turned to Karanja with eyes tense with malice. "He has saved you," Mwaura said, and swiftly moved away. (p.260)

Mugo (now the village scapegoat) is brought to trial by the elders of the village and led away to face the consequences. Another villager tells him, " 'You—No one will ever escape from his own actions' " (p.270). Gikonyo and Mumbi make a fresh attempt to come to grips with the past too:

> "Will you go back to the house, light the fire, and see things don't decay?"
> She considered this for a while, her head turned aside. Then she looked at him, directly, in the eyes.
> "No, Gikonyo. People try to rub out things, but they cannot. Things are not so easy. What has passed between us is too much to be passed over in a sentence. We need to talk, to open our hearts to one another, examine them, and then together plan the future we want. But now, I must go, for the child is ill."
> (p.280)

*A Grain of Wheat** intellectually probes the nature of power, nationalism, and unity—themes that have been reiterated throughout all of Ngugi's writing. Symbolically, like Wole Soyinka in *A Dance of the Forests*, Ngugi is saying that

---

* The significance of the title is implied in the Biblical quotation prior to the last section of Ngugi's novel:

> "Verily, verily I say unto you, Except a corn
> of wheat fall into the ground and die, it
> abideth alone: but if it die, it bringeth
> forth much fruit." (St. John 12:24)

the politics of the present can only be built on an understanding of the past, that each man must come to a realization of his past in the best way he can, and that in the process there are bound to be those who will be hunted and pursued because they themselves have tried to distort their own past lives by shrugging their responsibility to the group—to the nation. Like Ngugi's two other novels, *A Grain of Wheat* is fragmented and impressionistic, based on dozens of short individual scenes, each one contributing a vital part like a piece of a puzzle. Yet this novel, unlike the other two, probes more deeply into the very nature of every society—the individual citizen, his duty to himself, his family, his community, his nation. The characterization, as we will shortly see, is complex and manifold as Ngugi knits a brutal yet realistic picture of the African's relationship to his fellow man, his bravery in the face of the common enemy, his tradition for group solidarity, his sense of humanity which can only be harvested from the group-felt situation.

Characters and Modes of Characterization:

Chinua Achebe, James Ngugi, and Peter Abrahams

THUS FAR IN OUR ANALYSIS OF AFRICAN FICTION, we have ignored what many Western novelists and critics believe to be the novel's prime concern: character. We have noted, however, some of the identifying aspects of several individual characters and the de-emphasis of characterization in a number of African novelists: Achebe's tendency to rely on action for character revelation in *Things Fall Apart*; the "type" charcters (young adults and their parents) in the works of the Onitsha novelists, and the stagnant nature of characterization in these works; Tutuola's tendency to base characterization on the function of the person or creature within his tale; the situational plot wherein character may become secondary to the ideas or the historical patterns the writer is working with. There are vast differences in the characters themselves who appear in the works by these and other African writers, and also in the modes of characterization used by the individual writer. I suggest that many of these writers share certain basic similarities because of the African concept of group solidarity; but I believe, too, that characterization in African fiction may often be quite similar to what we think of its being in the West. In addition, the characters in African fiction and the modes of characterization may often be shaped by the traditions within the geographical area of the given writer, for there are decided differences in these matters in West, East, or South African fiction.

West African Anglophone fiction, especially by the novelists who began their writing careers in the 1950's and the early 1960's, is almost totally devoid of what in the West has been referred to as "character growth." Instead, in whole groups of novels, the characters are basically the same at the end of the story as they were at the beginning. For the non-African reader, this may present a problem. I, for example, find it easy to identify with the situations Chinua Achebe's characters are involved in; but rarely do I identify with the characters themselves. This identification does not take place because of the absence of what I have been trained to see in Western fiction: character development. My empathy extends instead to the situations, the forces operating upon these characters. I am certain, however, that the African reader does make an identification with Achebe's characters, at least on a basic level—though I feel that it may be the situation the character is placed in that leads to the identification as much as anything else. The tendency toward non-developing characters does not seem to be as prevalent, however, in East or South African fiction. Here the Western reader is likely to find characters who do change as the story develops, characters with whom he can readily make an identification.

Another geographically oriented difference is the importance that women have in East and South African fiction compared with their relatively minor importance in much West African fiction. In many early West African novels, the female characters play almost no significant part; if they are present, they are mere objects, performing a function.* Yet, in East African fiction—as we have already noted in Ngugi's *A Grain of Wheat*—female characters are often more important, frequently playing an integral part in the development of the story. In South African fiction, because of a more lengthy exposure to the West, heterosexual love plays a more important part than it does in West or East African fiction. The love story, which is almost totally missing from West African fiction, is often of prime importance with the South African novelist. All of these aspects can be noted only by examining the fiction related to these areas. Our examples here will be limited to Chinua Achebe (Nigeria), James Ngugi (Kenya), and Peter Abrahams (South Africa).

The primary method of portraying character that Achebe uses in *Things Fall Apart*—characterization by action—is important in all of his other novels. We have already noted that Okonkwo's character is developed almost entirely in this manner. Achebe uses very little dialogue, and there are only two or three very brief passages of introspection. Okonkwo is the same at the end of the story as he was at the beginning, for the revelation of character was not Achebe's prime concern in writing *Things Fall Apart*. This does not mean, however, that the reader learns little about Okonkwo—it simply means that what he learns is learned in another way and one certainly not unknown to Western fiction. Okonkwo's friend,

* There are some partial exceptions to this: Elechi Amadi's *The Concubine*; S. A. Konadu's *A Woman in Her Prime*; and Flora Nwapa's *Efuru*. To a certain extent, these three novels are in-depth character portraits of the African woman in her society. The weakness of each book is the relative lack of interaction of the heroine with the other characters in the story.

Obierika, is characterized by more typically Western methods, though he too is of secondary importance to Achebe's objective: recording the destruction of a traditional culture.

Destruction of the traditional culture is also of prime concern in Achebe's third novel, *Arrow of God*. Here Achebe relates the story of Ezeulu, the Chief Priest of Ulu, the God of the six villages of Umuaro, and his attempt to regain the power which he feels has slowly been slipping away from his position. Because of a misunderstanding with the white District Officer, Captain Winterbottom, Ezeulu is exiled from his village and placed in jail for more than a month. When he returns, the period of the year for harvesting the new yams is near, and only Chief Priest Ezeulu can announce the New Yam Festival which must precede the harvest. His exile from Umuaro, however, has thrown off his reckoning of the yearly cycle, and when Ezeulu refuses to announce the New Yam Festival, and the yams begin to rot in the land, the villagers *en masse* make their sacrifices to the Christian god instead, and the old traditional religion loses its last vestiges of power almost overnight.

Achebe's methods of characterization in *Arrow of God* are somewhat different from those in *Things Fall Apart*. Ezeulu is a much more significant person than Okonkwo, though Ezeulu too is characterized in great part by what he does rather than by lengthy authorial commentary or description. There is more introspection, however, both in the form of dreams and in conversations Ezeulu has with himself. Yet, Ezeulu is still an enigma—and this is clearly Achebe's intention. A much less gregarious individual than Okonkwo, Ezeulu bears a closer affinity to Obierika of the earlier novel. Misunderstood by his family and friends, proud, obstinate, quick-tempered and determined not to bend—these are the characterstics he shares with Okonkwo. His wisdom, however, connects him every bit as much with Obierika's pensive probing of the future. Achebe has increased the importance of dialogue in this novel—especially dialogue which makes use of materials drawn from traditional oral literature such as the proverb. Hardly a page of his story passes without the presence of a proverb or two; sometimes there will be as many as half-a-dozen, piled one upon another. Telling the elders of Captain Winterbottom's request to see him, Ezeulu says,

> "I was thanking you for what you have done. Our people say that if you thank a man for what he has done he will have strength to do more. But there is one great omission here for which I beg forgiveness. A man does not summon Umuaro and not set before them even a pot of palm wine. But I was taken by surprise and as you know the unexpected beats even a man of valour. . . ." Then he told them the story of the Court Messenger's visit to him. "My kinsmen," he said in conclusion, "that was what I woke up this morning and found. Ogbuefi Akuebue was there and saw it with me. I thought about it for a long time and decided that Umuaro should join with me in seeing and hearing what I have seen and heard; for when a man sees a snake all by himself he may wonder whether it is an ordinary snake or the untouchable python. So I said to myself: 'Tomorrow I shall summon Umuaro and tell them.' Then one mind said to me: 'Do you know what may happen in the night or at dawn?' That is why, although I have no palm wine to place before you I still thought I should call you together. If we have life there will be time enough for palm wine. Unless the penis dies young it will surely eat bearded meat. When hunting day comes we shall hunt in the backyard of the grass-cutter. I salute you all." [1]

Sometimes the oral illustration is related to a more personal desire or need. When released from jail, Ezeulu says,

> "I cannot stay another day. . . . I am the tortoise who was trapped in a pit of excrement for two whole markets; but when helpers came to haul him out on the eighth day he cried: Quick, quick: I cannot stand the stench." (p.204)

The use of these oral examples is a primary means of characterization, and it is the adults in Achebe's novel who make the greatest use of these materials—giving the impression of great wisdom. The majority of the proverbs in *Arrow of God* are spoken as dialogue rather than as a part of authorial commentary. The unique aspect of Achebe's characterization, then, is his use of oral literary materials—far more frequently than almost all other African writers.

There are more numerous examples, too, of authorial commentary in *Arrow of God* than in *Things Fall Apart*. The most revealing of these comments are often presented through a second character, reflecting upon another. In such a manner, Ezeulu's son, Edogo, thinks about his father:

> The trouble with Ezeulu was that he could never see something and take his eyes away from it. . . . That was what their father could never learn. He must go on treating his grown children like little boys, and if they ever said no there was a big quarrel. This was why the older his children grew the more he seemed to dislike them. (pp.103–104)

And later Edogo—

> . . . remembered what his mother used to say when she was alive, that Ezeulu's only fault was that he expected everyone— his wives, his kinsmen, his children, his friends and even his enemies—to think and act like himself. Anyone who dared to say no to him was an enemy. (p.105)

The total impression one gets of Ezeulu—and it is clear that this opaque presentation is intentional because of his very position as Chief Priest—is that of an extremely lonely man, a man of the strongest moral convictions who ultimately must stand alone in his decisions. Ezeulu's inability to be understood by his family and friends is of a dual nature, making it impossible for him to understand them too. Ezeulu is presented as the strong-willed elder, half man, half spirit, surrounded by jealous and quarrelling wives, by children who either fear or ignore him. Achebe's concluding picture of the insane Ezeulu is indeed poignant, yet not unexpected.

Perhaps the most interesting contrast that Achebe makes in *Arrow of God* is between Ezeulu and the white District Officer, Captain Winterbottom. Ironically, they are quite similar, and the descriptive terms that apply to Ezeulu— obstinate, misunderstood, lonely, quick tempered and brash—

all apply to Winterbottom, too. However, Achebe's European characters in *Arrow of God* are generally a little less convincing than they could be, for, in truth, they are examined only from the outside, are stereotyped and one-dimensional, efficient little machines meant to do a job in the British Foreign Service, and, necessarily, I suppose, are in too many ways typical of the men who were in the colonial service. The following comment on Winterbottom, who is given to judging the Africans in rather generalized concepts, is typical:

> Thinking of this incident Captain Winterbottom could find some excuse for the overseer. He was a man from another clan; in the eyes of the native, a foreigner. But what excuse could one offer for a man who was their blood brother and chief? Captain Winterbottom could only put it down to cruelty of a kind which Africa alone produced. It was this elemental cruelty in the psychological make-up of the native that the starry-eyed European found so difficult to understand. (pp.64–65)

Achebe's tendency to stereotype his expatriates in *Arrow of God* is an indication, I believe, of the direction in which he was moving by the time his third novel was published—in 1964. His African reading audience was rapidly increasing and by the time his fourth novel, *A Man of the People*, appeared in 1966, it can truly be said that Achebe was writing for the African reader first and the foreign audience second. Almost all—if not all—of Achebe's characters in *A Man of the People* are stereotypes, because with this novel Achebe moved into a new area: satire. In many ways the novel is his weakest so far, and I am convinced that its popularity with the African reading audience bears little correlation to its literary merits; however, the novel accomplishes exactly what it set out to do—satirize life in Nigeria in the mid-1960's. Many of the situations satirized can only be appreciated by someone who lived in Nigeria during those years: political corruption, the increasing bureaucracy, the postal strike, the census, the means of communication, the daily news media.

It probably is not fair to criticize Achebe's cardboard

characters in *A Man of the People*, since satire rarely is built on believable characters. Even the fact that the story is told in the first person results in no great insight into Achebe's narrator, Odili Samalu, or any of the other characters. The thin story thread is more reminiscent of the novels of Cyprian Ekwensi than of Achebe's earlier works: when Chief Nanga, the country's Minister of Culture, seduces Odili's girl, Odili swears to end Nanga's political career. He runs a race for Nanga's seat in parliament and another race to win Nanga's intended second wife. When the story line gets out of control, Achebe conveniently draws his political morality to an end by having the nation succumb to a military coup. In spite of the de-emphasis on character development, there is certainly more dialogue than Achebe has ever used before, especially in dialects such as Pidgin English, as a means of characterization. The conversation at times is witty, but the whole affair— Odili's entering politics because he has lost his girl—is unconvincing and rather overdrawn. Everybody gets satirized, however, educated and uneducated Africans, the British and the Americans, even the Peace Corps. The following dialogue is typical:

> "So you see, Mr . . . I'm sorry I didn't catch your first name?"
> "Odili."
> "Odili—a beautiful sound—may I call you by that?"
> "Sure," I said, already partly Americanized.
> "Mine is John. I don't see why we should call one another Mister this and Mister that—like the British."

* * *

> "America may not be perfect," he was saying, "but don't forget that we are the only powerful country in the entire history of the world, the only one, which had the power to conquer others and didn't do it." [2]

A Man of the People should be acknowledged for exactly what it is: an entertainment, written for Africans. Achebe no longer tries to explain the way it is, to apologize for the way things are, because this is exactly the point: this is the way things are. The characters are ineffectual, and Achebe's satire itself will be short-lived. The story and the characters have none of the magnitude or the nobililty of those in *Things Fall Apart* or *Arrow of God*.

The most noticeable difference in methods of characterization between James Ngugi and Chinua Achebe is Ngugi's use of impressionism, the internal rendering of his character's emotional reactions to the external world. The result is a much more introspective approach to character than in the novels by Chinua Achebe, in spite of the fact that Ngugi, too, generally uses the third person narrator for his tales. We have already noted Ngugi's use of the second person "you" as an extremely effective device for drawing the reader into his narrative. Ngugi's use of the third person is no less effective, with frequent insertions of internal monologue, which give us direct access to the character. Most of *Weep Not, Child,* for example, is told from Njoroge's point of view, although Njoroge is not the narrator of the story. The alterations which take place in his perceptions as the novel advances and as he grows from a young boy to an adult—his emotional development—are impressionistically rendered from the beginning to the end of the novel.

The opening pages of *Weep Not, Child* are typical of Ngugi's use of the third person to depict Njoroge's feelings. The reader immediately reacts to Nyokabi as Njoroge does— as if he were Njoroge. The italicized passages almost immediately inject the reader into Njoroge's mind—a technique scarcely found in Achebe's fiction—into the introspection of the young child's mind:

> *Oh, Mother, I'll never bring shame to you. Just let me get there, just let me.* The vision of his childhood again opened before him. For a time he contemplated the vision. He lived in

it alone. It was just there, for himself; a bright future . . .
Aloud he said, "I like school." [3]

Often Ngugi's use of the second person merges with Njoroge's
thoughts: "You did not know what to call the Indian. Was he
also a white man? Did he too come from England?" (p.27).
These thoughts are the reader's, the communal center's (the
second person's) and those of the young boy named Njoroge
—a merging of the three points of view into one, lyrically
rendered so the reader experiences situations along with the
child, so that the reader grows along with Njoroge. There is
a definite development in Njoroge as the story progresses
and this alteration in character is another marked difference
between Ngugi's characters and Achebe's. Nowhere in West
African Anglophone fiction is there quite the same thing—
the African child's growth into adulthood, presented impressionistically from his own ever-changing point of view.

Ngugi's use of impressionism for the depiction of Njoroge's
character can be seen most clearly in the scattered passages
throughout the novel that are concerned with Njoroge's experiences in school, fittingly because this is the new world into
which he has been catapulted. Colors and sounds are merged
to record the child's growing awareness of the unfamiliar
educational world:

> The teacher wore a white blouse and a green skirt. Njoroge
> liked the white and green because it was like a blooming white
> flower on a green plant. Grass in this country was green in wet
> weather and flowers bloomed white all over the land, especially
> in Njahi season. Njoroge, however, feared her when two days
> later she beat a boy, whack! whack! ("Bring the other
> hand!") whack! whack! whack! The stick broke into bits.
> Njoroge could almost feel the pain. It was as if it was being
> communicated to him without physical contact. (pp.34–35)

The impressionism in some of these scenes is achieved by
Ngugi's use of the dramatic—episodes are rendered as if
Ngugi were writing a drama (complete with stage directions)

instead of a novel, and the dramatic is mixed with the authorial use of what Dorrit Cohn has called "narrated monologue" [4]— the internal depiction of a character's thoughts by use of the third-person narrator and the tense of narration:

> The children laughed. It was so funny the way he said this. He made yet another mark on the board. Njoroge's heart beat fast. To know that he was actually learning! He would have a lot to tell his mother. (p.58)

There is also considerably more authorial commentary in the depiction of character in Ngugi's *Weep Not, Child* than in Achebe's *Things Fall Apart* or *Arrow of God* and this is particularly fitting because Njoroge is not a man of action but an extremely sensitive young child increasingly given to fantasies and daydreams. At times these authorial comments have a staccato-like effect in their brevity, such as the following three statements which occur on the same page of the text: "He clung to books and whatever the school had to offer. . . . Education for him, as for many boys of his generation, held the key to the future. . . . The Bible was his favorite book" (p.77). For Njoroge, school slowly becomes a means of escape and Ngugi depicts Njoroge's loneliness as an intellectual isolation from his family and friends, a theme that has found an increasing importance in African fiction, and that illustrates the African child's reaction to Western education. Even Njoroge's friend, Mwihaki, as we have already seen, is unable to understand the gradual alteration that is taking place within Njoroge's mind:

> Whenever he was with Mwihaki, he longed to impart some of these things to her. Yet when he tried to define them in words, he failed. So he kept them all to himself, walking alone in the fields and sometimes finding companionship with the nights. (p.78)

In *Weep Not, Child*—which is essentially a one-character novel—the female characters play more of a role than they

generally do in Achebe's fiction, but still are basically under-
developed and used functionally. There is certainly a drastic
difference between Ngotho's wives and Ezeulu's but as far as
their characterizations go or their functions within the story,
there is little difference at all. Even Mwihaki is little more
than a sounding board for Njoroge's ideas. Other characters
in *Weep Not, Child*, though depicted with sensitivity and
compassion, are essentially secondary when compared to the
completeness with which Ngugi renders Njoroge. And although Ngugi's white characters in *Weep Not, Child* are a
little less stereotyped than Achebe's, they are for the most part
undeveloped.

Ngugi's methods of characterization in *The River Between*
are essentially the same as they are in *Weep Not, Child*. This
novel, however, moves toward being what we in the West
think of as a love story—though the depiction of the lovers'
relationship is rendered not in Western concepts but in those
which are fully African. In some ways it may be argued of
Ngugi's protagonists that it is Waiyaki's involvement with
Nyambura that leads to his downfall; or, in other words, the
inter-involvement of Ngugi's characters leads to Waiyaki's
downfall instead of the more abstract conflict of character
with concept or an exterior force as in *Weep Not, Child* or
the novels of Chinua Achebe. Proverbs and other oral literary
materials are also occasionally used in the presentation of
character in *The River Between*, no doubt because this novel
is set in an Africa for the most part uninfluenced by the West.

A Grain of Wheat, Ngugi's third novel, is particularly
interesting when compared to Chinua Achebe's later works,
for while Achebe has plainly been moving in the direction
of the African reader, Ngugi, it seems to me, has written fiction which probably appeals to a more Westernized reading
audience. I have already noted the elaborate technical innovations in *A Grain of Wheat*, and Ngugi's characters here also

are presented in more conventional Western patterns. They are much more fully realized than in almost any of the works by his West African counterparts, much more fully developed. The total effect is a more personalized account of African life than we are likely to find in Achebe or other early West African Anglophone writers or even in Ngugi's two earlier novels, for here it may be said that the characters are truly complex personalities, often presented psychologically—a mode almost completely absent in other West African Anglophone fiction. It is the interaction of his six main characters—Mugo, Kihika, Gikonyo, Mumbi, Karanja, John Thompson—and the many lesser ones that gives this novel the scope of humanity and personal flavor that it has. No longer are characters simply mouthing the author's ideas, instead they are voicing their passions and their innermost thoughts; no longer are characters fighting the big bogy man of the West, instead they are gnawing at each other.

The presentation of internal character in *A Grain of Wheat* is rendered in a variety of ways: authorial commentary, extended sections of dialogue where a character tells to another the story of his involvement in the Emergency, or the stream-of-consciousness technique. The latter is especially effective for depicting Mugo's thoughts to the reader, since he is not the kind of person who can articulate his feelings to someone else. The third person authorial commentary frequently merges into stream-of-consciousness presentation of thought:

As soon as Gikonyo had gone, Mugo rushed to the door, flung it open and cried out: Come back. He waited for an answer, and getting no response went back and sat down to think. His mind lightly hopped from one episode to another. Gikonyo had wanted him to say something. He felt he should have said something. Twice he had moistened his lips with spittle and cleared his throat ready to speak. But his mouth was dry; thoughts and words refused to form. What could he have told him? Gikonyo's outburst against Karanja's betrayal and his unforgiving anger at Mumbi had made Mugo recoil within. Every time Gikonyo talked about Mumbi and Karanja, Mugo felt sharp irritation as if acid was eating away at an ulcer in his stomach. He now shivered at the recollection. He became restless. He stood up and walked about the room. Suppose I had told him . . . suppose I had suddenly told him. . . . Everything would have been all over . . . all over . . . the knowledge . . . the burden . . . fears . . . and hopes. . . . I could have told him . . . and maybe . . . maybe . . . Or is that why he told me his own story? At this thought he abruptly stopped pacing and leaned against the bed. A man does not go to a stranger and tear his heart open. . . . I see everything . . . everything . . . he pretended not to look at me . . . yet kept on stealing eyes at me . . . see if I was frightened . . . see . . . if. . . . No. He recalled the agony on Gikonyo's face. His voice had sounded sincere and trusting.[5]

The text weaves from the third person presentation of Mugo's thoughts in the past tense (the narrated monologue) into the first person, present tense, interior monologue.

It should at least be mentioned that often Ngugi's minor characters in *A Grain of Wheat* are also quite striking in spite of their brief appearances in the novel. The brief portrait of Gatu—whom Gikonyo meets in one of the detention camps —is one such portrait: terse, vivid, and horrifying. There are also extremely effective moments when Ngugi presents his European characters internally instead of externally.

A novel written by a black South African is often remarkably different from a West African or an East African one. The ties that South Africa has had with Europe go back considerably further than do those of most areas of tropical Africa, and in this century at least it has been possible for the black or Coloured South African to grow up in an urban milieu where English is his first language. In spite of the politics of separation, educational possibilities for the black South African, including the significant factor of advanced education, are of longer standing than are those in tropical Africa.

In South Africa it has been possible for a writer to grow up in a family where English is the most commonly spoken language, and in an environment conducive to writing. Many tropical African writers have lived in households where the printed word was almost nonexistent. Because their South African counterparts have often experienced a more bookish atmosphere, the shaping of their materials has been clearly influenced in two areas especially: South African writing tends to be almost totally devoid of anthropological background, and the influence from oral literary materials is usually quite negligible.

The fact that South Africa is multi-racial, as well as that it has been a white-dominated society for so many years, has also had a major influence on its writers. Ezekiel Mphahlele has commented on the frequent autobiographies of South African writers, and the small amount of fiction in relation to the total published writing:

> During the last twenty years the political, social climate of South Africa has been growing viciously difficult for a non-white to write in. It requires tremendous organization of one's mental and emotional faculties before one can write a poem or a novel or a play. This has become all but impossible.[6]

The South African race situation, Mphahlele says, has conditioned the South African writer—forced him to concentrate on the shorter fictional work (the short story) or the more obvious form of protest, the autobiography. The social conditions are related to those that led to the great number of slave narratives in the United States in the nineteenth century, well before the development of black American fiction. The overriding theme of black South African writing—in all forms —is indeed the inhuman life imposed upon the Africans by the European population.

As a result of these and other conditions, characterization in South African fiction is more closely aligned with characterization in Western fiction than with that in writing from tropical Africa, and the novel itself is in many ways an extension of the traditional English novel because there are few African innovations. In South African black writing, there is hardly any distinction between the importance of male and female characters, for example, and the love theme is often portrayed as it is in the West. If anything, the African woman in South African writing may play a more dominant role than the male—in large part because of the emasculation of the African male by the white population—again a theme found in black American writing.

The most prolific novelist from South Africa is Peter Abrahams; and his early novel, *Mine Boy*, which was published in 1946—earlier than any of the other writings we have been concerned with—is representative of the South African novel as a whole. The story itself is relatively uncomplicated—an account of a young man's exposure to life in Johannesburg and his work as leader of one of the work crews in a gold mine. The concentration, however, is on life in Johannesburg itself; thus *Mine Boy* is a novel with urbanization as its theme.

When the story begins, Xuma, the main character, has just arrived in the Malay Camp section of Johannesburg. Almost immediately he meets Leah, a "Skokiaan Queen," a woman who brews and sells illicit beer (for alcoholic beverages other than a mild so-called Kaffir beer which is legalized are prohibited for Africans in South Africa). Leah takes Xuma into her house temporarily, and it is here that much of the story takes place. Living with Leah are a number of other people, and they along with Xuma and Leah play central roles in the story. The concluding paragraph of Abrahams' first chapter sets the scene of the novel and the fate of his characters:

> A strange group of people, these, he thought. Nothing tied them down. They seem to believe in nothing. But well, they had given him a bed. She had given it to him. She who was the

strangest of them all. And in the other room the old one they call Daddy was sleeping against a wall with an open mouth and with nothing to cover him. But life is strange. Yes, and these people are life. . . . Of course. . . .[7]

Life in Johannesburg, Xuma shortly learns, is very transitory. The Africans have been completely cut off from their traditional life, and nothing in the new one can be thought of as a replacement because of the South African racial situation.

There is little plot in *Mine Boy*. Rather, Abrahams' story is one of character and atmosphere, for, like Cyprian Ekwensi's Lagos, Abraham's picture of Johannesburg's Malay Camp is in many ways the prime concern of his novel. Blacks, Coloureds, and whites are all in the novel, but it is only the sections of the story that are set in the Malay Camp among the African characters that are truly alive. The brief sojourns that Xuma makes in the segregated white areas of the city are flat and considerably less realistically drawn; Abrahams' white characters are often given to mouthing ideas of racial equality—rather than living these ideas as the African characters do. Xuma is, of course, the center-most character in the story. Shy, alone, withdrawn, almost a country bumpkin at the beginning, he is wiser, a little more mature and scarred, by the time the novel ends; his story is a little like the Pilgrim's Progress into the city of chaos and sin. The parts of the story which deal with Xuma are essentially about his effectiveness as a mine leader in the Johannesburg mines, and his involvement with the two women who love him, Eliza and Maisy. Although for the greater part Xuma is presented from the outside by action and authorial commentary, there are places where the reader is thrust into Xuma's innermost thoughts via the use of the internal monologue.

If Xuma is essentially naive and optimistic about Johannesburg, the other characters are almost all shown as victims of the pressures of Johannesburg ghetto life. Leah, the most

important, is referred to again and again as a "strong" woman
—the pillar upon which her unorthodox "family" leans. Of
Xuma's first contact with her, Abrahams notes,

> Xuma looked at the woman. She was tall and big, with that
> smooth yellowness of the Basuto women, and she had sharp dark
> eyes. A strong woman, he decided, and those eyes can see right
> through a man. (p.11)

She is practical in business, shrewd, almost calculating—her
every move is against the city which constantly attempts to
beat her down. It is Leah who takes care of all the other
characters in the story, but in the end, she too, becomes a
victim of the city's repression, and she is taken off to jail for
brewing the illicit beer. Two other characters, Daddy and
Drunk Liz, have learned that the only way they can endure
the city is by being in a constant drunken stupor. Daddy,
especially, is no more than a shell of a man, yet when he dies
after being knocked down by an automobile Leah tells Xuma
that the man he saw was nothing like the man Leah knew in
earlier years:

> "You scorn him, heh? Yet when he first came to the city he
> was a man. Such a man! He was strong and he was feared and
> he was respected. And now you scorn him. You may think I am
> an old woman but I tell you, Xuma, he was a man such as I
> have never seen." (p.88)

Much of the story of Xuma's life in Johannesburg concerns his relationship with two other women, Eliza and Maisy.
Xuma falls in love with Eliza shortly after he comes to
Johannesburg, but Eliza is slow to return this love. It is difficult for her to love Xuma because she is educated and he is
not. Of all the characters in the novel, she is most torn by the
false values of the white world. As she tells Xuma,

> "I am no good and I cannot help myself. It will be right if
> you hate me. You should beat me. But inside me there is some-
> thing wrong. And it is because I want things of the white people.

I want to be like the white people and go where they go and do the things they do and I am black. I cannot help it. Inside I am not black and I do not want to be a black person. I want to be like they are, you understand, Xuma. It is no good but I cannot help it. It is just so. And it is that that makes me hurt you. . . . Please understand." (p.68)

By the end of the story, when she runs away from Xuma and Johannesburg—as another one of its victims—she has become little more than a pathetic creature, unable to attain her objectives in the black world. Maisy, the other woman in Xuma's life, is totally opposite, and Abrahams' contrast of the two women is especially effective. "This one knew how to be happy," Abrahams tells us, "She knew how to laugh. And it was so good that she made other people laugh and be happy as well" (p.101). Patiently she waits for Xuma who is blinded by his love for Eliza. The triangular love story here is of particular interest compared to the plots of most tropical African fiction. Xuma thinks, "The only thing that is bad is if a man loves a woman and she loves him not" (p. 126). The result for Xuma is a different kind of loneliness from that usually expressed in fiction from tropical Africa—loneliness because of a love which is not returned. This loneliness is also articulated more explicitly than in the fiction we have examined from tropical Africa: "The life around him made Xuma more conscious of his isolation, of his loneliness, of the absence of Eliza and his great need for her" (p.164).

But if Xuma is lonely and isolated because of his unfulfilled love and and the debilitating life in Johannesburg, there is still companionship. Again and again Abrahams illustrates the growing friendship Xuma shares with Leah, Ma Plank, and Maisy. This is of crucial importance since *Mine Boy* differs so greatly from other African fiction where the family still plays a significant part. In *Mine Boy* the family has been completely destroyed, there is no sense of the communal consciousness. People band together out of a common need. There is no sense of the basic filial unit which plays such an important function in tropical African fiction. Nor are there any children to give the novel warmth and humor and the happiness we have seen in other African novels. Abrahams has created an adult world instead—in a city which eventually destroys its inhabitants. The strong characters, other than Xuma, are all women, and in spite of the optimistic and overly didactic ending, one cannot foresee much of a future for Xuma. He is still young; the city will eventually count him in its toll.

7

Assimilated Négritude:

Camara Laye's
Le Regard Du Roi

THE FRENCH COLONIAL POLICY OF ASSIMILATION was designed to make the African into a black Frenchman. The African was told that he had no worthwhile traditions of his own, that his own culture was not worth clinging to. Instead, the black man in the French colony was supposed to immerse himself so completely into what the French felt was the superior culture that he would lose all vestiges of his former "uncivilized" life. For the potential African writer this was an especially difficult predicament; he was told to emulate the French classics in his own writing, to learn French so well that his own vernacular language was forgotten: "Think French! Think *in* French!" Assimilation was thus based on the assumed belief that the dominant world language and culture were French. The effects were of an eclectic nature. When asked why he chose to write his poetry in French, Léopold Sédar Senghor wrote:

Parce que nous sommes des métis culturels, parce que, si nous sentons en nègres, nous nous exprimons en français, parce que le français est une langue à vocation universelle, que notre message s'adresse *aussi* aux Français de France et aux autres hommes, parce que le français est une langue "de gentillesse et d'honnêteté."

[Because we are cultural half-castes, because, although we feel as Africans, we express ourselves as Frenchmen, because French is a language with a universal vocation, because our message is addressed to the Frenchmen of France as well as to other men, because French is a language of 'graciousness and civility'.] [1]

The assimilation policy eventually backfired. In the early 1930's, a group of black students in Paris, from Africa and the Caribbean—with French as the only language of communication among them—laid the groundwork for the first modern African literary movement: négritude. Above all, négritude was to be a revolt against the French colonial policy of assimilation, for these students felt that if they simply mocked the French classics in their own writing, they were, in truth, contributing nothing new to world literature. As Ellen Conroy Kennedy and Paulette J. Trout have written:

The *témoins de la négritude*, as they dubbed themselves, became convinced that there were actual differences in perception, in the fundamental apprehension of reality, between the white and black races. Their credo, and the new literature through which it was to be expressed, would find its sources in what they thought of as the Negro's "special" sensibility, his feeling for rhythm, myth, nature, the erotic and emotional life, group solidarity. . . .

. . . *les témoins* discarded the French classics in favor of new models. The stylized beauty of African masks, the natural humor and wisdom of ancient tales and legends, American "blues" and the spontaneity of Negro American poets such as Claude McKay, Langston Hughes, and Countee Cullen were fervently admired. Senghor experimented with translating oral poems from his native Serer, Birago Diop "recorded" legends gathered from his village *griot*, Ousmane Socé Diop published *Karim* (1935), a novel which viewed transitional Senegalese society through the eyes of its confused young hero. [2]

On the one hand, cultural assimilation had failed—it led to open revolt and négritude. Stated conversely, assimilation succeeded in producing through this revolt the major African poetic movement in the twentieth century. It is exactly this revolt that Jean-Paul Sartre seemed somewhat surprised about in "Orphée noir," his introductory essay to the 1948 Senghor collection, *Anthologie de la nouvelle poésie nègre et malgache de langue française*. Read today, the most upsetting aspect of Sartre's essay is his inability to hide his surprise, a little as if he were saying, "My goodness—they even write poetry?" This condescending tone is present throughout much of his essay.

The intended result of assimilation has been illustrated fictively in a number of Francophone African novels portraying the cultural half-caste, as Senghor expressed it, trapped between two cultures, belonging to neither. One of the best examples of this is undoubtedly *Mission terminée* (*Mission to Kala*) by the Cameroonian novelist, Mongo Beti. The story concerns a student named Jean-Marie Medza, who has just failed the oral part of his *baccalauréat* exams. Sent up-country to the "backwards" village of Kala to retrieve the errant wife of one of his relatives, Medza soon realizes that his French education has failed him in more ways than one. When the villagers question him about his education (such as a request to "explain geography") he realizes how thoroughly inadequate his education has been. The oral examination they give him is much more grueling than the one he failed at his school. Other, more personal matters, such as his naiveté in regard to the sexual patterns of his culture, are made blatantly clear to him. By the time he returns to his home, Medza realizes that his real education began only when he arrived in Kala. The solution would not have been simply a matter of staying in Kala, however, where he was esteemed by the villagers because of the amount of his education—for by the end of his stay in the up-country village, Medza has realized that he is cut off from both cultures. The final picture we see of him is that of the outsider, fated to wander the world looking for an ideal which had been at least hinted at during his stay in Kala. As Medza himself explains it,

> le drame dont souffre notre peuple, c'est celui d'un homme laissé à lui-même dans un monde qui ne lui appartient pas, un monde qu'il n'a pas fait, un monde où il ne comprend rien. C'est le drame d'un homme sans direction intellectuelle, d'un homme marchant à l'aveuglette, la nuit, dans un quelconque New-York hostile. Qui lui apprendra à ne traverser la Cinquième Avenue qu'aux passages cloutés? Qui lui apprendra a déchiffrer le "Piétons, attendez"? Qui lui apprendra à lire une carte de métro, à prendre les correspondances?

> [The tragedy which our nation is suffering today is that of a man left to his own devices in a world which does not belong to him, which he has not made and does not understand. It is the tragedy of man bereft of any intellectual compass, a man walking blindly through the dark in some hostile city like New York. Who will tell him that he can only cross Fifth Avenue by the pedestrian crossings, or teach him how to interpret the traffic signs? How will he solve the intricacies of a subway map, or know where to change trains?] [3]

This "trapped" portrayal of the African who has been assimilated, and then found it imposible to accept his own traditional culture, has played a part in a number of other significant Francophone African works: Ousmane Socé Diop's *Karim* (1935), Bernard B. Dadié's *Climbié* (1956), Cheikh Hamidou Kane's *L'aventure ambiguë* (1961), and Camara Laye's autobiography, *L'Enfant noir* (*The African Child*) (1953), works for the most part published prior to African independence. Several of these African novelists and one or two others (Ferdinand Oyono and Birago Diop) all but ceased writing and publishing once independence was attained, implying that there was nothing more to write about other than the colonial experience—which is directly or indirectly the concern of all of these works. The result has been the vanishing Francophone African novelist.

Of the writers mentioned here, only Camara Laye has

published an additional work since independence (*Dramouss*, [*A Dream of Africa*] 1966), and it is with Laye that the picture of the "assimilated" novelist takes on its most significant twist: the négritude novel. Usually négritude is thought of as a poetic movement, but in the works by Camara Laye, African cultural values have been so thoroughly woven into the novel's form that the result is a kind of assimilated presentation of African values, African traditional life: négritude. The result is a much more unified introduction of anthropological materials into the texture of the novel itself, rather than the inclusion of ethnographical background in isolated passages. The African cultural values have been so deftly handled in the works of Camara Laye that the reader is almost unaware that they are there. It is this use of what I call "assimilated anthropology" that, I believe, is the major distinction between the Francophone African novelist and the Anglophone African novelist, for the Francophone writer has remained much closer to the French classical tradition, changing the novel in fewer ways than his Anglophone counterpart, and, as a result, has produced a more intellectualized concept of African traditions, values, and life.

Laye's first work, *L'Enfant noir*, which was published in 1953, has often been regarded as a novel but is, in actuality, an autobiographical account of his childhood and adolescence, growing up in Guinea. The narrative ends as Laye boards an airplane for departure to Paris to continue his studies. *L'Enfant noir* is undoubtedly one of the most significant works by an African writer and certainly the most readable autobiography by a writer from tropical Africa. It is also, I feel, an illustration of Laye's early attempts at unifying cultural materials into a coherent artistic achievement. Anthropological materials are introduced into the narrative, yet, for the most part, they are left unexplained. Laye wants the reader to accept them at face value, and admits that he often has no explanation for the unusual happenings he has recorded. For example, after explaining his mother's totem, the crocodile, which protects her from crocodile-infested waters during flood times, Laye comments, "le monde bouge, le monde change; il bouge et change à telle enseigne que mon propre totem—j'ai mon totem aussi—m'est inconnu." ["I, too, had my totem, but I no longer remember what it was."] [4] Earlier, Laye had written concerning his mother's mystical control over animals,

> J'hésite un peu à dire quels étaient ces pouvoirs et je ne veux même pas les décrire tous: je sais qu'on en accueillera le récit avec scepticisme. Moi-même, quand il m'arrive aujourd'hui de me les remémorer, je ne sais plus trop comment je les dois accueillir: ils me paraissent incroyables; ils sont incroyables! Pourtant il suffit de me rappeler ce que j'ai vu, ce que mes yeux ont vu. Puis-je récuser le témoignage des mes yeux? Ces choses incroyables, je les ai vues; je les revois comme je les voyais. N'y a-t-il pas partout des choses qu'on n'explique pas? Chez nous, il y a une infinité de choses qu'on n'explique pas, et ma mère vivait dans leur familiarité (p.71).

> [I hesitate to say what these powers were, and I do not wish to describe them all. I know that what I have to tell you will perhaps be greeted with sceptical smiles. And to-day, now that I come to think about them, even I hardly know what to make of them. They seem to me incredible; they *are* incredible. Nevertheless, I can only tell you what I saw with my own eyes. How could I disown the testimony of my own eyes? I saw those incredible things. I seem to see them again as I saw them then. Are there not things everywhere around us that are incapable of explanation? In our country there were mysteries without number, and my mother was familiar with all of them.] (p.58)

The clear, matter-of-fact tone records incident after incident in the child's growing awareness of the Islamic/animistic world around him. By the end of the narrative, the reader feels an immense sense of personal loss at a way of life which has rapidly come to a halt. *L'Enfant noir* is a beautiful account of traditional African life, as delicately wrought as a Dürer engraving, a detailed tableau of the paradise Laye knew in his youth and later lost.

Dramouss, Laye's third book, published in 1966, is a sequel to *L'Enfant noir*, and the most striking element, that immediately jolts the reader, is the harshness of the book when it is compared to Laye's first work. The softness, the sense of oneness and wholeness expressed in the earlier book is missing in *Dramouss*, which is ostensibly concerned with Laye's life in France and his return to Guinea after living several years in Paris. Laye's interest here is in politics in post-independent Guinea—in the failures of the African regime to live up to the pre-independence promises. As such, this work moves beyond the sense of the personal, which was so vitally important in *L'Enfant noir*, to a concern with problems of nationhood, nationalism, and political charlatanism, resulting in one of the most scathing commentaries on African political institutions written by a Francophone African writer. The publication of *Dramouss* also led to Laye's forced exile from Guinea to Senegal.[5]

Le regard du roi, (*The Radiance of the King*) which was first published in 1954, is, in the view of several critics of African literature, the greatest of all African novels. The novel has won this distinction, it seems, because of Laye's ideal assimilation of African materials into the novel form. As has so frequently been the concern with African novelists, Laye too is outwardly at least concerned with the conflict between African and Western civilization, yet his treatment in *Le regard du roi* is unlike any other we have seen. His main character is not African but European, and instead of recording the conflicts that an African encounters in his exposure to the West, Laye, in this lengthy novel, has reversed the usual pattern and presented a European and his difficulty in coming to grips with Africa. Laye's story goes far beyond this, however, for it is not simply a confrontation which ends in confusion or tragedy, but a story which begins in chaos and ends in understanding, grace, and beauty. The white man may be the protagonist, but Africa is the antagonist. It is the hero's ability to comprehend the magnitude and the complexity of the African experience—to realize that his own culture has little significance at all—which leads us to a basic aspect of what Senghor has seen as the final evolutionary stage of cultural syncretism—"reformed négritude," a kind of world culture which embodies the best of all cultures. Instead of being destroyed in the process, or trapped forever between two cultures like Medza in *Mission terminée*, Laye's hero becomes assimilated into the African culture and through this process achieves salvation. He learns the lesson of Senghor's reformed négritude that for the white man the African experience may lead to a kind of rebirth, or as Senghor has written in his poem "Prière aux masques" ("Prayer to Masks"), Africa will contribute to the rebirth of the world, being "Ainsi le levain que est nécessaire à la farine blanche," ["the leaven that the white flour needs"] [6] for its very existence, that the future harmony of the world can only be attained by a linking of Africa to the West, and that the individual's humanity can only come from accepting Africa for what it is—not from trying to change it into something it was not meant to be.

Clarence—Laye's main character—finds himself stranded in an African city. He has gambled away his meager resources and been thrown out of his hotel after being unable to pay his bills. It is a day of celebrations, when the king is making an appearance outside of his palace, and Clarence believes if he can only secure an audience with the king that he will be given a job because he is a white man. The crowd surrounding the king, however, is so dense that Clarence is not able to get near him—he can only see him from a distance. A beggar tells Clarence that the king will eventually go south, and that if Clarence goes south, too, his chances of meeting the king will probably be greater. This Clarence does, travelling with the beggar to the village of Aziana. It is in Aziana that Clarence learns to wait for the king, eventually meeting him, feeling the great radiance of his being.

Le regard du roi is divided into three sections with a total of ten chapters. Part One, which is composed of the first five, is called "Adramé," beginning with "L'Esplanade" ("The Esplanade"). Clarence is standing on the esplanade, surrounded by a thick crowd of Africans. He is almost completely without possessions except for the clothes he wears, his razor and his shaving soap; in this manner almost immediately Laye strips Clarence of the accouterments of Western civilization. He stands as the lone white figure in the midst of a huge crowd of black people. The racial stereotypes that white people frequently use to play up the differences between themselves and black people are introduced almost immediately—in the second paragraph. Clarence is aware that "il émanait de ces hommes étroitement agglomérés sous le ciel d'Afrique une odeur de laine et d'huile, une odeur de troupeau qui plongeait l'être dans une espèce de sommeil." [A "herd-like odour that seemed to dull the senses into a kind of trance, emanated from these men packed tightly together under the African sky."] [7] The odor is so overpowering that Clarence feels he will fall asleep. In this manner, Laye introduces one of the basic motifs in the novel: that of the sleepwalker, the somnambulist, stumbling through an alien culture, unable to comprehend it or appreciate its differences. The reader is bombarded with the sounds and smells of Africa in this tourist-like view of a strangely "uncivilized" scene, for Laye's descriptive passages are most frequently presented as if Clarence were the one writing them, from Clarence's point of view.

Clarence's pilgrimage—until the time he meets the king—is a re-education as he is slowly stripped of the accretions of Western civilization, its false values, its prejudices and hang-ups, for at first he can only evaluate in terms of his past life.

At first, the results are snap judgments without any attempt to understand the experience behind the African's way of doing things. Noting, for example, that all of the tallest people in the crowd are standing in front, making it difficult for the shorter ones to see the dances that are going on, Clarence thinks: "ce qui était proprement stupide, et à l'inverse de ce qui aurait dû normalement se passer, puisque ces géants du premier rang auraient pu, sans beaucoup se gêner eux-mêmes, se retirer à l'arrière-plan et offrir ainsi aux plus petits une chance de voir" (p.10). ["This was really very stupid, the exact opposite to what should have been the case, for these giants in the front row could easily have stood at the rear and so have given the smaller ones a chance to see."] (p.22) Clarence must come to realize that what is logical for him, may not be logical for an African.

Clarence tries to pass through the crowd to the front so he can see better, and in the process he meets a beggar:

> —Le roi ve-t-il bientôt venir? demanda Clarence.
> —Il sera là à l'heure fixée, dit le noir.
> —A quelle heure? dit Clarence.
> —Je vous l'ai dit: à l'heure fixée.
> —J'avais compris. Mais quelle est cette heure?
> —Le roi le sait! dit le noir.
> Il le dit d'un ton cassant, qui coupait court à l'interrogatoire (pp.11–12).

> ["Will the king be here soon?" asked Clarence.
> "He will be here at the appointed time," answered the black man.
> "What time will that be?" asked Clarence.
> "I've just told you: at the appointed time."
> "Yes, I know. But exactly what time will that be?"
> "The king knows!" replied the black man. He spoke the words abruptly, cutting short the interrogation.] (p.24)

It is here that Laye introduces a second concept differing from the West's: that of the African's way of regarding time. We have already noted a difference, in Tutuola; in Laye, time is presented as something completely antithetical to Western measurements. It is only the stupid white man who has to know exactly when the king will arrive, for, as the beggar tells him, the king knows and that is the most important thing. Time in *Le regard du roi* does not exist in a Western sense at all, and Clarence must learn that he will meet the king only when he least expects him, only when he is most unworthy of his coming.

Clarence talks to the beggar, telling him that he wants to speak to the king, and the beggar asks him if he thinks the king receives just anybody. Clarence replies, " '—Je ne suis pas n'importe qui. . . . Je suis un blanc!' " (p.12). [" 'I am not "just anybody" . . . I am a white man.' "] (p.24) Clarence's sole reason for feeling that the king will give him an audience resides in his belief in white superiority. White men have always been granted special privileges in Africa, he knows, simply because of their color. Clarence takes it for granted that the king will automatically give him a job, and, by implication, that the king also believes in the superiority of the West. The beggar suggests that he might be able to put in a good word for Clarence, and Clarence replies:

> —Vous? fit Clarence
> Il regarda son voisin avec stupéfaction: c'était un vieil homme misérablement vêtu; certes, un homme de haute taille, comme tous ceux qui étaient au premier rang, mais déguenillé; une espèce de mendiant.
> —Vous êtes un mendiant! dit-il. (pp.13–14)

> ["What—*you!*" cried Clarence.
> He looked at his neighbour in amazement: he was an old man, poorly clothed; a tall man, no doubt, like all those in the front rank, but dressed in rags—a sort of beggar.
> "But you are a beggar!!" he said.] (p.26)

Clarence's assumption that the beggar is insignificant is based on his equating beggars in Western society with beggars in Africa, assuming that both are the same, without status. In this deeply ironic incident, Clarence has failed to notice that *he* is the beggar, the one who is begging. It is this kind of blindness, this inability to understand cultural differences that Clarence must cleanse himself of. Laye notes, "Il se proposerait au roi pour un travail ou l'autre, n'importe quel travail honorable, et il recevrait le juste prix de sa peine; il ne se présenterait pas en quémandeur!" (p.14). ["He would offer his services to the king; he was willing to do some kind of work, provided it was honest and he received adequate remuneration for his services. *He* wasn't going begging!"] (p.26) Clarence assumes that his Western education has prepared him for a position with the king. Later he will learn that his education has taught him nothing that can be of use to Africa.

Soon Clarence and the beggar are joined by two young boys who are dancers, and Clarence is again aware of an overpowering odor. And, then, as Clarence feels he is about to fall asleep, the king arrives: "Clarence aperçut alors un adolescent vêtu de blanc et d'or, monté sur un cheval dont le caparaçon traînait sur le sol . . ." (p.19). [". . . an adolescent boy dressed in white and gold, mounted on a horse whose caparisonings trailed on the ground . . ."] (p.31) Laye makes extensive use of pictorial description:

Sitôt que le roi eut mis pied à terre, deux pages danseurs se portèrent à sa droite et deux autres à sa gauche, et ils lui relevèrent les bras; alors Clarence découvrit que ces bras étaient cerclés de tant d'anneaux d'or que le roi n'aurait pu les lever sans aide; l'impression de pesanteur venait de cette invraisemblable profusion d'anneaux. En même temps que les pages avaient levé les bras du roi, la robe royale s'était entrouverte sur un mince torse d'adolescent.

. . . c'était la fragilité qui frappait le plus, elle frappait plus que la jeunesse et elle frappait comme douloureusement; on se demandait comment le roi pouvait supporter le poids de tous ces anneaux, comment ses bras ne se rompaient pas sous le faix, et on comprenait qu'il n'eût pu faire un pas sans l'aide de ses pages. Il était si extraordinairement fragile qu'il en devenait comme sans défense; oui, et en dépit de sa suite, en dépit de ses innom-

brables pages, de ses timbaliers, de ses joueurs de trompe, en
dépit des superbes guerriers qui l'avaient précédé, en dépit même
du respect dont toute cette foule l'entourait. (pp.20–21)

[As soon as the king reached the ground, two of the pages or
dancers placed themselves at his right hand, and two at his left,
and slowly lifted his arms. It was only then that Clarence discovered that these arms were encircled with so many golden
bracelets that the king would never have been able to lift his
arms without help: and it was this extraordinary profusion of
gold bracelets that gave the impression of heaviness. At the same
time as the pages were lifting the king's arms, the royal robe
was falling open to reveal the slender black torso of an adolescent boy.

. . . It was his fragility that was most striking; it was even
more striking than his youth, and painfully so. One wondered
how the king, such a slender boy, could bear the weight of all
those bracelets, why his arms were not broken by such a load;
and one understood that he could not have taken a single step
without the support of his pages. He was so extraordinarily frail
that he seemed utterly defenceless—yes, defenceless, in spite of
his innumerable pages and drummers and trumpeters, in spite of
the superb warriors who had ridden so proudly before him, in
spite of the reverence of the immense crowd that stood all round
him.] (pp.32–33)

The description given here appears to be based on Laye's
knowledge of African art. This detailed description of the
king and later ones describing the frescoes on the king's
palace indicate that Laye is familiar with Benin (Western
Nigeria) bronze plaques of the middle period, which according to William Fagg of the British Museum, date roughly
from "the century or so from about the middle sixteenth to
the late seventeenth centuries. . . ." [8] Several of the plaques
depict the king in elaborate regalia, weighted down with
necklaces and bracelets, seated or standing, but supported by
other chiefs, or attendants. The descriptions which Laye
gives here are almost unique in African fiction for their detail
concerning physical stature and personal raiment, for the incorporation of artistry from the golden age of African art.

The beggar tells Clarence that the king is young but also very old and the gold bracelets hold him captive: "—S'il était moins chargé d'or, rien sans doute ne pourrait le retenir parmi nous" (p.37). [" 'If he were not so heavily weighed-down with gold, there would be nothing to keep him among us here.' "] (p.33) They are a sign of love, "—si l'amour atteint à sa pureté; c'est d'un or de cette sorte que le roi est prisonnier, c'est pourquoi ses bras sont si lourdement chargés" (p.37). [" 'The purest kind of love. That is the sort of gold that holds the king a prisoner, and that is why his arms are so heavily laden.' "] (p.33) Then the king, supported by his attendants, returns to the palace. Frenzied, Clarence again tells the beggar that he absolutely must see the king, stressing the fact that he has no time to waste. Clarence does not yet realize that the one thing he does possess is time—a superabundance of it. The beggar informs him that many people wait years to see the king. Yet the beggar suggests a solution to Clarence's problem—that Clarence go south where the king is bound to go some time in the future. First, however, the beggar leaves Clarence and the two boys who have joined them to see if it is possible for Clarence to gain an audience with the king.

Meanwhile the king has gone into his palace, and shortly thereafter Clarence believes he hears some screams. The two boys, who constantly contradict one another throughout the novel, explain to him what the screams indicate. One tells Clarence that the screams are from the king's faithful vassals being sacrificed; the other tells him the sounds are from the sacrifice of his unfaithful vassals. The boys names are Nagoa and Noaga, and they play a kind of Tweedledee/Tweedledum act throughout the narrative. Clarence, of course, cannot hear any difference in the pronunciation of their names and, initially, at least, believes that they both have the same name. Nor can he tell the two boys apart—all Africans, of course, look the same to him. Nagoa and Noaga add a great amount of merriment to the story, yet there is a basically contradictory relationship between them, which further prevents Clarence from comprehending the African experience. The king appears briefly again, climbing a staircase to the central tower of his palace. He makes a salutation to the sky. Clarence's final image of the king is as follows:

Mais l'impression n'en demeurait pas moins, d'une marche en plein ciel, comme si les bracelets et les anneaux, comme si tout cet or et tout cet amour, fussent devenus tout à coup impuissants à retenir plus longtemps le roi sur le terre. . . . (p.34)

[One still had the impression that the king was walking off into space, as if the bracelets and the rings of gold, as if that gold, and all that love had suddenly become powerless to hold the king to the earth. . . .] (p.46)

Then the palace itself slowly fades away.*

The beggar returns, informing Clarence that there is no post available for him within the palace.

—J'aurais pu . . . dit-il
Mais qu'aurait-il pu? Le savait-il seulement?
—Un simple emploi de timbalier, par example . . .
—Ce n'est pas là un simple emploi, dit le mendiant; les timbaliers sont de caste noble et, chez eux, l'emploi est hérédi-taire; certes, vous auriez battu du tambour, seulement ce n'est pas ce qui compte: vos battements n'auraient eu aucun sens. Là aussi, il faut savoir . . . Vous êtes un homme blanc! (p.37)

["I could have been a simple drummer boy . . ."
"That is not a simple occupation," said the beggar. "The drummers are drawn from a noble caste and their employment is hereditary. Even if you had been allowed to beat a drum, your drumming would have had no meaning. You have to know how . . . You see, you're a white man!"] (p.48)

* The most significant literary influences on Laye's writing have been the works of Franz Kafka. The origin of many of the incidents in *Le regard du roi*, some of the characters, the surrealistic passages, and the basic quest may be traced in large part to Kafka's *The Castle*. For a detailed comparison see Patricia Deduck's unpublished thesis, *Franz Kafka's Influence on Camara Laye's "Le regard du roi,"* (Indiana University, 1970.)

Laye begins to suggest that African traditions are not as simple as the white man believes they are. This is the first of any number of such illustrations of the fact that African life has a definite complexity—the leaven the white bread needs—a perfect example of cultural materials being assimilated into the text of the novel. For the first time Clarence has an intimation that his own culture has inadequately prepared him for Africa. As the chapter ends, Clarence resigns himself to the fact that he has no choice except to go along with the beggar and the two boys. Indeed, the four of them are all alone, for everyone else has disappeared—just like the king and the palace. Clarence, the sleepwalker, begins his walk toward consciousness.

Chapter Two is called "L'Auberge" ("The Inn"). Clarence, the beggar, and the two boys go to an inn for a meal. Clarence is concerned about the piles of rubbish that are all over the place—the squeamish Westerner will need a period of adjustment before he can adapt to less sanitary conditions than he has been used to. An idea is developed from the first chapter—that of one's rights and favors in a given society— for Clarence has automatically been assuming that his whiteness gives him certain rights in an African society. The beggar tells him,

> —Je n'ai parlé de "faveur", dit le mendiant. Vous vous trompez certainement en m'attribuant des propos sur un "droit" quelconque. Pour ma part, je n'ai jamais revendiqué aucun droit, je me suis toujours borné à quémander. C'est assez dire que je ne saurais attendre que des faveurs. (p.42)

> ["I spoke only of 'favours' . . . You are quite wrong to think I said anything about 'rights' of any kind. As far as I'm concerned, I have never claimed any kind of 'rights.' I have always restricted myself to soliciting favours. I'll say no more than that I expect these favours to be granted."] (p.53)

Clarence must learn that as an outsider he has no rights at all in Africa—there can only be favors, and these are certainly not granted on the basis of one's color.

When they sit down to eat, Laye gives us another example of the Westerner's total inability to cope with African culture. Clarence does not know how to eat without a knife and a fork; the rice slips off his fingers, and, of course, the food itself bothers him. He asks the beggar, "—Ces pâtes ne font-elles pas tomber les dents?" (p.47). ["'Don't these sticky mixtures make the teeth fall out?'"] (p.58) After a few minutes, Clarence more or less gives up trying to eat. Instead, he begins drinking palm-wine like the others. Laye allows the reader to partake of Clarence's introspection—over and over again we see what is going on in his head; and frequently, as if he, too, can read his mind, the beggar makes a comment apropos of what Clarence has been thinking. The beggar proposes that Clarence make the journey south with him, and as they are ready to leave the inn, Clarence is reminded of the fact that he has no money to pay the bill. He gives the innkeeper his jacket instead; then Clarence and the beggar leave—the two boys dragging, for the moment, behind.

The sleepwalking motif is re-introduced at the beginning of the third chapter, "La veste volée" ("The Stolen Coat"). The chapter opens with another extended passage of pictorial description, portraying the sounds and smells of an African street. The point of view is clearly Clarence's—once again verging on the tourist's superficial look at Africa, with the overtones of cultural shock. It is all Clarence can do to keep awake; the street odor has a narcotic effect on him; and, as the beggar and Clarence are walking along the street, Clarence is suddenly seized from behind by the innkeeper who yells to some guards, "—Je veux ma veste! Je ne retirerai pas ma main avant que l'homme blanc ne m'ait restitué ma veste" (p.64). ["'I want my coat! I won't take my hand away until the white man has given me back my coat!'"] (p.74) In the bizarre scene which follows, Clarence, with the beggar following him, is dragged off to court by the innkeeper and the guards, as Clarence yells, "—Comment pourrais-je la lui rendre? . . . Je le lui ai déjà donnée" (p.64). ["'How can I give

it back to him? . . . I've already given it to him.'"] (p.74)
In a Kafkaesque scene in the courtroom, Clarence is brought
to trial by the innkeeper, and Laye splendidly illustrates the
difficulties of communication between two cultures:

—Permettez, monsieur le premier président, dit le garde à
la cordelière. Quand je l'ai interpellé, l'homme blanc a prétendu
qu'il n'avait plus revu l'hôtelier depuis qu'il avait quitté l'hôtel.
Or, il l'affirmait alors que l'hôtelier était devant lui! Aussi nous
sommes-nous tous mis à rire.
    —Volà qui ne plaide assurément pas en faveur de votre
sincérité, dit le juge à Clarence.
    —On m'a mal compris, dit Clarence. Je disais. . . . (p.69)

["If you will excuse my interruption, my lord president,"
said the guard, "when I questioned him, the white man claimed
that he had not seen the inn-keeper since leaving the hotel. And
all the time, while he was speaking, the inn-keeper was standing
right in front of him! So then we all burst out laughing."
    "That is something which certainly does not say much for
your truthfulness," the judge said to Clarence.
    "They misunderstood me," said Clarence. "What I meant
was . . ."] (p.78)

Clarence tries to explain what he means, but he is completely
misunderstood. This scene, according to Janheinz Jahn, illustrates the way Africans were treated in colonial courts [9]—
neither party, of course, fully understanding the other. The
trial itself is a mockery of the kind of justice Clarence has
been familiar with in the West.

The innkeeper wins his case, and since Clarence does not
have the coat, it is suggested that his shirt and trousers be
given as a substitute. The cultural differences are again brought
to the surface. Clarence asks the judge, "—Me voyez-vous bien
me promenant nu dans les rues?" The judge replies, "—Il n'y
a pas de loi qui le défende . . ." (p.72). ["'Can you see me
walking naked in the streets?'" The judge replies, "'There
is no law against that. . . .'"] (p.82) The concern with clothing throughout the entire novel is extremely important; these

outer vestiges of Clarence's culture must give way before there can be any inner changes within the man himself. The beggar whispers to Clarence to make a run for it, that they will meet at the city gates. Clarence succeeds in his escape, yet once outside the courtroom he finds himself in a maze of corridors and empty rooms. His flight from reality takes him deeper and deeper into the somnambulist's dream-like world.

When he eventually escapes the palace of justice, Clarence finds himself in a dense mob of people, yet his one fear is that he will be captured by the guards again. Shortly, however, he is helped by a dancing girl, who leads him into another building which immediately reminds him of the palace of justice from which he has just fled. The girl informs Clarence that he is in her house, and when she finally opens a door to a room, Clarence is united with the beggar and Nagoa and Noaga, sitting around a table, drinking palm-wine:

Clarence . . . découvrit le juge, assis au milieu du groupe.
—Ciel! cria-t-il.
—Je vais vous présenter à mon père, dit la danseuse.
Et elle conduisit Clarence devant le juge.
—Prenez place, dit le juge, et buvez un coup de vin. Je vois que vous avez beaucoup couru; un coup de vin ne vous fera pas de tort.
—Je vous remercie, monsieur, dit Clarence.
Il avait failli dire: "Merci, monsieur le premier président," mais quelque chose l'avait retenu: la crainte de commettre une incongruité peut-être. Il prit place dans le cercle avec la danseuse.
—Est-ce que votre père n'est pas juge au tribunal? dit-il à l'oreille de la danseuse.
—Pensez-vous! fit la danseuse. Je ne tolérerais pas cela chez moi: mon père est un homme honorable! (p.79)

[Clarence . . . suddenly saw the judge sitting at the centre of the group.
"Heavens!" he cried.
"Allow me to introduce you to my father," said the dancer.
And she led Clarence to the judge.
"Sit down," said the judge, "and have a drink of palm wine.

I can see you've been running: a drop of wine won't come amiss."

"I thank you, sir," said Clarence.

He had almost said: "I thank you, my lord president," but something had stopped him—perhaps the fear of saying or doing something incongruous. He took his seat in the circle next to the dancer.

"Isn't your father a high court judge?" he whispered in the dancer's ear.

"I should think not!" said the dancer. "I wouldn't allow such a thing in my house. My father is an honourable man!"] (p.88)

Once again, Clarence is not certain if he is dreaming or whether the judge and the dancing girl's father simply look alike. In his confusion, Clarence chastises the beggar for not supporting him during the trial, and the discussion returns to the subject of rights and favors. The beggar says,

—Ne pouvez-vous comprendre qu'un droit ne se quémande pas? J'aurais pu quémander une faveur, je veux dire: une chose que n'est pas due; je ne pouvais quémander un droit, qui vous est dévolu d'office. D'ailleurs je n'ai pas appris à quémander les droits: cela ne s'enseigne nulle part. Comprenez-vous à présent?

—Vous me cassez la tête, dit Clarence.

—Tenez, un exemple: rien ici ne m'interdit de quémander une calebasse à notre hôte, mais . . . Merci! fit-il en s'inclinant devant l'hôte qui lui tendait une calebasse. Mais, acheva-t-il, je ne la quémande pas comme un droit, même pas comme un droit de l'hospitalité. Comprenez donc que c'est faire injure, que de quémander un droit! (p.81)

["Can't you get it into your thick head that one cannot beg the favour of receiving something that is one's 'right'? I could have asked for any favour, I mean something that is *not* due to you; I could not possibly have asked for something that is your 'right,' something which devolves upon you officially. Anyhow, I never learned how to beg for 'rights'—that sort of thing can't be taught. Now do you understand?"

"My head's reeling," said Clarence.

"Look, take this example: there is nothing to prevent my asking our host for a calabash of wine, but . . . Thank you!" he said, bowing to his host who was holding out a fresh calabash for him. "But," he resumed, "I do not ask for it as if it were my 'right,' or even one of the simple rights of hospitality. You must understand that it is highly insulting, to ask for something that is one's 'right.' "]   (p.90)

Of course, the beggar is not above taking advantage of a given circumstance to gain certain "favors." When Clarence looks at the two boys rather carefully, he notices that they have his coat.

The fourth chapter, "L'odeur du sud" ("The Odour of the South"), is concerned with the trip south that Clarence makes with the beggar and Nagoa and Noaga. In this chapter, Laye again makes extensive use of pictorial description, not at all typical of the descriptions of jungle and bush we have seen in West African Anglophone writing, because Laye's descriptions are much more than simple functionalism. The forest that Clarence walks through becomes a symbol of the chaos of his mind, the maze that he is becoming more deeply entrapped in:

> Le soleil s'était levé sur une campagne magnifiquement ordonnée et sur des terres plus riches qu'on ne s'y serait attendu. Il y avait des champs de mil et d'arachides, de riz et de maïs, le tout facilement reconnaissable. Puis une variété de plantes exotiques dont Clarence peut-être n'ignorait pas les noms, mais qu'il hesitait néanmoins à déterminer; dans le nombre, il y avait du manioc et du sorgho, très vraisemblablement; et encore des graines d'un rouge lumineux qui, même si elles n'étaient pas comestibles, ce qui n'est pas prouvé, constituaient, au lever du jour, un régal pour les yeux; enfin, des palmiers en abondance, destinés ou non, mais certainement destinés en partie, à l'industrie du vin.   (p.85)

[The sun had risen on a magnificently cultivated landscape and on fields richer than one would ever have expected. There were fields of millet and groundnuts, of rice and maize, all looking just as they do in other lands. Then there was an abundance of exotic plants whose names Clarence was perhaps not unfamiliar with but which he could not identify exactly. Among them there were some very like cassava and sorghum, as well as

corn of a luminous red colour which, even if it was not eat-
able—and why shouldn't it be?—provided, in the light of the
rising sun, a feast of unparalleled splendour for the eyes. Finally,
there were whole forests of palm trees, in part certainly, if not
entirely, devoted to the wine industry.] (p.93)

Laye's description is highly impressionistic like Ngugi's,
though the olfactory element is much more important for
Laye:

> L'approche en fut signalée par une odeur qui mérite d'être
> décrite, non seulement pour le fait que Clarence était spéciale-
> ment attentif aux odeurs, et très curieusement affecté par elles,
> mais encore, mais surtout, parce que cette odeur était hautement
> représentative des caractères du Sud. (pp.85–86)

> [They were made aware of its proximity by an odour which
> ought to be described, not merely because Clarence was espe-
> cially sensitive to smells, and very curiously affected by them,
> but also, and above all, because this odour was particularly
> representative of the whole character of the South.] (p.94)

The sleepwalking motif continues as Clarence penetrates
deeper and deeper into the heart of darkness, further and further into his own ethnocentric psyche. He believes that the
beggar and the two boys are leading him around in circles;
he can see no paths in the forest at all. The beggar tells him,

> —Il y a des sentiers. Si vous ne les voyez pas—et pourquoi les
> verriez-vous?—n'accusez que vos yeux. Un homme blanc ne
> peut pas tout voir; et il n'a pas non plus besoin de tout voir, car
> ce pays n'est pas un pays de blancs. (p.87)

> ["There *are* paths. If you can't see them—and why should you
> see them?—you've only got your own eyes to blame. A white
> man can't see everything: and he has no need to see everything
> either, because this land is not a white man's land."] (p. 95)

The idea expressed here—the ontological gap again—is paramount for an understanding of the mystical world expressed
in négritude poetry, especially the physical world which sur-

rounds one. In Birago Diop's short story, "Sarzan," for example, Diop states in a poem which is part of the story:

> Ecoute plus souvent
> Les choses que les êtres,
> La voix du feu s'entend,
> Entends la voix de l'eau.
> Ecoute dans le vent
> Le buisson en sanglot:
> C'est le souffle des ancêtres.
>
> [Listen to things
> More often than beings
> Hear the voice of fire
> Hear the voice of water
> Listen in the wind to
> The sighs of the bush
> This is the ancestors breathing.] [10]

It is the unseen animistic world which Clarence, as a white man, is incapable of understanding. The paths which Clarence cannot find in the forest are symbolic of the jungle in his own mind and the African's acceptance of the universe.

By the end of the trip, Clarence has been reduced to little more than a child being led by the two young boys—he is not at all like the typical explorer in the latter's account of himself in Africa. Laye's objective is precisely to show that the white man in Africa has been concerned only with a physical exploration of the continent—and not with any attempt to explore the mystical or the spiritual aspects of African life.

> Clarence sent l'immonde torpeur l'engluer, et il tend docilement la main.
> Il avance en aveugle, et c'est d'abord à un aveugle qu'il fait penser, la main tantôt dans celle de Noaga, tantôt dans celle de Nagoa. Mais, pour peu qu'on observe ses traits, c'est à un enfant qu'on pense; à un enfant que ses parents traînent par des rues de

banlieue, un dimanche soir, au retour d'une promenade. (pp. 91–92)

[Clarence begins to feel the unclean and cloying weakness stealing over him, and he quietly holds out his hand to the boy.

He walks along like a blind man, and it is of a blind man one thinks as he stumbles along, his hand holding Noaga's hand, now Nagoa's. But if one were to look at his face, one would think it belonged to a child being dragged through suburban streets by his parents on a Sunday evening, after a long walk.] (p.99)

It is necessary that Clarence lose his Western prejudices and misconceptions, that he be reduced to this childlike state before his re-education may commence. The fact that Laye makes no references to time in this chapter is of extreme importance, for Clarence believes that the trip through the forest is taking forever and ever, that it will never end. For the beggar and the two boys, the trip is a thing accepted, taken for granted. They will have reached the south when they reach the south.

The fifth chapter, "Le troc" ("The Exchange"), begins as the four travelers arrive in the south, at the village of Aziana. Clarence immediately notices a vivid contrast with the north; the village of Aziana is scrupulously clean, and the women are immediately appealing. Clarence thinks of them,

peut-être celles-ci avaient-elles les mêmes jolis minois—sûrement elles devaient avoir de jolis minois,—seulement il était impossible de le découvrir, car il y avait dans leur poitrine, et quand ce n'était pas dans la poitrine c'était dans la croupe, quelque chose de si provocant qu'on en perdait—que Clarence tout au moins en perdait—le loiser, ou la volonté, de lever les yeux sur le visage. (p.109)

[Perhaps they, too, had pretty faces—surely they must have pretty faces—only it was impossible to find out, because in the formation of their breasts—and if it was not in their breasts it was in their hips—there was something so utterly provocative that—for Clarence at least—all opportunity, or all desire to raise one's eyes to their faces was completely lost.] (p.116)

The village chief, the naba, we learn, is Nagoa and Noaga's grandfather, and there is a celebration the night they arrive in Aziana. The beggar suggests to Clarence that he wait in this village for the king:

—Mais pourrai-je rester ici? demanda Clarence.
—Pourquoi n'y resteriez-vous pas?
—On ne m'y gardera pas pour rien.
—Peut-être pourriez-vous rendre de menus services. Et, en retour, on vous garderait . . .
—Y a-t-il vraiment des services que je puisse rendre?
—Vous devez le savoir, dit le mendiant. Il n'y a généralement pas d'homme si dépourvu qui ne puisse, à l'occasion, rendre quelques menus services. Par exemple, j'ignore absolument quels services vous rendriez, mais je puis m'en informer; je puis, le cas échéant, proposer qu'on vous garde à l'essai. (p.116)

["But shall I be able to stay here?" asked Clarence.
"Why shouldn't you stay here?"
"They won't keep me for nothing."
"Perhaps you could offer some small services. And in return, you would be kept . . ."
"Are there really any services I can perform?"
"You should know best yourself," the beggar replied. "Men are hardly ever quite so lacking in ability that they cannot, on occasion, perform some small task or other. I am completely in the dark about the sort of services you might be called upon to perform, but I can find out. I could even, if it so came about, propose that you should be taken on for a probationary period."] (p.122)

Clarence later thinks,

Il était à Aziana, il allait longuement se reposer à Aziana, en échange de menus services; tous les menus services qu'un homme de sa sorte peut rendre à des villageois: par exemple, éloigner des champs de mil les oiseaux, à l'époque des semailles ou de la moisson; ou poursuivre les mulots aux approches de la moisson; ou détruire les chenilles; ou enfumer les nids de guêpes. . . . (p.122)

[He was now at Aziana; he was going to enjoy a long rest in Aziana, in exchange for doing a few small services—every kind of small service which a man like himself could perform for village people. For example, he could scare away the birds from the millet-fields at seed-time and harvest; or catch field mice when the corn was reaped; or kill caterpillars; smoke wasps out of their nests. . . .]   (p.128)

The image that Clarence has of himself has become extremely childlike.

Shortly thereafter, Clarence is introduced to Samba Baloum, and the beggar and Samba Baloum have an argument that Clarence does not understand. Baloum argues that Clarence is "an old hen," while the beggar refers to Clarence as a "fighting-cock." All Clarence knows is that he is revolted by Samba Baloum's feeling him "comme on tâte un poulet" (p.122), ["as one would feel a chicken"] (p.128), and even more upset when Baloum gives his behind a swat.

As the dancing, drinking, and other nightly celebrations continue, Clarence has a parting glimpse of the beggar:

> Le vieil homme était juché sur un âne, et une femme conduisait la bête par la bride. L'âne paraissait malingre. Ou était-ce le mendiant qui était trop grand pour la bête? La femme, par contre, était bien nourrie; elle avait de la croupe et de la poitrine. (p.129)

> [The old man was perched on a donkey and a woman was leading the beast by its bridle. The donkey seemed to be a sickly, puny beast. Or was it the beggar who was too big for it? The woman, on the contrary, was well upholstered; she had luxuriant buttocks and breasts.]   (p.135)

In the deeply ironic conversation that concludes Part One of *Le regard du roi*, Clarence's innocence becomes even more evident:

> —Qu'est-ce que le mendiant à troqué? dit Clarence. Avait-il quelque chose à troquer?
> —N'a-t-on pas toujours quelque chose à troquer? dit Nagoa. Et il lorgna imperceptiblement Clarence.
> —En somme, ce n'est qu'un tout petit fourbe, dit Noaga. Un apprenti.

—Ce n'est pas vraiment un tatoué, dit Nagoa.

Ils pouffèrent brusquement.

—Vous riez comme des fous, dit Clarence.

—Mais vous, pourquoi ne riez-vous pas? demandèrent les garçons.

Et ils pouffèrent de plus belle. (p.130)

["What has the beggar bartered?" asked Clarence. "Did he have something to sell?"

"Haven't we all got something to sell?" said Nagoa, eyeing Clarence rather narrowly.

"After all, he's just a little twister," said Noaga. "An apprentice."

"He doesn't really know what's what," said Nagoa.

They suddenly roared with laughter.

"You laugh like a couple of lunatics," said Clarence.

"But why aren't *you* laughing too?" asked the boys.

And they started laughing even louder.] (p.136)

Nagoa and Noaga will be Clarence's companions throughout much of the rest of the story. If Clarence cannot understand these young boys, how will he ever understand Africa?

If Part One of *Le regard du roi* is concerned with pitting Clarence against an alien culture and demonstrating the inadequacies of his own for coping with the African experience, Part Two, "Aziana," is concerned with stripping Clarence of his built-in stock responses to cultural situations which will in turn prepare him for a more complete benefit from the African experience. Slowly Laye is building up his case for the beauty which can only result from cross-cultural fertilization, and implying what is already a foregone conclusion: nothing can be more important than the merging of cultures, than the individual's ability to appreciate another culture. Africa is the yeast the white flour needs for its development, to be whole.

The first chapter in this section is named after Clarence's African wife—"Akissi." Although like the rest of the novel in being without any direct references to time, Part Two begins, we can be relatively certain, many, many months after Clarence has arrived in Aziana, perhaps even some years later. Clarence, at least at the beginning of this section, is still a sleep-walker in a foreign world. As the passage begins, it is morning and he has just gotten up and yelled at Akissi for bringing a sheaf of flowers into his hut during the night. "Cette lourde odeur de fleurs et de terreau, c'était l'odeur même de la forêt; une abominable, une inavouable odeur!" (p.135). ["That heavy odour of flowers and leaf-mold was the odour of the forest—an abominable, unmentionable odour!"] (p.139) As Akissi walks away from the hut toward the public water fountain, Clarence thinks, "Drôle de femme! . . . Pas un jour elle n'est la même" (p.135). [" 'Queer woman. . . . Never the same for two days on end.' "] (p.139)

Clarence has been in the south long enough to become bored—he believes he has been doing nothing, that the naba has not called upon him to render any services. As Laye says, ". . . tout se passait comme si l'on eût tenu Clarence pour incapable de jamais tenir un emploi" (p.137). ["Everyone seemed to consider Clarence incapable of doing any work."] (p.141) Yet, in a somewhat ludicrous passage, Clarence realizes he has left his mark on the village of Aziana, perhaps a little like Mark Twain's Connecticut Yankee in King Arthur's Court:

> Akissi apporta le tabouret et grimpa dessus. Elle remit la jarre sur sa tête et l'inclina au-dessus de Clarence. . . .
>
> L'eau tomba, comme une vraie douche. C'était très agréable. Clarence avait inventé le système; et maintenant beaucoup de gens, à Aziana, se lavaient ainsi.   (p.138)

> [Akissi brought the stool and stepped on to it. She put the jar on her head again and tipped it towards Clarence. . . . The water poured over him like a real shower. It was very pleasant. Clarence had invented the system and now many people in Aziana washed themselves in this way.]   (p.142)

He has also influenced the local weaving:

Akissi commença d'essuyer Clarence. Elle se servait pour cela d'une sorte de serviette-éponge. Avant que Clarence n'apprît à tisser, on ne connaissait pas ce genre de tissu à Aziana; on s'es-suyait avec des toiles affreusement rèches et qui arrachaient la peau. Mais Clarence avit appris à tisser avec du fil qu'on laissait tout exprès très mousseux; à présent, on avait de ces tissus qui étaient comme des serviettes-éponges; l'usage s'en était répandu rapidement. (pp.140–141)

[Akissi began to dry Clarence. She used a kind of spongy towel. Before Clarence came to Aziana and learnt to weave, this kind of material was quite unknown; people dried themselves with horribly rough cloth which nearly skinned them alive. But Clarence had learnt to weave with yarn which had been deliber-ately made very soft; now people used these towels all the time.] (p.144)

These are all minor alterations, because Clarence does not yet realize the biggest change he has brought to Aziana. Samba Baloum tells Clarence that the naba is pleased with him; Clarence cannot understand why, or that his subconscious feelings of hate for himself are in some way related to his "services" for the naba:

Il savait bien qu'il était devenu un autre homme, depuis qu'il sé-journait à Aziana; mais il détestait cet homme, il refusait de donner audience à cet homme qui, à la nuit, se déchaînait pour l'odeur de quelques fleurs. (p.144)

[He knew quite well that he had become a different man since he had come to live in Aziana. But he detested this new man, he refused to countenance this new man who at night so utterly abandoned himself because of the odour of a bunch of flowers.] (pp.147–148)

Samba Baloum persists in calling Clarence a fighting-cock and swatting him on the posterior. Clarence wonders,

qui aurait pu dire ce qui s'était passé? Clarence lui-même ne le savait pas. L'odeur de la forêt, sans doute; certainement cette odeur frôleuse qui est l'odeur même du Sud, aguicheuse et cruelle, lascive, inavouable. Mais Clarence la respirait avec dégoût, il y pensait avec dégoût. De la croupe et des seins, c'était ce qu'on voyait; c'était cela peut-être aussi q'on respirait. Et là, Akissi était commes les autres; Clarence n'aurait pas pu la différencier des autres. Il ne voyait pas mieux son visage que celui des autres; il ne la différenciait avec certitude que dans les moments où elle se montrait aux hublots de la case: Akissi posait son visage dans l'encadrement du hublot, et Clarence la différenciait. Mais, sitôt qu'il la voyait toute, il ne voyait plus son visage: il voyait de la croupe et des seins; la même croupe haute et les mêmes seins piriformes que les autres femmes d'Aziana . . . . (pp.144–145)

[who could tell just what had happened to him? Clarence himself did not know. The odour of the forest had probably had something to do with it; certainly that caressing odour which is the very odour of the South itself—provocative and cruel, lascivious and unmentionable—that had something to do with it all. But Clarence breathed this odour with great distaste, and he always thought about it with disgust. Buttocks and breasts—that's all one saw, and perhaps that's what one breathed, too, the odour of buttocks and breasts. In this respect Akissi was no different from the others; Clarence could not have distinguished her from any of the others in this respect. He could not recognise her face any more than he could recognise the faces of the other women; the only time he could be sure it was her face was when she showed it in the porthole of the hut: Akissi would put her face in the porthole's oval frame, and Clarence would be able to recognise it as hers. But as soon as he saw her whole body, it was as if he could no longer see her face: all he had eyes for were her buttocks and her breasts—the same high, firm buttocks and the same pear-shaped breasts as the other women in Aziana. . . .]   (pp.148–149)

When the naba's number one assistant, the master of ceremonies, visits him, Clarence begins to question himself, wondering if his licentiousness has been detected by the villagers. The master of ceremonies asks Clarence which woman he was with the night before; Clarence assumes, of course, that it was Akissi. Samba Baloum sends the master of ceremonies away before Clarence can pursue the topic. Yet, he thinks, "il était vraiment comme un étalon. Il y avait des nuits, ces nuits où l'odeur de la forêt emplissait la case, où il était un immonde étalon. . . ." (p.150). [". . . he really *was* a stallion. There were nights, those nights when the odour of the forest filled the hut, when he was simply a foul, filthy stallion. . . ."] (p.154) Clarence asks himself questions about his nocturnal activities, but for the time being, not to any great depth. Laye's presentation of Clarence shows him to be increasingly introspective.

The second chapter of Part Two is called "Le maître des cérémonies" ("The Master of Ceremonies"), and it is here that the reader begins to get a clearer picture of the services Clarence has rendered the naba. The chapter begins with the repetition of an idea already expressed—that it is still difficult for Clarence to distinguish one African woman from another, that his eyes never quite get to their faces. Laye writes,

Il voyait le visage seulement, mais il se représenta brusquement le corps d'Akissi et il pensa à la façon dont leurs corps, le sien et celui d'Akissi, se tendaient. Il sendit un feu sombre le parcourir, un feu aussi sombre que la peau d'Akissi. Et il eut honte . . . Mais avait-il toujours honte? . . . "Parfois je n'ai pas honte," s'avoua-t-il. "Il y a des nuits où je n'ai pas honte, des nuits où je suis comme fou, où je suis réellement fou." Il soupira. . . . Comment un feu semblable, un feu si brûlant et si sombre, pouvait-il parcourir les veines? Comment pouvait-on à la fois abominer une chose et le convoiter? . . . (pp.151–152)

[in his imagination he suddenly saw Akissi's naked body, and he thought of the way in which their two naked bodies, his own and Akissi's, would lock together. He felt a dark fire smouldering through his legs, a fire as dark as Akissi's naked flesh. And he was ashamed. . . . But did he always feel ashamed? . . . "Sometimes I do not feel ashamed," he admitted to himself. "There are nights when I am without shame, when I seem to go mad." He sighed. . . . How was it that such a fire, such a dark and burning fire, could shoot through all his being? How was it that he could at one and the same time abominate, and yet so frantically lust after such a thing? . . .] (p.155)

An even more marked change is now illustrated in Clarence's appearance in the village. Although he is beginning to show some embarrassment about his lust for Akissi, frequently he goes aound naked: "on ne pensait pas non plus à voiler sa nudité. Les gens d'Aziana ne voilaient pas davantage la leur: ils n'y songeaient pas, ils se laissaient vivre" (p.152). ["The people in Aziana did not veil their nakedness any more than he did: they never thought about it; they just enjoyed life."] (p.155)

This is quite a contrast to the Clarence who was once shocked when the judge suggested that there was no law against going about naked. However, Clarence often wears an African *boubou* now also. He is beginning to feel a sense of harmony with the village. Slowly he begins to enjoy his friendship with Samba Baloum, not quite realizing that as the naba's harem keeper, Baloum is a eunuch.

In their typical prankish fashion, Nagoa and Noaga lead Clarence into the naba's inner palace where he can secretly watch a trial that is taking place. Clarence, of course, is not supposed to witness the trial, for the master of ceremonies is being brought to court for having revealed to Clarence what his "services" to the naba have been. If the reader has not detected what these services are, he does when Clarence overhears the master of ceremonies state his case: "—Il fait parfaitement la différence entre Akissi et les femmes du sérail qui lui rendent visite pendant la nuit" (p.160). [" 'He is perfectly well aware of the difference between Akissi and the women of the harem who visit him during the night.' "] (p.163)

Samba Baloum then states,

—Je répète que l'homme blanc ne s'apercevait de rien, et qu'il ne pouvait s'apercevoir de rien, car chaque épouse, en entrant dans sa case, déposait à la tête du lit une gerbe de fleurs forestières: l'odeur aussitôt se répandait et rendait l'homme blanc inconscient. (p.160)

["I repeat that the white man was never aware of anything, and that he could not be aware of anything, for each woman, on entering his hut, placed a sheaf of forest flowers beside his bed; their odour filled the hut at once and rendered the white man unconscious."]   (p.163)

But Clarence, still the sleepwalker, fails to realize that he is actually responsible for the trial, and he passes the whole thing off by saying, "—Quelles fables stupides!" (p.161). [". . . a lot of silly lies!"] (p.164) Clarence makes so much noise mumbling to himself that Nagoa and Noaga fear they will be discovered. As they lead Clarence away from the trial, Clarence has a strange feeling of *déjà vu*, wondering if he has returned to the palace of justice in Adramé. Samba Baloum catches up with them, and Clarence manages to talk him into giving him a peek at the naba's harem:

A l'ombre de la muraille, il y avait une quantité de femmes, entourées chacune d'une ribambelle d'enfants; presque toutes tenaient dans leurs bras, ou juchés sur le dos, ou à demi-enfouis dans des pagnes, des enfants plus petits, dont la coleur café-au-lait était celle des mulâtres.
  —D'où viennent ces petits sang-mêlé? demanda Clarence.
  —Ce ne sont pas des sang-mêlé, dit Samba Baloum.
  —Alors pourquoi sont-ils café-au-lait?
  —Beaucoup sont café-au-lait quand ils naissent, dit Samba Baloum. Ils foncent par la suite.
  —Tu veux dire qu'ils deviennent noirs comme toi?
  —Tout juste! Viens maintenant, car il y a plus d'une seconde que tu regardes.
  —Je regarde seulement les petits sang-mêlé, dit Clarence.
  —Mais je t'ai dit que ce ne sont pas des sang-mêlé! Allons, viens. Ne reste pas planté là.
  —A quel âge noircissent-ils?
  —Le soleil les noircit. Mais à présent, viens. Je ne peux pas te laisser ici plus longtemps.
  —Je viens, dit Clarence. J'aurais juré que c'étaient des sang-mêlé. (pp.164–165)

[In the shadow of the wall, there were a number of women, each one surrounded by a swarm of children; nearly all of them held in their arms or carried on their backs or in swaddling clothes much smaller children, whose *café-au-lait* complexions proclaimed them to be mulattos.

"Where do they come from, the little half-castes?" asked Clarence.

"They are not half-castes," said Samba Baloum.

"Then why have they got such light skins?"

"Many are born with that colour skin," said Samba Baloum. "It gets darker as they grow older."

"You mean they become as black as you?"

"Exactly! Come on, now, you've been looking at them for longer than a second."

"I'm only looking at the little half-castes," said Clarence.

"But I've told you they are *not* half-castes! Come on, let's go. Don't just stand there."

"How long does it take for them to turn black?"

"The sun turns them black. But come along now. I can't leave you here any longer."

"I'm coming," said Clarence. "I could have sworn that they were half-castes."] (pp.167–168)

Subconsciously not wanting to admit his lust, Clarence still remains the sleepwalker incapable of understanding his "services" to the naba. (Laye has made use of the sexual overtones of black/white racial stereotyping in a more than ironic way.)

As they leave the inner confines of the naba's palace, Clarence and Samba Baloum and the two boys encounter the naba and his dignitaries sitting in a courtyard. The master of ceremonies is there too, stripped and tied face downward on the ground. Having lost his trial, the master of ceremonies is receiving his punishment—a beating. Once again Laye makes his case about the danger of making value judgments about culture. Clarence is appalled at the brutality of the beating; sickened when he sees the spectators spit on the master of ceremonies' inflamed buttocks. "—Dis au naba que c'est assez," he tells the harem-keeper. Samba Baloum replies, "—Je ne peux pas. . . . Le naba est un homme juste" (p.169). [" 'Tell the naba that this man's had enough,' " he tells the harem-keeper. Samba Baloum replies, " 'I cannot. . . . The naba is a just man.' "] (p.172)

Clarence swears, and he calls the Africans savages; but the beating continues:

—Prenez un peu de vin, dit Noaga. Vous pourrez cracher une gorgée sur le derrière du maître des cérémonies.
—Pour qui me prends-tu? fit Clarence.
—Vous n'avez donc pas pitié? dit Noaga. Une bonne gorgée de vin, voilà qui rafraîchirait pourtant bien les fesses du maître des cérémonies.
Clarence prit une gorgée à la calebasse, mais il l'avala presque aussitôt.
—Non, je ne pourrais pas, dit-il.
—Vous êtes sans pitié, dit Noaga. Vous prenez une gorgée et vous l'avalez; vous l'avalez alors que le derrière du maître des cérémonies est brûlant, gonflé à éclater. Après cela, vous me reprocherez de manquer de coeur! Mais regardez donc comme le derrière est devenu gros! . . . Il est bien deux fois aussi gros qu'il était. (p.171)

["Have some wine," said Noaga. "Then you can spit a mouthful over the backside of the master of ceremonies."
"What do you take me for?" cried Clarence.
"Have you no pity?" replied Noaga. "A good mouthful of palm wine would help to cool off the master of ceremonies' burning cheeks."
Clarence took a mouthful of wine, but swallowed it almost at once.
"No, I couldn't do it," he said.
"You are completely without pity," said Noaga. "You take a mouthful and swallow it; you swallow it, when the master of ceremonies' cheeks are burning and inflamed and swollen to bursting point. And you have the nerve to call me heartless! Just look how enormous that behind has grown! . . . It's easily twice its original size."] (p.174)

At Clarence's request, however, the beating finally stops. Clarence has yet to realize that justice in one culture is not necessarily the same in another. Several days later he will learn that even the master of ceremonies holds it against him for having the beating stopped. The master of ceremonies knows that in the eyes of his villagers he has lost face because the beating was interrupted.

The scene in the courtyard ends with Clarence's making an even larger faux-pas than stopping the punishment. Still raving about the beating, Clarence begins to remove his *boubou* to give it to Nagoa and Noaga as his part of the agreement for taking him to the master of ceremonies' trial. Samba Baloum tells him, "—Mais tu ne peux pas te mettre nu devant la naba! Ça ne se fait pas!" (p.178). ["'. . . you can't let the naba see you naked! It's not done!'"] (p.175) However, in his disgust at the beating he has just witnessed, Clarence removes his *boubou* in front of the naba and stands naked until the old chief gives him another. Samba Baloum lets Clarence know that he has committed the biggest social blunder that a man could possibly make. Even Akissi, who is usually so understanding, is completely shocked, and Clarence's respect in the village is at its lowest level.

The third chapter in Part Two, entitled "Les femmes-poissons" ("The Fish-Women"), halts the downward trend in Clarence's fall and begins the more positive stage of his regeneration. Clarence is beginning to comprehend that he has no rights at all—nobody owes him anything. He is not bringing light to the dark continent; instead, he will be the one illuminated, but only through his hard-won understanding of African culture. Though still a sleepwalker, he is soon to face a total awakening, once he has acknowledged his own unworthiness. The chapter begins with a dream and ends with a second more significant dream for Clarence, who is abruptly awakened to face the shock of reality. It is a little as if Laye were forcing Clarence to undergo shock treatment under the guidance of a psychiatrist.

In the first dream, the odor of the south is all but overpowering, for Clarence's subconscious is beginning to gnaw more readily through to his consciousness. Just before he wakes up, a crowd of women have been rushing toward him, each one presenting him with a half-caste child. "'Dis bonjour à ton fils!' criaient-elles" (p.178). ["'Say hallo to your son!'

they kept crying."] (p.180) It is the beginning of his self-realization: Clarence increasingly feels disgusted with himself; the naba has reduced him to little more than an animal, a stud.

—"Vous n'êtes pas sot, Clarence. Vous faites parfaitement la différence entre Akissi et les femmes du sérail qui vous rendent visite au cours de la nuit . . . Alons! avouez; abattez enfin ce jeu que tout le monde connaît! . . . Que pourriez-vous faire, sinon avouer? Tous ces petits sang-mêlé, dans la cour du sérail, ne sont pas tombés du ciel!"

La colère alors reprit Clarence. L'effroi l'avait figé, mais la colère le fit bondir. Il lança le poing sur cette bouche, il le lança avec toute la violence dont il était capable. Il aurait voulu écraser ces lèvres et briser ces dents. Mais son poing ne rencontra rien, rien que le vide. Entraîne par l'élan, Clarence tomba à côté de sa couche.   (p.180)

["You're not silly, Clarence. You know quite well the difference between Akissi and the women of the harem who visit you during the night . . . Come on, admit it! Stop putting on this act which deceives no one! . . . What else can you do now but confess? . . . All those little half-caste brats in the courtyard of the harem didn't just drop from the clouds!"

Then Clarence was again convulsed with fury. Terror had made him freeze, but now anger made him jump into action. He gave the mouth a punch with his fist; he punched it with all the strength he could summon. He would have liked to pound those lips and smash those teeth. But his fist met nothing, nothing but air. Carried away by the force of his projected blow, Clarence lost his balance and fell down by the side of his bed.]   (pp.182–183)

Later in the morning, as he begins to take off his *boubou* to join the bathers in the stream, he feels his modesty for the first time since he has been in Aziana. "Non, il n'était pas possible que Clarence se mît nu devant tant de gens; en tout cas, pas devant toutes ces femmes qui attendaient leur tour de puiser à la fontaine" (p.184). ["No, he could not possibly strip himself naked in front of all these people; not, at any rate, in front of

all these women who were waiting their turn at the fountain."]
(p.186)

Aimlessly, Clarence wanders the streets, eventually going to
see Diallo, the blacksmith. They discuss the beating of the
master of ceremonies on the day before, Diallo taking the side
of the naba, and then the subject changes to Diallo's work.
The blacksmith is forging an axe which he hopes will be the
finest one he has ever made, because the naba intends to present it as a gift to the king. Once again Laye illustrates the
African's differing concept of time. Clarence asks Diallo if the
king will be coming soon. Diallo replies,

—Lui seul le sait. Il ne viendra pas absolument à l'improviste,
mais ce sera tout comme: il nous surprendra comme s'il était
venu inopinément.
—Comment cela? dit Clarence.
—Eh bien, nous l'attendons. Chaque jour et chaque heure,
nous l'attendons. Mais nous nous lassons aussi de l'attendre. Et
c'est quand nous sommes le plus las qu'il survient. Ou nous
l'appelons—à chaque seconde nous l'appelons; mais, malgré nous,
nous ne l'appelons pas toujours; nous oublions de l'appeler, nous
sommes distraits, l'espace d'un quart de second—, et soudain il
apparaît, il choisit ce quart de seconde pour apparaître. Ou même
nous l'attendons et nous l'appelons constamment, notre vigilance
n'est jamais en défaut, mais sa venue ne nous surprend pas moins
en plein désarroi, car elle est telle qu'elle nous précipite im-
manquablement dans la [sic] désarroi. Quand bien même nous
serions irréprochables—et le roi sait si nous le sommes peu—,
sa venue nous ferait tout de même trembler.   (pp.188–189)

["He alone knows. He will not come without any kind of
warning at all, but it will be very sudden. He'll take us by surprise, just as if he had not been expected."

"How is that?" asked Clarence.

"It's like this: we are waiting for him. Every day and every
hour we wait for him. But we also get weary of the waiting.
And it is when we are most weary that he comes to us. Or we
call to him—every moment we are calling him; but however
hard we try, we do not call to him all the time—we keep for-
getting to call to him; we are distracted for a fraction of a

second—and suddenly he appears, he chooses that very fraction of a second in which to make his appearance. Or even when we are waiting and calling to him constantly, even when our vigilance is perfect and unremitting, his arrival nevertheless finds us in great confusion, because it is of such a nature that it inevitably throws us into confusion. Even if we were without reproach— and the king knows how far from being irreproachable we are— his arrival, his sudden coming would make us tremble all the same."]   (p.191)

This is not the first intimation that Laye has given concerning the godlike aspects of the king, and Clarence begins to realize that the king is more than a king: he is release from all the burdens of life, a purification which is attained only when it is most unexpected, when one is most unlikely to expect the king's coming. Laye's comments here, spoken through Diallo, are perhaps the most significant in his novel. The African is at a oneness with his world, his environment. Life and death are inevitable—just as the king's coming is inevitable. In essence, there is *no* ontological gap—for life and death are fused together, and a man is a part of everything that surrounds him. It is only the Westerner who feels a sense of separation from his environment.

The conversation continues as Clarence asks Diallo if his axe will be ready by the time the king arrives:

—C'est probable, dit Diallo; enfin je l'espère. . . . Mais qu'est-ce qu'une hache? J'en ai forgé des milliers, et celle-ci assurément sera le plus belle; toutes les autres ne m'auront servi que d'expériences pour finalement réussir celle-ci; si bein que cette hache sera le somme de tout ce que j'ai appris, sera comme ma vie et l'effort de ma vie même. Mais que voulez-vous que le roi en fasse? . . . Il l'acceptera; j'espère du moins qu'il l'acceptera, et peut-être même daignera-t-il l'admirer; mais il ne l'acceptera et ne l'admirera que pour me faire plaisir. En fait, quel plaiser y prendrait-il? Il aura toujours des haches infiniment plus belles et plus meurtrières que toutes celles que je pourrais forger. . . . Pourtant je la forge. . . . Peut-être ne puis-je faire autre chose, peut-être suis-je comme un arbre qui ne peut porter qu'une espèce de fruit. Certainement je suis comme cet arbre. . . . Et peut-être, en dépit de tant de défauts, peut-être parce que je suis comme cet arbre et que je manque de moyens, le roi malgré tout considérerat-il ma bonne volonté. (p.189)

["Probably. . . . Anyhow, I hope it will be. But what is an axe. I have forged thousands of them, and this one will undoubtedly be the finest of them all; the others will have been no more than experiments I made in order to forge this one perfect axe. So that this will be the sum of everything I have ever learnt; it will be like my life, and all the effort I have made to live it well. But what does the king want with an axe? . . . He will accept it; at least I hope he will accept it, and perhaps he will even deign to admire it: but he will accept it and admire it only in order to give me pleasure. After all, what sort of pleasure could he take in it? There will always be axes that are finer and more deadly, more murderously sharp than any I can fashion . . . Yet I go on forging it . . . Perhaps I can do nothing else, perhaps I am like a tree which can bear only one kind of fruit. Yes, I am like that tree . . . And perhaps, in spite of having so many faults, perhaps because I am like that tree and lack the means to do anything but this; in spite of everything, the king will give me credit for my good will. . . ."] (pp.191–192)

It little matters if the axe is finished; what is important is that each axe be better than the previous one, that life be a constant pathway toward perfection. Like Allah, the perfect axe is probably unattainable, yet that is no reason for giving up. Diallo's answer is the reply of a skilled artisan who takes extreme pride in his work. There is the same inevitability in his axe-forging as there is in the coming of the king, and the two are, indeed, related. What is important here is the work itself: life. In the attempt toward perfection with the perfect axe, Diallo is coming closer to a oneness with his God. Diallo is truly at one with his work—a part of his work—for his work is his life, a part of everything else. It is difficult to tell where the axe-maker ends and the axe begins.

The conversation returns to the master of ceremonies' beating of the day before, and the wise blacksmith explains to Clarence the magnitude of his error in calling off the punishment:

—Ne comprenez-vous pas que tout monde maintenant regardera son derrière avec suspicion? Ce n'est qu'un demi-mal, de recevoir des coups dont on peut exhiber la trace; mais les recevoir, les sentir au profond de sa chair, et sentir la peau qui vous cuit, sans qu'on puisse rien exhiber du tout, c'est vraiment souffrir pour des prunes. Personne finalement ne sera content, ni le maître des cérémonies, ni les gens.

—Vous voulez dire que, par suite de mon intervention, les gens auront le sentiment que la justice est insatisfaite? demanda Clarence.

—Exactement. . . . (p.192)

["Don't you understand that now everyone will look upon his backside with the greatest suspicion? It is only like feeling half the pain, to receive strokes the marks of which one can display to the public; but to have received them, felt them bite into one's flesh, and to have felt the flesh smart like fire, and then not be able to display one's weals is to suffer meaninglessly. In the end, no one will be satisfied—neither the people, nor the master of ceremonies himself."

"You mean that, because of my intervention, people will feel that justice has not been done?" asked Clarence.

"Exactly. . . ."] (pp.194-195)

As Clarence leaves the blacksmith, he realizes the scope of his misjudgments, and it leads to a realization of himself:

Clarence était tout plongé en lui-même, Clarence récapitulait tout ce qu'il avait surpris depuis son arrivée à Aziana. En vérité, il avait tout surpris, il s'était aperçu de tout, et il n'avait rien compris à ce qu'il surprenait; il n'avait pas cessé d'être averti, et les avertissements les plus précis lui avaient échappé. Mais, à présent que tout s'était éclairci, il voyait enfin, il voyait jusqu'à la nausée, de quels menus services il payait l'hospitalité du naba. (p.193)

[Clarence was sunk deep in thought; he was going over everything that had happened since his arrival in Aziana. Actually there was nothing he had *not* been aware of; he had been alive to everything that was going on; he had never ceased being aware of what was happening, and yet the most obvious warnings had passed him by. But now that everything had become clear, he could see it all at last, with sickening clarity—he realised now what the "small services" had been with which he had paid for the naba's hospitality.]   (p.196)

Clarence continues his walk, almost in a trance, toward the river, once again becoming obsessed with the odor of the south. His thoughts return to the king: "Le roi se détournerait de cette bête immonde, il s'en détournerait avec horreur. . . . Un jour, le roi viendrait, et ce serait comme s'il n'était jamais venu" (p.195). ["The king would turn away from this unclean beast, he would turn away in horror and disgust . . . One day, the king would come; but it would be as if he had not come at all."] (p.198) He has a sudden premonition that only death will deliver him from his vileness.

The chapter ends with the second dream—which is also an awakening and the end of his sleepwalking. In the dream, the odor becomes overpowering and an immense feeling of disgust comes upon him. He slips into the water and is carried along by the current, past islands populated with fish-women, calling him, thrusting out their breasts at him. The current carries him along, just as Clarence has permitted his life in Aziana to be one of continual drifting, without meaning or purpose. As his revulsion increases toward the siren-like fish-women, Clarence consciously realizes the depths of his degradation, for he is suddenly awakened by Samba Baloum and the two boys and the subconscious thoughts become a reality. He tells them that he does not want to go back to Akissi or to his hut, that everything is changed. Samba Baloum tells Clarence he will feel all right once he has drunk some palm wine. Clarence replies, "—Jamais je ne changerai! Tu m'entends, Baloum? Jamais je ne changerai!" (p.202). [" 'Never! . . . I'll never feel any differently! Do you hear, Baloum. I'll never change my mind!' "] (p.205) The encounter with the fish-women has jolted Clarence into an awareness that his life in Aziana has been one of continual revelry in search of fulfillment for one side of his being only—the pleasure principle, temporary eroticism. Henceforth, Clarence will search for a balancing with the more mystical or spiritual side of life.

Part Three of *Le regard du roi,* "Le roi" ("the king"), begins with a chapter called "Dioki." In this section Clarence has a vision of the king's coming. Laye creates the effect of a photographic still portraying the actual event before it happens, a little as if he were stopping the narrative, controlling the temporal element, and presenting the scene in which Clarence will later directly participate. This controlled image of the king's arrival is fitting for the surreal world through which Clarence has been walking as the sleepwalker. Instead of a flashback we have a flashforward, heightening our anticipation of the actual event, and the result is that both Clarence and the reader are ready for the final scene involving the king.

At the beginning of the chapter, we learn that Clarence has remained faithful to the promise he made after seeing the fish-women. He has, indeed, changed, and now, even though he still continues to service the harem, he does so with disgust, for his one concern is in escaping. His feelings toward the king have altered too: "Pourtant c'était au roi malgré tout que Clarence pensait; c'était malgré tout sur le roi qu'il comptait, pour être déliveré. Oui, le roi viendrait et le délivrerait. . . ." (p.210). ["He was counting on the king to give him his freedom . . . the king would come and . . . deliver him. . . ."] (p.211) No longer does he see the king simply as someone who will give him employment as something he deserves; rather, the king is now looked at as a kind of release—an escape. When Clarence asks Nagoa and Noago when they believe the king will come, they tell him that Dioki knows, "—Elle voit tout et elle fait découvrir tout. . . ." (p.211). [" 'She finds out

things and lets you see them happening.' "] (p.212) The two
boys lead Clarence to the entrance of Dioki's dwelling, and
since they are afraid of the strange witchlike woman, they let
Clarence go the rest of the way alone. He descends a flight of
stairs into her cave, and when he asks the old woman when the
king will come, she tells him she will consult her snakes.

Dioki's snakes immediately surround her, and when she an-
nounces that the king is coming, Clarence replies, "—il y a des
années qu'on ne cesse de me le répéter. . . ." (p.219). [" 'People have been telling me that for years and years.' "] (p.219)
Clarence's reference to time here is the only one in the novel,
and it is difficult to tell if he literally means what he has said.
It is almost impossible to tell how long Clarence has been in
Aziana. The only real evidence we have of any extended
period of time is the fact that the harem is filled with half-
caste children. Dioki assures Clarence that the king is on his
way, and she goes on to describe the king's appearance. Clarence is somewhat put off by Dioki's withered look and by her
snakes, and he thinks how ugly she is:

> Elle se roulait dans la poussière et parmi les serpents, et ceux-
> ci s'enroulaient autour de son corps en sifflant. Ils l'étreignaient,
> ils l'enlaçaient; et elle, elle gémissait. Mais quelle étreinte était-ce
> là? Quel enlacement était-ce là? C'étaient les convulsions mêmes
> de l'amour! (p.220)

> [She was rolling in the dust, among the serpents and these
> were hissing and rolling themselves round her body. They were
> embracing her, enfolding her: and she—she was crying out. But
> what sort of embrace was this? Clarence could hardly believe
> what he saw. These were the passionate convulsions of love
> itself!] (p.220)

Clarence is also disgusted by her open show of passion, though
his own actions in Aziana have not been any more subtle. Then
Clarence has his vision of the king: "Il semblait que le scène
entière, à laquelle Clarence avait assisté sur l'esplanade, se fût
déroulée de nouveau, mais cette fois dans le sens contraire"

(p.222). ["It seemed as if the entire scene which Clarence had witnessed on the esplanade had taken place all over again, only in reverse."] (p.223) The king's eyes notice nothing—he is far removed from all worldly events—and Clarence, realizing that he has little right to expect anything at all from the king, is chilled to the bone. We are reminded of what the beggar said much earlier; man has only favors and not rights. By assuming he has rights in this African society, Clarence has assumed a superiority over the culture itself and he has broken the un-written laws of hospitality; just as he now makes a value judg-ment about Dioki. As he leaves her cave, Dioki tells him, "—Sache qu'il n'y a pas de femme si vieille qu'on ne puisse la maltraiter!" (p.224). [" 'Remember there's no woman so old that she cannot be ill-treated!' "] (p.224) Clarence's super-cilious attitude toward Dioki is indicative of the way he has treated the whole African experience, based on the false as-sumption that Africa has nothing to contribute to his educa-tion. The opposite is actually the case: Clarence has nothing he can offer Africa. For Clarence is like the *témoins de la négritude,* only in a negative sense. What the *témoins* rebelled against, Clarence has upheld; what they rediscovered was the importance of the African experience. Clarence is still only on the verge of making this discovery.

As he returns to the village after leaving Dioki, Clarence talks to Diallo once again. Clarence tells him to hurry up, the king is on his way, and Clarence confesses, too, that his waiting for the king is now different from before: "—Je ne l'ai pour-tant pas toujours attendu avec la même ferveur" (p.226). [". . . I haven't always waited for him with the same ardent longing, with the same fervour."] (p.226) As he recalls his nocturnal activities, he is once again filled with a sense of disgust:

La bête qui était en lui, la frénésie de la bête; une attirance comme irrésistible pour l'inavouable. . .
   —Je ne l'ai pas attendu comme je l'aurais dû, dit-il.
   —Personne ne l'attend comme il devrait, dit Diallo.   (p.227)

[There was the beast inside him, the lustful frenzy of the beast, and an irresistible appetite for the unmentionable. . .

"I have not always waited for him as I should have done," he said.

"No one waits for him as they ought to," said Diallo.] (p.227)

Once again, the wise blacksmith becomes Laye's mouthpiece. Clarence's self-realization that he has not always waited for the king as he should have indicates the basic alteration that has now been made in his thinking. It is again related to the African's sense of time and rights and favors. Diallo prophetically says that no one can be completely ready for the king, a comment which should recall the beggar's earlier question: "—L'imaginez-vous fait pour des êtres comme nous?" (p.21). [" 'Do you suppose he [the king] was intended for the likes of us?' "] (p.33) If the king, who represents the final oneness of the African experience, the ultimate perfection, had to wait for complete purity in his followers, he would have no subjects. There is a hint here basic to Islamic thought: salvation is not determined solely by the individual's acts—ultimately, it is only Allah who can grant this salvation.

The chapter ends with the talking drums announcing that the king is, indeed, coming, that he will be in Aziana the next day. At this news, Diallo states that, just as he had said, the king is coming without any warning. He is concerned that his axe will not be ready and concludes that he will offer the king all of his axes instead. "—La quantité, alors suppléera peut-être, à la qualité" (p.228). ["Then perhaps what is lacking in quality will be made up for in quantity."] (p.228) The boys tell Clarence that the king will arrive the next day—at the stroke of noon. Clarence comes to a fuller realization: "Son visage n'avait pas cessé de rayonner. Il rayonnait comme si le roi eût déjà posé le regard sur lui. Oui, comme si véritablement un autre visage, un visage plus haut, plus grand, déjà se fût emparé du sien . . ." (p.228). ["His face still shone with rapture. He was glowing as if the king had already laid his eye upon him. Yes, as if another face, a loftier, greater gaze had already become part of his own. . . ."] (p.228)

The final chapter of *Le regard du roi* could only be called "Le roi" ("The King"). It begins on the following day—the day of the king's arrival—and Akissi is scrubbing Clarence's back. Clarence believes that by this act he can purify himself so that he will be more worthy of the king. His plan is short lived, however, for even before he has finished his ablutions, the master of ceremonies arrives and informs Clarence that "—Le naba vous fait dire de ne bouger de votre case, aujourd'hui, sous aucun prétexte" (p.231). ["'The naba has given orders that you are under no circumstances to leave your hut today.'"] (p.230) This is, of course, a brutal blow, for Clarence now believes that the king will complete his purification, cleanse him of his animalistic past—give him release. Samba Baloum visits him shortly thereafter, however, and states that the message of the master of ceremonies was erroneous. The naba merely requests that Clarence not walk on the carpets. Once again Clarence's hopes arise, yet after Samba Baloum leaves, the master of ceremonies returns and strongly hints that it would be best if Clarence did not attend the ceremonies.

In the most severe condemnation in the story, the master of ceremonies tells Clarence that he is unworthy of seeing the king:

— . . . je vais dresser le bilan de ton attente et le bilan de ta conduit. . . . Ton attente, c'était des bavardages sans fin avec Pierre ou Paul; c'était des beuveries à n'en plus finir et le chapardage du vin du naba; c'était les escapades avec les deux polissons et les paresseuses stations à la forge; c'était le tissage, de loin en loin, d'une malheureuse serviette-éponge et la jarre-douche à la vue des passants; c'était . . . Mais que n'était-ce pas, cette prétendue attente? . . . C'était le moulin; c'était ta case, qui est comme un moulin ouvert à tout venant; et c'était l'in-

avouable farine de ce moulin; c'était, la nuit, la sale promenade
de deux limaces! (pp.238–239)

["I'm going to reckon up what you've been doing and how
you've been doing it while you've been kicking your heels here
in Aziana. . . . It's been nothing but idle chatter with any Tom,
Dick or Harry; it's been nothing but guzzling and wine-bibbing
and pinching the naba's calabashes, foolish escapades with those
two scamps and long idle hours gossiping at the forge; you took
months to weave a horrible little towel; you performed your
ablutions naked in full view of the passers-by; you. . . . But
what did it all amount to? . . . Your house became like a
public flour mill, open to all and everyone. And what sort of
flour did you grind? The unmentionable things that went on
here! . . . Every night, you were with someone different, like
two snails out on a filthy crawl!"] (p.238)

When Clarence tells him to shut up, the master of ceremonies
continues,

—Pourquoi me tairais-je? Ai-je rien dit que tu ne saches
déjà? Tout ne parle-t-il pas suffisamment? Même si je me
taisais, l'odeur qu'on respire dans ta case parlerait. Ne sens-tu
pas cette odeur? . . . Mais non, tu ne le sens même plus! Elle
a si intimement pénétré ta peau, elle est entrée si profond dans
ton sang, que tu ne la sens plus. . . . Et crois-tu jamais t'en
débarrasser? Ce n'est pas Akissi, en te ponçant le dos, qui pourrait la laver, cette odeur; rien ne la lavera jamais! Le roi la sentira
de la galerie; tu ne te seras pas approché de lui, que déjà il le
sentira! . . . (p.239)

["Why should I shut up? Have I said anything you don't
know already? Doesn't it speak for itself? Even if I were to
shut up, the odour of your hut would speak for itself. Can't you
smell that odour? . . . No, you can't even smell it any longer!
It has entered into your flesh and bones, and you can't smell it
any more! . . . And do you think you'll ever get rid of it? You
won't get rid of it by making Akissi scrub your back with
pumice-stone; nothing will ever wash it away! The king will
smell it from the arcade; as soon as you go near him, he'll smell
it!"] (p.238)

The master of ceremonies reveals to Clarence, also, that the beggar sold him to the naba:

—Peut-être ignorais-tu que tu ne t'appartiens plus, que tu appartiens au naba; à présent, tu le sais; tu sais que, même si tu voulais servir le roi, tu ne le pourrais pas. Mais quelle est cette prétention de vouloir servir le roi? Alors même que le naba consentirait à te lâcher—et rien ne prouve qu'il lâcherait son bien, rien ne prouve qu'il surmonrait sa pingrerie—, qu'est-ce que le roi ferait d'un coq? . . . (p.240)

["Perhaps you didn't know that you are no longer your own master, that you belong body and soul to the naba; well, now you know: you know that even if you wanted to serve the king, you could not possibly do so. But what right have you to serve the king? Even if the naba consented to let you go . . . and there is no reason to suspect that he would give up what belongs to him . . . that he would be able to overcome his miserliness . . . what would the king want with such a cock?"] (p.239) *

The master of ceremonies goes away, informing Clarence, "—Impur comme tu l'es, tu n'es bon qu'à être enfermé dans le sérail!" (p.240). [" 'Foul as you are, you are good for nothing but the harem!' "] (p.239)

For Clarence, this is the final revelation—the final stage of his education—not that he will be a more worthy man by seeing the king, but that he is *beyond* purification. As the magnitude of this revelation begins to grasp him, Clarence tells Akissi that he will not put his *boubou* on, that he will voluntarily remain in his hut. When she asks him if he does not want to go outside, he replies, "—Je le veux encore. . . . De toutes mes forces, je le veux. . . . Mais je ne peux plus; à présent je ne peux plus. . . ." (p.241). [" 'I still want to. . . . With all my heart, I want to go out. . . . But I can't now, I can't go out

---

* Although I believe that it is possible to make a Christian interpretation of Laye's novel—with the king as God and the naba as the devil— I do not believe that that was Laye's intention.

any more. . . .' "] (p.241) Clarence tells Akissi to leave him alone and her reply hints at something Clarence has yet to comprehend, "—Sais-je combien de temps je te verrai encore?" (p.242). [" 'How do I know how much longer I shall see you?' "] (p.241)

As the king's arrival is announced, amidst the fury of the drumming, Clarence thinks back to his arrival in Africa, and the rolling waves which constantly threatened the shore, battering it, but never subduing it. It is a motif which Laye has repeated several times in his story, and the waves are symbolic of Clarence's own inability to grasp the African situation. As his mind recalls an image of a small craft being repelled by the shore, Clarence remembers that the sea

> n'oubliait pas de ramener la barque, car il jugeait que, leur curiosité satisfaite, les gens de la barque n'avaient rien de plus à attendre de la terre d'Afrique. Il jugeait, avec sa vielle sagesse, qu'il leur en cuirait d'en apprendre davantage. (p.243)

> [did not forget to draw the bark away from the shore, for it knew that once their curiosity was satisfied, the crew of the bark had nothing more to expect from the red earth of Africa. It knew, with age-old wisdom, that it would be their undoing if they were to learn any more.] (p.242)

It is in this constant fashion that Clarence, too, has been repelled by an African he has tried too infrequently to understand. Laye implies, however, that the age-old wisdom of Africa can be comprehended, but, as we will shortly see, only if a price is paid, if something else is given up.*

Clarence sits dreaming of the past, the wall of waves, and the other African walls he has been unable to scale. As he thinks of the odor—which he now recognizes is not Africa at all, but his own impurity—he blushes in sudden shame, at his

---

* The motif of the waves and their blocking Clarence from Africa is also related to several other motifs: the thickness of the forest and its walls, the mists of the air, and the dreamlike atmosphere present in much of the novel.

great stupidity in believing he was worthy of the king. The introspection continues as Clarence admits that there are impurities which nothing can cleanse. Nagoa and Noaga visit Clarence, telling him that when the king leaves the next day, they will go with him. He asks the boys, "—Ne sentez-vous pas cette odeur qui est sur moi?"(p.246). [" 'Can you not smell the odour that clings to me?' "] (p.245) Then Diallo visits Clarence also, and Clarence confesses that it is too late, implying that it is too late for him to expect any form of assistance from the king. Diallo answers,

> —Il est toujours trop tard, dit Diallo. A peine sommes-nous nés, qu'il est déjà trop tard. Mais le roi ne l'ignore pas, et c'est pourquoi aussi il est toujours temps.
> —Est-ce là ce que tu disais hier? demanda Clarence.
> —Hier? dit Diallo. Est-ce que hier compte encore? Ce jour seul et cette heure seule comptent. Il suffirait d'un millième de second.
> —Tu ne sens donc pas l'odeur? dit Clarence.
> —L'odeur? dit Diallo.　(p.246)

> ["It is always too late," said Diallo. "We have barely finished being born, before it's already too late for something or other. But the king knows that, and that is why there is always time."
> "Is that what you said yesterday?" Clarence asked.
> "Yesterday?" said Diallo. "What's yesterday got to do with to-day? It is only this day and hour that count."
> "Can't you smell the odour?" said Clarence.
> "What odour?" said Diallo.]　(p.245)

The wise blacksmith again shows his oneness with his world; one must make the best of the present moment; the past (and the future) simply do not exist.

Clarence refuses to go with the others to see the king. Diallo, he says, at least possesses an axe to present to the king, something he himself has made. Of himself, Clarence says, "—Moi, je n'ai rien. Ou plutôt. . . . Ah! si je n'avais rien, s'il était possible que je n'eusse rien! . . . Mais j'ai cette odeur, cette indétachable odeur. Ne la sens-tu pas?" (p.247). ["I haven't anything. Or rather . . . Oh, if I *did* have nothing, if it were only possible for me to have nothing! . . . But I have this odour, this ineradicable odour. Can't you smell it?' "] (p.246) It is the final admission of his own unworthiness—that he has nothing to offer—and it is this admission that places Clarence on equal terms with his environment, with Africa. Stripped of all his beliefs of superiority, Clarence is at last admitting the significance of the African experience: that Africa, too, may teach the white man something, if he will only take the patience to listen, to learn. This is an idea which is paramount, also, in Ezekiel Mphahlele's powerful autobiography, *Down Second Avenue:*

> I admire the white man's achievements, his mind that plans tall buildings, powerful machinery. I used to want to justify myself and my own kind to the white man. I later discovered that it wasn't worth it. It was to myself and to my kind I needed to justify myself. I think now the white man has no right to tell me how to order my life as a social being, or order it for me. He may teach me how to make a shirt or to read and to write, but my forebears and I could teach him a thing or two if only he would listen and allow himself time to feel. Africa is no more for the white man who comes here to teach and to control her human and material forces and not to learn.[11]

Only when the white man is willing to learn as well as to teach can he reap the benefits of cultural syncretism. Clarence repeats his decision not to leave the hut. Diallo reiterates one of the major ideas of the novel, "—Si tous ceux qui se présentent devant le roi devaient être dignes de lui, le roi vivrait dans un désert" (p.248). [" 'If all those who present themselves to the king had to be worthy of him, the king would live alone in the desert.' "] (p.246) Clarence feels that the naba will never release his hold on him.

And then the king arrives, and Clarence wakes up, after fainting: "Quand il reprit connaissance, il était seul, tout à fait seul. Un grand silence, un silence opaque, régnait dans la case" (p.250). ["When he regained consciousness, he was alone, utterly alone. A great silence, a dense silence, reigned in the hut."] (p.249) Clarence asks himself, "—Est-ce ainsi quand on meurt?" (p.250). [" 'Is this the way one dies?' "] * (p.249) Clarence has noticed that the radiance has even entered his hut. Going to his window, he sees the king:

> Toute sa vie, lui semblait-il avait attendu cette scène. Maintenant qu'il la voyait, il ne savait pas si elle était réelle ou si elle n'était qu'une image que ses yeux projetaient; une image depuis si longtemps formée et si souvent répétée, que les yeux finalement la voient en dehors de toute réalité. (p.251)

> [It seemed that he had been waiting all his life for this moment. Now that he saw this longed-for scene, he did not know if it was real, or if it was some mirage, some hallucination, an image projected by his own eyes upon the courtyard wall; an image that had taken shape so long ago, and that had been conjured up so often that the eyes finally seem to see it, divorced from all reality.] (p.249)

This time, however, it is not a mirage. Clarence is no longer the somnambulist. It is the daylight world in all its splendor.

The king pays no attention to the presents which are being piled up in front of him; he is oblivious to the material world. Clarence sees Nagoa and Noaga, too, looking at him:

> Plus Clarence regardait le roi, plus il measurait l'audace, l'étendue d'audace, qu'il eût fallu s'orroger pour s'avancer vers lui.
> Et ce n'était pas son dénuement seulement, ce n'était pas son avilissement seulement qui empêchaient Clarence de s'avancer, c'était bien autre chose; et bien d'autres choses. C'était la grande fragilité du roi, la fragilité autant que la puissance, la même adorable fragilité, la même redoutable puissance que Clarence avait observées sur l'esplanade. . . . Mais surtout tant de pureté, tant d'éclatante pureté. (pp.251–252)

> [The more Clarence looked at the king, the more he realised what courage, what audacity would be needed to go up to him.

---

* Some critics have suggested that this question is an indication that Clarence has died and that the rest of the novel takes place after his death.

And it was not just his nakedness, it was not just his vileness which prevented Clarence from going up to him; it was something else—many other things. It was the fragility—the fragility as well as the great strength of the king—the same adorable fragility, the same formidable strength that Clarence had observed on the esplanade. . . . But above all, so much purity, so much blazing purity. All these prevented Clarence from going up to him.]   (p.250)

As he continues to look at the king, Clarence has a feeling that all has been lost, that he will remain "pour toujours enchaîné au Sud, enchaîné à sa case, enchaîné au naba et au sérail, enchaîné à tout cela à quoi il s'était si inconsidérément livré" (p.252). ["for ever chained to the South, chained to his hut, chained to the naba and to the harem, chained to everything he had so thoughtlessly abandoned himself to."] (p.251) He thinks of his weakness, realizing that he would have liked to throw off his inertia, his listlessness. And in the final catharsis, he weeps. And then the king looks at him: *

Mais alors le roi tourna imperceptiblement la tête, et son regard se posa sur Clarence. Ce regard n'était ni froid, ni hostile. Ce regard . . . Est-ce que ce regard n'appelait pas?

—Hélas! Seigneur, je n'ai que mon bon vouloir, murmura Clarence, mon très faible bon vouloir! Mais vous ne pouvez pas l'accepter. C'est un bon vouloir qui me condamne plus qu'il ne me disculpe.

Pourtant le roi ne détournait pas le regard. Et son regard. . . . Son regard semblait malgré tout appeler. Alors brusquement, Clarence s'avança. Il aurait dû se heurter à la paroi, mais la paroi devant lui s'effondra, la case derrière lui s'effondra, et il s'avança.

Il s'avançait et il n'avait aucun vêtement sur lui. Mais la pensée ne l'effleura pas qu'il aurait dû, au préalable, mettre son boubou; le roi le regardait, et rien, plus rien n'avait d'existence

* The title of the English version of Laye's novel *The Radiance of the King*, is slightly misleading. It is not the *radiance* which is important in this scene, but the fact that the king has actually looked at Clarence, that is, glanced at someone as base as Clarence. Note too, the quotation from Kafka at the beginning of Laye's novel: ". . . Le Seigneur passera dans le couloir, regardera le prisonnier et dira:—Celui-ci, il ne faut pas l'enfermer à nouveau; il vient à moi."

en dehors de ce regard. C'était un regard si lumineux et où il y avait tant de douceur que l'espoir, un fol espoir, naissait en Clarence. Oui, l'espoir à présent le disputait à la crainte; l'espoir devenait plus fort que la crainte. Et bien que le sentiment de son impureté dissuadât Clarence de s'approcher, néanmoins Clarence s'avançait. Il s'avançait en chancelant; il foulait l'épais tapis en chancelant; il lui semblait à tout moment que ses jambes ou que le sol allaient soudain se dérober sous lui. Mais non, il avançait, il continuait de s'avancer, et ses jambes ne le trahissaient pas, le sol ne s'ouvrait pas. Et le regard. . . Le regard ne se détournait pas.

—Seigneur! Seigneur! murmura Clarence. Est-il vrai que vous m'appelez? Est-il vrai que l'odeur qui est sur moi ne vous fait pas reculer d'horreur?

Et parce que le regard demeurait posé sur lui, parce que l'appel demeurait sur lui, ce fut comme un trait de feu qui le transperça.

—Personne pourtant n'est plus vil que moi, plus dénué que moi, pensait-il. Et vous, Seigneur, vous acceptez de poser le regard sur moi! Ou était-ce son dénuement même? . . . Ton dénuement même! semblait dire le regard. Ce vide effrayant qui est en toi et qui s'ouvre à moi; ta faim qui répond à ma faim; ton abjection même qui n'existait pas sans ma permission, et la honte que tu en as. . . ."

Quand il fut parvenu devant le roi, quand il fut dans le grand rayonnement du roi, et tout meurtri encore par le trait de feu, mais tout vivant et seulement vivant de ce feu, Clarence tomba à genoux, car il lui semblait qu'il étàit enfin áu bout de sa course et au terme de toute course.

Mais sans doute ne s'était-il pas assez approché encore, sans doute était-il trop timide encore, car le roi lui ouvrit les bras. Et dans le temps qu'il lui ouvrait les bras, son manteau s'entrouvrit, son mince torse d'adolescent se découvrit. Sur ce torse, dans la nuit de ce torse, il y avait—au centre, mais pas tout à fait au centre, un peu sur la droite—un léger battement qui faisait frémir la peau. C'était ce battement qui appelait, ce léger battement! C'était ce feu qui brûlait et cette lumière qui rayonnait. C'était cet amour qui dévorait.

—Ne savais-tu pas que je t'attendais? dit le roi.

Et Clarence posa doucement les lèvres sur le léger, sur l'immense battement. Alors le roi referma lentement les bras, et son grand manteau enveloppa Clarence pour toujours. (pp.252–254)

[But at that very moment the king turned his head, turned it imperceptibly, and his glance fell upon Clarence. That look was neither cold, nor hostile. That look. . . . Did it not seem to call to him?

"Alas, lord, I have only my good-will," murmured Clarence, "and it is very weak! But you cannot accept it. My good-will condemns me: there is no virtue in it."

Still the king did not turn his eyes away. And his eyes. . . . In spite of everything, his eyes seemed to be calling. . . . Then, suddenly, Clarence went up to him. He ought to have bumped into the outer wall, but as he approached it the wall melted away, the hut behind him melted away, and he walked on.

He went forward and he had no garment upon his nakedness. But the thought did not enter his head that he ought first of all to have put his *boubou* on; the king was looking at him, and nothing, nothing had any more meaning beside that look. It was so luminous a look, one in which there was so much sweetness that hope, a foolish hope, woke in Clarence's heart. Yes, hope now strove with fear within him, and hope was growing stronger than fear. And though the sense of his impurity seemed to be holding him back, at the same time Clarence was going forward. He went on with stumbling steps; he stumbled as he trod on the rich carpet; every moment it seemed to him as if his legs or the ground beneath him were going to disappear. But he kept moving forward, forward all the time, and his legs did not betray him, nor did the ground open up under him. And that look. . . . That look still did not turn away from him. "My lord! My lord!" Clarence kept whispering, "is it true that you are calling me? Is it true that the odour which is upon me does not offend you and does not make you turn away in horror?"

And because that look still calmly rested upon him, because the call was still going out to him, he was pierced as if by a tongue of fire.

"Yes no one is as base as I, as naked as I," he thought. "And you, lord, you are willing to rest your eyes upon me!" Or was it because of his very nakedness? . . . "Because of your very nakedness!" the look seemed to say. "That terrifying void that is within you and which opens to receive me; your hunger which calls to my hunger; your very baseness which did not exist until I gave it leave; and the great shame you feel. . . ."

When he had come before the king, when he stood in the great radiance of the king, still ravaged by the tongue of fire, but alive still, and living only through the touch of that fire, Clarence fell upon his knees, for it seemed to him that he was finally at the end of his seeking, and at the end of all seekings.

But presumably he had still not come quite near enough; probably he was still too timid, for the king opened his arms to him. And as he opened his arms his mantle fell away from him, and revealed his slender adolescent torso. On this torso, in the midnight of this slender body there appeared—at the centre, but not quite at the centre . . . a little to the right—there appeared a faint beating that was making the flesh tremble. It was this beating, this faintly-beating pulse which was calling! It was this fire that sent its tongue of flame into his limbs, and this radiance that blazed upon him. It was this love that enveloped him.

"Did you not know that I was waiting for you?" asked the king.

And Clarence placed his lips upon the faint and yet tremendous beating of that heart. Then the king slowly closed his arms around him, and his great mantle swept about him, and enveloped him forever.] (pp.251–253)

These final paragraphs of *Le regard du roi* constitute one of the most beautiful passages in all African literature. The reader coming upon this ending for the first time cannot help being deeply affected, deeply startled. The ending of Clarence's searching can only be salvation—death—yet in a totally positive way. After Clarence has acknowledged his baseness, Laye merges the elements of purification by fire, passion, and love— fusing Clarence into total oneness with Africa, a total unity with the mystical world of his environment. For the white man willing to cleanse himself of his past, Africa may somehow become the final fulfillment in life—grace. And the king, who represents all of Africa, everything that the continent consists of and symbolizes, is the total fulfillment of the African experience, the total embodiment of the dark world négritude. Salvation has been granted because Allah gives it only to those whom he chooses.

Camara Laye's *Le regard du roi* is the supreme achievement in African fiction. Like the syncretic world he writes of, Laye's novel is a totally harmonious unity of form and content, structure and idea, for the novel unifies the intellectualized concepts of the African experience in a form and structure which cannot be separated from one another. Outwardly, Laye works with the same ideas with which his Anglophone counterparts have been concerned: the differences between the African way of life and Western life, the inevitable clash which, initially, at least, results when the two come together. Yet, unlike his Anglophone counterparts, Laye not only reverses the usual story of the African's difficulty in coping with the Western experience—to that of the white man's inability to come to grips with the African experience—but he goes on far beyond that, indicating that it is possible for the fruits of the two cultures to go together, that things may fall apart, but it is possible—though never easy—for them also to begin to go back together again, that Africa and the West may sometime even reconcile their differences. In this sense, too, Laye's novel begins where many African novels end; there is chaos and misunderstanding at the beginning, but understanding and appreciation at the end, an indication that the Western world may gain something positive from the African continent. It is this hope, this hint of cultural unity that gives *Le regard du roi* a far greater scope, a much deeper penetration into the usual conflict we have seen presented in other African novels, for Camara Laye's canvas is not only larger than those most other African novelists have dared to paint, but more brilliantly hued in the nuances of acculturation, the mystical, and the beautiful.

It is this scope of the novel and its total unity that make it especially difficult to talk about the individual characteristics that we have examined in other African novels. Certainly one can say, for example, that Laye uses anthropological materials as do most of the rest of his fellow African writers. Yet, in

Le regard du roi these materials are never isolated bits and pieces, rarely ever even background; they are the very stuff on which the total African experience is dependent, and as such they are skillfully fused into the intellectual meaning of his story, its spiritual and mystical overtones. If time, space, and description are also utilized in such a fashion that makes their extraction from the narrative impossible, so too can they be seen only as part of the African experience. For example, we have already noted that Laye makes no significant references to time in his story—for time is in one sense the very substance out of which the story has been constructed—and only when Clarence has developed, through the passing of time, an attitude toward waiting for the king comparable to that of the African characters, does the significance of this basic difference become completely apparent.

Characterization in *Le regard du roi* is also something woven into the texture of the narrative. It is surprising how little we actually know of Clarence, and yet it is possible to think of the book as a one-character novel. We know almost nothing of Clarence's past life, before he came to Africa—there is only one instance where Laye makes a comment about this life—when Clarence visits Diallo the first time and is reminded of a blacksmith in his youth who made shoes for horses. Of course, this too is a subtle indication on Laye's part that no matter *what* the Western experience is, it is totally inadequate as a preparation for African life. Other characters, although vividly drawn, are also unified into the négritude theme of the novel (that is, made important only by their function in the story): Diallo, the blacksmith; Dioki, the witch-like priestess; the beggar and his ironic humility;—even the two boys and their persistent shenanigans reveal to Clarence things he has not comprehended about the African experience. The king, more than any of the other African characters, typifies the wholeness of the work. In contrast to Clarence, who represents all the temporal aspects of Western life (its concern with material things, the heaviness of earthly existence, and death), the king represents the mystical aspects of the animistic/Islamic background—spirit, continuity, weightlessness. In his fragility, too, he represents Allah's unattainability.

If Laye spells out his meaning a little too clearly at the end—and I do not believe that he actually does—this, too, as the reader thinks back over the entire novel, may be interpreted as part of a wider fabric textured with ideas of grace and salvation which are present almost from the very beginning of the narrative. There are any number of indications throughout the story that death can be the only fulfillment for Clarence, a final union with the king and Africa. The only major differences I see in Laye's *Le regard du roi* when it is placed next to Anglophone African fiction are an absence of direct transformation of oral literary materials into the text of the story, and a more limited sense of the situational aspect of African fiction. Nevertheless, it can be argued that Camara Laye's *Le regard du roi* is of all African novels that which fits best into the situational category, since Clarence, who is archetypal of Western man in particular, is symbolic of everyman and his difficulties in adjusting not only to a different culture, but to life itself.

$$\underset{\underline{}}{\wedge\!\wedge\!\wedge}$$

8

$$\overline{}\\ \vee\!\vee\!\vee$$

Lenrie Peters'
The Second Round:
West African Gothic

THE COMPLEXITY AND AESTHETIC TEMPER OF
Camara Laye's *Le regard du roi* have restricted its popularity
among African readers. An African student of mine argued
against the importance of the book because, as he said, it fails
to deal openly with a situation which can be comprehended by
the average African reader—it is too obscure, and it fails to
deal with a problem socially relevant to Africa today. He continued his argument by citing passages which he felt were not
faithful to African life, episodes which he said simply do not
depict the African way of life.* In further discussions he
agreed, however, that Laye's book is extremely well-written
and skillfully constructed. The problem, as he saw it, was

---

* The incident where the dancing girl leads Clarence to the beggar
and the two boys was mentioned as an example of this, with the African
informant arguing that the dancing girl would never sit drinking with a
group of men.

essentially one of relevance to the African way of life and relevance to the African reader.

Similar statements about other black writers' relevance to the black man's condition have found frequent articulation within the last few years, as black artists and black cultural groups have begun to gain the recognition their work has long deserved. In his introduction to Peter Abrahams' novel, *This Island, Now*, the Caribbean novelist, Austin C. Clarke has commented:

> Any work of fiction written these days by a black author is automatically inspected to see what the author's social commitment is to the problem, the people, or the country with which his work deals. There is a growing concern about the author's accountability to his people that is not strictly literary. This accountability is almost a prerequisite to any writing being done in this country by black authors, and it is certainly an essential dimension of the prevailing black consciousness in art, literature and politics.[1]

A similar belief is the thesis of a recent essay by the South African critic, Louis James, who begins his essay with the following statement: "In situations as explosive as that of Africa today there can be no creative literature that is not in some way political, in some way protest." [2]

The problem is apparently that there is a more heightened demand being placed on black artists that their work be a frontal attack on the race situation as it involves them—depending on their culture—that is, protest, and protest in a manner which may be appreciated by the masses. The implication is that any work by a black artist which ignores the problems of black people today is of no value to black people themselves; or, as it has also been expressed, any work which tries solely to be a work of art is of no use to black people. This kind of statement, although perhaps made more frequently in relation to black American writing, attests to the functional value of African literature we have already noted.

In relation to this, the most frequently articulated belief here is that art need not be universal at all, since, as these black artists and critics have expressed it, the concept of universality is Western, that is, a white concept, having no bearing on African art, or in this case, on African literature. And by implication, critics (usually European and American) who try to find universals in African literature are looking for the wrong thing. By these criteria, Camara Laye's *Le regard du roi*—which certainly deals with a universal situation in its treatment of the outsider experiencing a new culture—cannot be regarded as a significant piece of writing, at least in African terms.

Similar statements have been made about Lenrie Peters' novel, *The Second Round*. I remember a panel at the African Studies Convention in Los Angeles in 1968 where I commented that I had been particularly impressed with Peters' novel.[3] Dennis Duerden, of the Transcription Centre in London, an organization which has been responsible for recording many African writers for broadcast in Europe and Africa and therefore for encouraging African writing in general—dismissed Peters' novel and Peters himself as not meriting any serious consideration because, as he said, Peters has been away from his African homeland for a long time. If I understood Duerden correctly, exile negated any validity (or perhaps "accountability" to use Clarke's term) in Peters' work. I think, however, that this was not exactly what Duerden meant; he knows of too many African writers who have long been in exile and continued to write material directly concerned with the African situation. Rather, I think what bothered Duerden is the nature of Peters' novel—its universality, its very limited concern with Africa itself.

Why do we (those of us who are not Africans) read African fiction? I have already suggested in the first chapter that for certain critics, the prime reason for their appreciation of African novels appears to lie in the cultural materials they are able to identify in a given book, ethnographical materials recorded by a writer about his own culture. A poor reason for reading fiction—if that is the only concern. All too often, however, this has been the pattern. Frequently when I have asked my own students why they take courses in African literature, most of them admit it is so that they may learn something about Africa. Rarely do they answer that they want to learn something about African *literature* or just literature itself. (One reads Western literature to do that!)

How are we to judge an African writer's novel which attempts to be first, a work of art, and, only secondly something accountable or faithful to an African way of life? How are we to judge a novel by an African writer which makes no attempt to be functionally relevant to Africa today? Is a work by an African writer which does not relate something to us about life in Africa "un-African"? Should a work by an African novelist in which Africa plays only an incidental (or even an accidental) part be totally rejected? These are questions which I feel have often been ignored in regard to African literary criticism, and questions which bear directly upon the significance, and certainly the appreciation, of a novel such as Lenrie Peters' *The Second Round;* for, indeed, this novel is for the most part as "un-African" as it could possibly be—if such a term can exist. That it is set in Africa appears to be accidental, for except for a few comments at the beginning, Peters' story might just as easily take place in the southern part of the United States or, say, in the southern regions of France or Italy. If a few names of characters and places were changed one would indeed feel that this was an American novel or a French or Italian novel. In short, Peters' story is universal. Or am I deluding myself in considering the work universal? Maybe what I really mean is that *The Second Round* is to a great degree Western and therefore scarcely African at all.

Before we begin an analysis of *The Second Round,* it should be noted that Lenrie Peters is first and foremost a poet. He has published one volume of poetry and many of his poems have been anthologized in collections of African writing. His concern in many of these poems is directly with the contemporary African situation, and therefore his poetry has been treated more seriously than his prose. It is this fact that Peters is a poet that strikes one most forcibly when one reads his single novel, for at its best, Peters' prose is never far removed from poetry. *The Second Round* is, on all counts, a lyrical novel, and this, too, I suppose, is one of the things which may have bothered a number of its African readers. Like the lyrical novel in the West, *The Second Round* is concerned primarily with human emotions—the expression of these emotions in the attempt to depict personality.

There is very little story or plot to *The Second Round*. Rather, Peters is concerned with a number of human relationships, centering on young Dr. Kawa, who at the beginning of the story has just returned to Freetown, Sierra Leone, after some years of medical school and practice in England. Preceding the first chapter, there is a five-page poem, a poetic evocation of Freetown. The poem describes the city in such terms as: a place "where elements fuse," a city of "change," where "habits and attitudes ferment between extreme polarities"—certainly nothing radically different from what we have already seen in a half-dozen African novels; for, indeed, the basic situation is typically African (though not untypically Western).

The opening chapters of the book are concerned with Dr. Kawa's first few days and weeks back home in Africa. We see him arriving on a mail boat from England and the excitement of a number of women who have looked forward to his return. We are told, also, that Dr. Kawa has been away from Africa for many years; people began to wonder if he would ever return. Kawa's father is dead, but his mother holds a grand welcoming party for him, and Peters tells us that "Even before he had begun to lay his professional hand on the community, the rumour had spread that he was the best doctor Freetown had seen for many years." [4] For a short time, the concern of the novelist is with settling his main character in his work in Freetown: getting his house, and his car, for instance. There are occasional comments about contemporary Freetown seen from Peters' point of view, often however, avowedly universalized, such as the following:

> He became overwhelmingly convinced that the trouble with the society into which he was snuggling like a roosting hen, was its weightlessness. Not light enough to take wings and soar but at the same time not heavy enough to settle on a firm foundation. A people at the middle way; the turning point. Hovering like evil ghosts and restless enough to be confused. . . .
>
> Europe was frightened because she too was at the middle way and could not see round the corner. The whole world was frightened. Not so much of science or of nuclear bombs. The fear was deep inside the spirit of Man. If Mephistophelean science should win the wager, then his soul was gone—and there was only deluge, chaos, worse than chaos. So the blind had finally abandoned the blind—each for himself. The problem was not unique to Africa; it was only in a different shade of black. What was different was that Africa had a chance to stem it. Perhaps a last chance to banish the fear. (pp.16–17)

As the novel begins, it is July, and by October Peters has already changed the course of what looked as if it might be a novel concerned with the inadequacies within the civil service, the government, or even medicine in Africa. True, there are a few sections which are given a distinctly African touch: such as Kawa's mother's concern with his getting married, and his subsequent visit by four women who hope to arrange the marriage for him. But these are quickly passed aside, as are direct scenes depicting Kawa in his new position, as the story increasingly begins to concentrate on Kawa himself, and not on his practice. He is a solitary figure, given to nightly walks along the river and the ocean, a man alone, removed from the communal aspect of life which has played such an important

part in many West African novels. Then suddenly his isolation
ends.

Kawa's next door neighbor, who is referred to throughout
most of the novel as Mr. Marshall, visits Kawa and opens up
his heart to him. Marshall, who is half Lebanese and half
African, has been married for ten years. Some time ago he had
sent his wife to London for a "brushing up," as he refers to
it, because until the two of them met, she had never spoken
a word of English. Clara, the wife, who is twenty-four years
younger than Marshall, has been carrying on an open affair
with Freddie, Marshall's nephew, ever since her return from
London to Freetown. Marshall, who is Catholic and unable to
think of divorce, is still passionately in love with his wife, and
lives for the moment when Clara will end her affair with
Freddie. Two children were born prior to Clara's trip to England, but only the daughter, Sonia, lives with the parents, because Clara is not exactly the ideal mother. All of these facts
are related to Kawa during the initial encounter between him
and Marshall. The reader may feel that the incident is somewhat artificial, somewhat melodramatic, but as the story
develops, we realize that Marshall is madly groping for friendship, for someone, anyone, to whom he can expose his burden.
In a particularly moving section of this first meeting between
the two of them, Marshall describes the time Sonia found her
mother and Freddie in bed together. After that, he says of
Sonia: " 'she behaved as if she had got a lot older. Not the
same child at all. She was quiet and reserved: too much so for
a girl of her age. Tell me, Doc. This is something that really
worries me. Do children commit suicide?' " (p.59)

After this rather complete account of Marshall's marital
problems, the narrative abruptly shifts to Kawa's own love
affair. When Kawa spends a day at his old high school giving
a physical examination to the students for sports day, he meets
a young student named Jonah. The two of them strike up a

friendship. Several nights later when Kawa is walking alone at night, he hears the cries of a young girl in distress. Her name is Laura, and she has just been raped by two boys. Shortly thereafter, Kawa learns that she is Jonah's sister.

> So they came together. . . . Dr Kawa entered into a world of happiness which he had not known existed. Laura was in her first spring of love but the harshness of her rape still hung like black clouds on the horizon of a clear sky. She loved him but could not yet involve her body and he respected her reluctance. He tried to be unselfish in his love; hers, he knew, was tinged with hate. (p.85)

Peters' most lyrical passages are those where he describes Kawa's early relationship with Laura, and his passion for words makes these passages unlike the descriptions of heterosexual love we have seen in other novels by African writers.

> Feathered by the intoxicating freshness of salt air they would walk several miles along the sea front to the cape where they linked tongues and bruised noses at the foot of the old light-house. Then when the sun lowered her sail and the strain of the glittering ocean lifted from their eyes, they would follow the changing wind through ankle-deep sands and under tall coconut trees and open palms to a stretch of beach where they would watch a whole phalanx of crabs disappear in an instant in the wake of receding waves. With minutes to lose they would break through the reeds which fringed the Lake of Aberdeen, and would run down to the swaying jetty to catch the ferry, the diamond sparkle of Laura's laugh ringing in his ears. Cramped by the silence of the other passengers, Laura would sit on his knees as the ferryman wafted them across on the yesterbound vessel of his ballads. (p.86)

It is this evocation of lyrical passion which makes Peters' account unfaithful to the traditional expression of African love. This is simply not the way it is, the African reader will say. Men and women do not fall in love in this manner.

The relationship is short lived. Kawa receives an anonymous letter, goes to one of the sleazier sections of Freetown, and entering a house without knocking, discovers Laura half naked.

> In a state of exhaustion a young man sat in a chair admiring her breasts. . . .
> "Who told you?" she mouthed drunkenly.
> "I received an unsigned letter," he replied
> "I am sorry. I am going to have a baby," she blurted out.
> The young man looked on sheepishly and uncomprehendingly. (p.90)

It is the end of the relationship, which has always been platonic, and Kawa withdraws into himself, afraid to get involved again. But the incident is not quite over, for some time later, Jonah visits Kawa at his house, and, drunkenly, he confesses to the doctor, " 'I loved her. I loved her when we were children, and I still love her. She is the only woman I have ever loved; my sister . . . I love her as a man loves a woman' " (p.100).

To deception and rape has been added incest, yet the horrors have only begun. Kawa begins to play the part of the observer, watching people around him crumble to pieces. His own profession—where pain and death are daily occurrences—has made him a freak, lonely yet incapable of becoming emotionally involved—an observer treating all human beings with the objectivity of a doctor. (Peters himself is a trained medical doctor and his imagery and vocabulary often reflect this training.)

> He was gnawed with bitterness that the icy shield of protective aloofness, which he had cultivated during his lonely years in England when he had felt only a superficial friendliness tolerantly accorded him, had now stained his personality under the guise of good breeding. . . . He could do his duty; he was a good doctor—that was easy enough. But when it came to moral alliance he felt like a run-down dynamo. (p.117)

When he goes turtle hunting with Marshall, who, he realizes, is slowly being destroyed by his love for Clara, Kawa thinks of himself as having more feeling for a dying turtle than for the people around him:

> Dr Kawa felt the wounding thrust of eternal suffering from its soft eyes. He had never seen such sadness in black and white: not from the eyes of all the people he had seen dying had he seen engraved so bleak a vision of the grave; and his heart was momentarily arrested by the timelessness of the expression in them. He watched the toothless jaws open and shut at the end of a voiceless throat, yet there was no anger or reproach in the black tenements of the eyes. The unquenching fire of life still burned in them and forced the creature on with regardless dignity. (pp.124–125)

The turtle becomes one of Peters' most important motifs in his novel, a symbol of Kawa's own sluggishness, his inability to get involved, for all of his relationships are belated, beginning when it is already too late. The turtle-hunting episode itself is a brilliantly lyrical account of the violence which lies just below the surface of Kawa's and Marshall's lives. In the brutal slaughter of the pregnant turtle, all of Marshall's own thwarted desires to harm his wife are given temporary release, and the turtle is depicted in more human terms than either Marshall or Kawa: Marshall, the masochist, who lives by the suffering he enjoys inflicting upon himself; Kawa who lives vicariously on the emotions of those around him. Only Sori, the semi-literate guide who takes them on the hunt, is capable of nobility and sanity. Sori will plug up the holes in the turtle shell and later deliver it as a trophy to Kawa; Marshall collects the eyes.

When they return to Marshall's house, after the turtle hunt, Kawa meets Clara for the first time, although he and Marshall have now been friends for some months. Her eyes remind him of the sadness he had seen in the turtle's. Kawa is immediately attracted to her; and in the conversation which follows, Clara reveals to Kawa and her husband that Freddie is dying of cancer.

The denouement is quick. Freddie dies within the month, constantly attended by Clara—in Marshall's own home. When Freddie—the cause of his jealousy and introverted love—is destroyed, Marshall goes mad. Kawa finds him in his basement eating his collection of turtle eyes. He has been morally blind to everything but his own suffering. In a moment of weakness at Freddie's death, Clara hysterically falls into Kawa's arms, and the doctor believes he is in love with her. There is a melo-dramatic scene at the funeral where Clara jumps into Freddie's grave, and there is further violence in a scene when Kawa visits Marshall, who is now in an insane asylum. Peters seems determined to shock his reader by dealing with subjects hither-to not depicted in African fiction—often taboo in Western writing as well—a little as if he were writing a casebook based on his medical internship. Yet the grotesqueness of his story must make a further descent.

Kawa visits Sonia who has been placed in the keeping of some nuns in a convent: "Sonia was sitting in an arm-chair like an old woman" (p.179). (She is barely ten years old.) Sonia refuses to stay in the convent any longer, so Kawa decides to take her home to her mother. When they reach the Marshall household, the child runs upstairs to see her mother, and minutes later when Kawa gets upstairs, he notices a look of anguish on Clara's face:

"Don't lean on Mummy; Mummy's not well," he said trying to pull Sonia away, but Clara clung to her child desperately. He seized Sonia in a fit of panic and wrenched her away. The little raffia handbag was stained with blood. Uncomprehending he tried to lift the bag but it was anchored firmly, and inside it he felt the handle of a knife. (p.181)

The knife had been stolen from the convent.

It is almost the end of the story, but Peters has not quite had his say. There is Clara's funeral in the last chapter, fol-lowed by the two brief incidents which unify Peters' novel. In the first, Sori, the guide who had taken Marshall and Kawa

on the turtle hunt, visits Kawa to bring him the turtle shell
which he has preserved. Sori has elaborately decorated the shell
with leather and symbolic designs. Kawa asks him what the
figures represent, and in his broken English, Sori attempts to
explain each of the figures:

"Dis; woman insaid hegg." *Woman inside egg.*

"Hegg is wold." *The egg is the world.*

"Why is it blue?" Dr. Kawa asked. To this Sori shrugged his
shoulders and pointed to the sky.

"Dis man wit spear." *Man with a spear.*

"Why red?"

"Cause man is sun," Sori said expanding his broad shoulders.

"Dis; is corn 'cause good cams from groun." *Green corn
sheaves; goodness comes from the soil.*

Dr Kawa raised his head and weighed the sense and depth of
the words.

"And this child reaching for the fruit is love," Dr Kawa
suggested, feeling pleased with his interpretation. But an in-
quiring perplexity, as a child's, came into Sori's expression.

"Loff? What is?" Sori asked, a little ashamed of his ignor-
ance. But he added;

"Child is friendship—all people friends." (p.187)

It is a revealing passage—Sori's inability to comprehend the
meaning of the word *love*—the missing piece to the puzzle. It
is love which has destroyed all of the people around Kawa and
very nearly him too—a sick love, unfulfilled, frequently mis-
directed—a Western concept which the fisherman is unable to
intellectualize. For it is with these supposedly educated people
that love has wrought perversion and violence—not in the
fisherman for whom love is something of an entirely different
sort; and Kawa, like Clarence in *Le regard du roi*, is choked
with the sudden realization of the price he has had to pay for
his education. The conversation between Kawa and Sori is one
of the more memorable passages of the novel. Sori leaves Kawa,
saying as he goes, " 'I solly velly bad' " (p.188). Kawa realizes
that the fisherman is capable of more feeling than he; that this

uneducated fisherman feels more deeply than he has ever felt in his life.

In the last few pages of the novel, Peters returns to his image of the solitary walker. Kawa has begun his nocturnal wanderings again. He runs into an old friend and confesses his intention to seek a transfer in his work; a transfer to Bo, up country, far away from Freetown. Kawa tells him,

> "One has to be drastic to survive. Just as kindness never won anything except a smile, so one's sensibilities repay only anguish. I need to get away like a turtle when she has laid her eggs. Perhaps one of the troubles with human beings is that they don't migrate enough these days. They hold on to a little piece of earth, an idea, an emotion, and are ready to see the rest of the world go up in smoke to keep it."
>
> "But Bo is a long way. Away from your own people."
>
> "My own people are just any who accept me." (pp.192–193)

The second round is about to begin—life in Bo. Or is it the second round which has just ended—back in Africa?

Rape, incest, madness, matricide, and other violence—a bit much for one book, we might conclude. Yet, we have only to look at our own literature—William Faulkner, Flannery O'Connor, and other Southern regionalists of the twentieth century, for example—to notice that our own writing is replete with these themes. Peters has simply written the first African horror story, the first African Gothic novel, and it is only the fact that we have not found treatment of these subjects before in African literature that makes his novel seem so different. Moreover, his book is not as melodramatic or sensational as this analysis would seen to suggest. In the context in which they appear, the events are believable—my African students admit that. They *could* happen, though perhaps it is unlikely that they would occur so closely together.

What makes this novel so far removed from African tradition? It is the depiction of the events in Peters' story, the manner in which they are presented, which appear to upset the African reader rather than the nature of the occurrences themselves: so full a treatment of love in Western conventions; male/female relationships untypical of Africa where marriage is for procreation, where such matters are usually left unspoken of (though an African admitted to me that the upper class in Sierra Leone is indeed much more thoroughly Westernized than the populace in many African cities, especially the Creole population with which Peters appears to be completely familiar). Peters in his presentation of lyrical passion, his depiction of human emotions, is atypical, unlike any other African novelist—his use of the poetic to describe his characters' feelings and the episodes in his story makes him a writer standing alone. Frequently his dialogue sounds British instead of African—an influence it was probably impossible to eradicate completely, since Peters lived in England for such a long time. Because of this, there are aspects of the writing which must surely confuse the African reader. On one occasion, Peters describes Kawa's medical case with its instruments as "a black box lined with blue velvet . . . nicely packed like chocolates" (p.70). The semi-educated housekeeper in the Marshall household says on one occasion, " 'As God is me witness you could 'ave knocked me flat wit' a feader!' " (p.158). She seems to be speaking Cockney rather than Pidgin English. The constant references to Marshall as *Mr.* Marshall and Kawa as *Dr.* Kawa are also awkward, much too formal—British. Granted, this sort of thing may be confusing to the African reader, but they are minor, certainly understandable considering Peters' cosmopolitan education.

Must we reject a novel such as this for being unaccountable to the current African situation? Is Lenrie Peters really being unfaithful to Africa by writing a story which may not appeal to the average African reader? Because he fails to incorporate oral literary materials or anthropological background into his writing should Peters' novel be excluded from the category "African writing" and placed, instead, with say, British fiction? In failing to deal with the usual African themes is Peters rejecting his African heritage and adopting that of the West? I fail to see how the attitudes that prompted these questions can have any true bearing on the significance of Peters' *The Second Round.* Certainly the history of literature is full of examples of writers who have been misunderstood or ignored by their own countrymen, and later rediscovered after having been appreciated by peoples from totally different cultures; for the history of art is, in many ways, a history of man ahead of his time, outside of his time, away from his time. I am not saying that Peters' novel will eventually be appreciated by the African reader. Rather, I am saying that the history of creative artists and writers is a history of exceptional men, and I rather suspect that African writers will in the future show a much more detailed concern with the individual in African society, as African society itself changes, for better or for worse, from a concern with the communal to a concern with the individual.

Peters' novel is not so much ahead of its time as his main character is a prophetic indication of things to come: a man (much like Clarence in Laye's *Le regard du roi*) deeply alienated from life on all sides of him. In his depiction of the alienated African, Lenrie Peters has created a haunting story of one man's attempt to hide from the demands of the culture and the people around him, to ignore the basic foundations on which all society is based. It is a fine novel—and the fact that its appeal at the moment seems to be limited to a non-African audience certainly does not weaken its power. Art cannot survive if it must conform to cultural restrictions. Just as it was logical that many African novelists would make changes in the form of the genre itself, so it is logical that some African writers may reject these Africanizations in their own work. All art must be accountable, but there is no reason to expect that all art must be accountable to everyone.

The Novel of the Future:

Wole Soyinka and
Ayi Kwei Armah

ALTHOUGH IN TIME ELAPSED THE AFRICAN NOVEL
is barely twenty-five years old—save for a few isolated exceptions—it is already far beyond a youthful stage. The oldest
novel we have thus far considered (Peter Abrahams' *Mine Boy*,
1946) was written twenty-five years ago, yet Peter Abrahams
and other novelists such as Cyprian Ekwensi, Amos Tutuola,
Camara Laye, and Chinua Achebe, who began writing somewhat later, belong to what we may now regard as the first
generation of African novelists. They began their writing
careers during the African independence movement which
reached its culmination in the early 1960's when the majority
of these nations achieved self-determination. In almost all
cases (with the exception of Peter Abrahams whose South
African condition is a completely different matter) the initial
fame that these writers achieved led to their being given positions of some importance within the civil service at the time
of independence. Cyprian Ekwensi worked for a while for
the Nigerian Broadcasting Corporation. Until the outbreak

of the Nigerian Civil War, Chinua Achebe was Director of External Broadcasting in Nigeria. In the case of the Francophone writers, several of them held important diplomatic or governmental positions shortly after independence: Camara Laye, Mongo Beti, and Ferdinand Oyono. The objective of these appointments was, of course, to give the writer a certain amount of security which his writing alone was not able to assure him. In practice, the result may often have been rather harmful; art rarely succeeds under part-time conditions. We have already noted the vanishing Francophone African novelist.

Besides civil service positions, the first generation of African novelists often shared similar educational backgrounds. More often than not, their education was acquired within the educational framework of their own respective nations. This has been true, especially, for the great majority of Anglophone African writers. Occasionally there was additional education overseas, but this tended to be for rather brief periods of time. James Ngugi, for example, attended Makerere University College in Uganda and later spent some time at the University of Leeds. While at Makerere, however, he wrote his first two novels, and after returning to Africa he taught at the University of Nairobi. Because of the belated appearance of the East African novel, Ngugi does not strictly belong to the first generation of African writers, and in the future he will probably be identified more closely with the post-independence or second generation of African novelists.

The case is more sharply delineated with two other African novelists whose work clearly places them in the second generation: Wole Soyinka and Ayi Kwei Armah. Both spent rather prolonged periods of their early writing careers overseas. Soyinka's plays were first produced while he was studying drama at the Royal Court Theatre in London. Armah's two novels appeared in American editions before their publication in England—a most unusual precedent for a writer who grew up in the Commonwealth, reflecting also the belated awareness of Africa on the part of American publishing houses. These two writers, in contrast with the earlier novelists, also reflect more seriously upon post-independent problems within their specific countries, and it is perhaps this concern which at the moment most strongly marks the content, at least, of the work by the second generation of African novelists.

It may be said that there has been a certain reserve or hesitance on the part of the first generation African novelists to deal directly with post-independent political conditions within their own countries. There are exceptions to this, of course. Cyprian Ekwensi's novel, *Iska*, ends with a military coup; but the coup is secondary to the story Ekwensi is telling once again: an up-dating of the Jagua Nana fable. Achebe's *A Man of the People* also ends with a military coup, and as already noted, the novel is clearly a condemnation of certain aspects of post-independent Nigeria; but this work is indeed secondary to Achebe's earlier novels, not nearly as serious an analysis as the two novels by Ayi Kwei Armah. Much the same may be said about Camara Laye's third book, *Dramouss*, and Laye frequently tries to disguise his criticism by resorting to allegory.

What marks Soyinka and Armah so strongly is their unwillingness to fall back on the past as a solution for present-day social and political problems, and their interest, instead, in the current-day scene, the immediate. When Soyinka's drama, *A Dance of the Forests*, was presented at the Nigerian Independence celebrations in 1960, it, indeed, denigrated the glorious African past and warned Nigerians and all Africans that their energies henceforth should be spent trying to avoid repeating the mistakes that have already been made. *Kongi's Harvest* (Soyinka's last play prior to the Nigerian Civil War) was a scathing condemnation of the recklessness of post-independent African political leaders, and Soyinka's two years in prison during the Nigerian Civil War typify the renewed political concern of the African writer as critic of his own independent society. Much the same political involvement, with an outcome approaching disgust, may be seen in the works by Ayi Kwei Armah, who appears literally to have renounced independent Ghana and exiled himself in the West.

Bitterness, disgust, and a lack of hesitancy to criticize the status quo, strongly identify the works of the most recent African novelists: the second generation. But there is also a continual lament that it is the West that continues to dominate African society as the last vestiges of African tradition are being destroyed, and the societal patterns these writers present in their novels become further removed from the older traditions which were written about by many of the first generation African novelists. The communal element has literally fallen apart and, hence, in most cases the situational pattern is no longer as predominant as it was. As the protagonist of Armah's novel, *Fragments* (1970), states when questioned about the old traditional ties,

". . . the hero idea itself is something very old. It's the myth of the extraordinary man who brings about a complete turnabout in terrible circumstances. We have the old heroes who turned defeat into victory for the whole community. But these days the community has disappeared from the story. Instead, there is the family, and the hero comes and turns its poverty into sudden wealth. And the external enemy isn't the one at whose expense the hero gets his victory; he's supposed to get rich, mainly at the expense of the community." [1]

The family now acts contrarily to the traditional communal ideals. But Armah shows too that the family itself is breaking into pieces. What is left is the isolated individual caught in a society moving in no clearly defined direction.

In the novels by Wole Soyinka and Ayi Kwei Armah there is one further marked distinction: the isolated individual is often the would-be artist, and the works by these two novelists are concerned with the pressing problem of the place of the artist in the independent African nation, the status and future of the intellectual who wants to be an artist only and not an appendage to the government and a part-time creator. In both instances the picture is that of the frustrated artist/intellectual whose society has made a commitment not yet to art but rather to the more utilitarian needs facing the newly-emergent society.

The Interpreters, Wole Soyinka's only novel, which was published in 1965, is one of the most impressive pieces of African fiction published in the last few years, and at the same time one of the most obscure African novels. The obscurity, however, is not due to culturally restricted materials. At the time of its publication, there was no precedent in African writing for this kind of work at all, and the critics were confronted with something totally different from what they had seen before. *The Interpreters* has no plot in a conventional sense; there is no real beginning or ending to Soyinka's story. The movement of the narrative instead of being temporal is figural, through space, and the pattern within the novel itself is based on a montage-like repetition of images, piled up on top of one another, overlapping upon one another, suggesting the works of Robbe-Grillet but only in the most generalized way. There is no conflict in the traditional sense of the well-made story; little, if anything, has been resolved by the end of the novel, and one has the impression that the arrangement of the scenes within the book itself could have been considerably different than it is without noticeably altering the impact or the meaning of the work itself. The fact that Soyinka is a playwright and a poet is apparent throughout much of the novel. Instead of basing his narrative on the orderly progression of events leading toward a suggested goal, Soyinka has given his narrative form and pattern by the repetition of certain scenes and images which are used as leitmotifs and short playlets incorporated into the texture of the novel. Soyinka's dialogue is especially effective and shows the influence of his years of work as a playwright. Many of the scenes read as if they were originally conceived as short plays and later incorporated into the novel.

Satire and social commentary are present in almost every incident of *The Interpreters*, and it is these aspects which especially relate Soyinka's only novel with Armah's two works, though Soyinka is not yet as bitter as Armah, nor as he himself is later, in his play *Madmen and Specialists,* written after the Nigerian Civil War. The interpreters are all educated Nigerians in their late twenties: intellectuals, who, for the most part, have been educated overseas (and consequently referred to as "been-to's"), cosmopolites, equally at home in the West and in Africa, though the linear action of the novel takes place almost entirely in and around Lagos (the capital of Nigeria) and Ibadan (the site of Ibadan University), in an academic and intellectually-charged atmosphere. The most significant characters are Sagoe, a newspaper reporter; Sekoni, an engineer; Egbo, a civil servant in the Foreign Office; Bandele, a teacher at Ibadan University; Kola, an artist, who also teaches at the University; and Lasunwon, a lawyer, the least important of the group.

As the story begins, these six characters and Sagoe's girl friend, Dehinwa, are drinking in a club in Lagos, but almost immediately (after barely more than a page of text), there is a flashback relating an earlier incident with several of the same characters riding in a canoe on a river at the site where Egbo's parents had drowned a number of years before. Egbo's obsession with the destructive aspects of water will be apparent throughout much of the novel, taking on the associations of rejuvenation, fertility, and the life force, becoming the most important motif within the story, often used almost ritualistically. The scene then shifts back to the club where they are all drinking, waiting for the rain to stop so they may go to their respective homes. Other characters are referred to in passing without any indication as to their importance within the story, though the concentration for the moment is on Egbo as his thoughts slide back to his childhood with his aunt, after his parents' death. Toward the end of the chapter, there is another flashback, relating Sekoni's return to Nigeria, after studying overseas and becoming an engineer. Upset with the first job he is given by the government—a routine desk position—Sekoni is sent up country to Ijioha where he builds a power station, which later is abandoned even before it is put into service. Because of the corruption in which his superiors are involved, Sekoni in his disillusionment has given up engineering and become an artist, a sculptor, working with his friend Kola. As the second chapter begins, the rain has let up enough and they all leave the club.

The use of multiple flashbacks (often flashbacks within flashbacks) and the juxtaposition and overlapping of several different time levels is apparent in almost every chapter of Soyinka's novel, though at the beginning this is much more confusing because the reader does not have enough information to piece together many of the incidents. By the time the first part of the novel comes to an end (after the tenth chapter), the reader has a fairly good understanding of Soyinka's main characters, though the emphasis has been most frequently on Sagoe and Egbo.

At the beginning of the second chapter, as they all leave the club after hours of drinking, Dehinwa drives Sagoe in his automobile, first to the beach where Sagoe ponders on the death of his employer, Sir Derin; and then to Dehinwa's apartment where Sagoe spends the rest of the night in her bedroom alone because Dehinwa's mother has shown up unexpectedly from Ibadan. Chapters Three and Four are devoted to two lengthy flashbacks. The first of these takes place at an embassy reception and introduces the marital squabbles of

Ayo and Monica Faseyi. Faseyi, who is a surgeon at Ibadan Teaching Hospital, is upset because his English wife has not only failed to wear gloves for the occasion, but has further embarrassed him by drinking palm wine. Sagoe, Bandele, and Kola are present at the reception also, and there is a good bit of satire at the expense of Faseyi who during his years of schooling overseas has become thoroughly British.* The flashback in the next chapter reveals Egbo's initial sexual experience many years before with the notorious prostitute, Simi. Then in Chapter Five the novel advances to the morning after the initial drinking scene in the club. Sagoe is hung over in Dehinwa's bedroom. He has an argument with Dehinwa—her mother has now left—and after Dehinwa goes to work, Sagoe slowly goes through a sobering-up period which, with its relation of multiple memories and dreams, recalls his return to Nigeria and attaining a job as a journalist on the *Independent Viewpoint*. The presentation often borders on the surreal, especially in Sagoe's continual dreams of his conversations with Sir Derin.

As in Armah's two novels, there are pictures of bribery and corruption and initial disillusionment on the part of the returned been-to. As the chapters continue, for example, Sagoe learns that an article he has written exposing the corruption involved in the abandonment of Sekoni's power plant will not be published, because the details of the corruption can be used to prevent a counter-exposure being made of those who control the newspaper Sagoe works for. Everyone, it appears, has something on someone else, and the result is that the general public never learns the truth about anything. In the seventh chapter, Dehinwa returns from work; Sagoe thinks of his employer, Sir Derin, and of attending his funeral later in the afternoon. As he leaves Dehinwa to attend the

---

* Soyinka's treatment of the British-affected Faseyi is satirical, for humorous purposes. When the same kind of imitation white man appears in Armah's work, the treatment is deadly serious.

funeral, he encounters the cortege of a second funeral leading up to the same cemetery, and he notices that the driver
of the hearse is an albino. Two weeks later, Sagoe again encounters the albino, who rescues a young thief from a crowd
about to tear him apart.

The remaining two chapters in Part One take place in
Ibadan. Egbo has continued his relationship with Simi and
also seduced one of Bandele's students when they went on a
picnic, but he failed to learn the girl's name. The tenth chapter depicts another marital squabble between Ayo and Monica
Faseyi, this time at a faculty party in Ibadan. The time of
the party in relationship to the previous chapter is not completely clear, but apparently it is some time later, because references are made to a student at the university who is pregnant;
later she will be identified as the student of Bandele's whom
Egbo seduced. Thus, all of the incidents in Part One seem
somewhat arbitrarily related—resulting from no articulated
conflict but instead giving an overview of a group of young
artists and intellectuals in contemporary Nigeria. The fragmented nature of these scenes is similar to the loose structure of the first half of Achebe's *Things Fall Apart*, but here
the experimentation is with time and space and not with the
introduction of anthropological and oral literary materials.

At the beginning of the second part of *The Interpreters*,
two months later, Sekoni has a fatal automobile accident with
a lorry. The others are deeply affected in a number of ways,
and the connecting thread of the remaining portion of the
novel leads up to an exhibition of Sekoni's sculptures as a
memorial to him. A fortnight after Sekoni's funeral, his friends
meet again in a bar and as they are drinking Sagoe notices
the albino he has already seen twice before. The albino joins
them, and we learn that he is a kind of self-ordained prophet,
and he invites Sagoe and the others to his church the following Sunday. He tells them also that he died sometime before,
and as he was being buried, he woke up.

"I do not know what I was before I died, or where I came from but what really frightened the villagers is that before they put me in the coffin, I was like you, like all your friends, black. When I woke up, I have become like this." [2]

Most of the twelfth chapter is devoted to the following Sunday when Sagoe, Dehinwa, Egbo, Lasunwon, Kola, and Bandele attend the prophet's service. He calls himself Lazarus, and his "church" is a shack on a lagoon near Lagos. A part of the service is satirical in the manner of Soyinka's uproariously humorous play, *The Trials of Brother Jero*, which also is concerned with indigenous religion in post-independent Nigeria, but Soyinka's intention in this scene is essentially serious, questioning the very nature of African religions which are offshoots of Christianity, the very nature of ritual and religion in contemporary African life. In the course of the service, Lazarus' latest apostle is baptized and Sagoe notices that he is Barabbas, the thief the albino rescued from the wild crowd the day he was caught stealing. Kola thinks he can use the new apostle, now called Noah, in a painting he is working on called "The Pantheon." Sagoe thinks he can write an article about Lazarus for his newspaper. When Egbo asks Bandele what he has gotten out of the visit to the service, Bandele answers, " 'Knowledge of the new generation of interpreters' " (p.193). A double interpretation of Bandele's reply is possible; it is not completely certain if he regards his own friends as the only interpreters or Lazarus and Noah also as interpreters, though in truth all relate to the title of Soyinka's work. Shortly thereafter, when asked if he believes in Lazarus' return to life, Bandele replies:

"It didn't matter whether I did or not. But at least one thing was obvious, this man did go through some critical experience. If he has chosen to interpret it in a way that would bring some kind of meaning into people's lives, who are you to scoff at it, to rip it up in your dirty pages with cheap cynicism, or Kola to. . . ." (p.194)

In spite of the fact that they all went to the albino's church prepared to ridicule him, they have all come away with the opposite reaction. All are drawn to Lazarus because of Sekoni's recent death.

The thirteenth chapter is concerned with an encounter between Sagoe and Joe Golder, an Afro-American (one-fourth black) who is a lecturer in African history at Ibadan. Sagoe is not aware that Golder is homosexual until Golder tries to get him to spend the night in his apartment. The following chapter suggests a growing relationship between Monica Faseyi and Kola, and that Monica will probably get a divorce from her husband. Chapter Fifteen begins with Kola's working on his canvas of the pantheon, recalling what Egbo told him of the creative act: the "medium was of little importance . . . the act on canvas or on human material was the process of living, and brought him the intense fear of fulfillment" (p.237). In the somewhat obscure passage which follows, Egbo and Kola return to Lazarus' church to pick up Noah so that Kola can use him for his pantheon. When they are unable to locate the church in the marshland, they separate to search for it. The technique that Soyinka employs at this point is typical of much of the writing in *The Interpreters:*

Egbo-o-o-o-o-o Egbo-o-o-o-o-o Egbo-o-o-o-o-o.
The voice was so distant, leaping, a reed-fly of sound, from surface to surface of the water, hardly disturbing it with a ripple. It sounded so distant and remote, like his aunt calling from nearly the length of the beach against the sea of recurrent surfs which beat about his ears and deafened him. Egbo-o-o-o-o-o Egbo-o-o-o-o-o . . . for it was his first glimpse as a child, there was his excited rush to bathe his feet in sea water, succeeding against the frantic caution of his aunt who lay tired under the moon and shut her eyes for too long a brief moment. And he had thought it strange that she who took to air so freely should live in such terror of the sea. "Just stay near me and let the white fringe come and lick your feet. Wait right here and the

water will come to you." But he ran far far away from the sleeping figure . . . "Help, help! Egbo, come back, Egbo-o-o-o-o-o." But he meant to catch two full pulses of the sea and he wanted the water up to his knees, not merely on his toes. As the water retreated the aunt caught up and her blow catapulted him into the very danger from which she sought to protect him. (pp.241–242)

(Egbo hears Kola calling him, and the voice reminds him of his aunt's cry many years before.) The chapter ends with Lazarus' losing his hold on Noah, suggesting the transitory nature of the new religious groups.

Chapters Sixteen and Seventeen deal with the final preparations for Sekoni's exhibit. Kola frantically works to complete his pantheon which will also be displayed at the memorial exhibition. He uses Noah, Simi, and Lazarus as additional subjects for his painting. The night before the exhibit, Joe Golder takes Noah up to his apartment on the eighth floor of a high-rise building and the youth, frightened, jumps from the balcony and dies.

As the last chapter begins, all the characters are once again together—for the exhibition of Sekoni's work and a vocal concert given by Joe Golder which marks its opening. It is the intermission during Golder's concert, and they are standing around looking at the art exhibit. There is a good bit of idle chit-chat here between the various major and minor characters, but it is difficult to think of the occasion as in any way a climax to the story, since there has been no conflict in a traditional sense. It is probably a logical place to end the story, since the characters are all together again. But there is no actual reason why the story could not go on and on. True, a number of things do happen. Sagoe states that he is going to marry Dehinwa; and it appears that an understanding will come about between Kola and Monica Faseyi. Even with Egbo there is the implication that his youthful days with Simi are coming to an end and that he will take responsibility for the student he has made pregnant. None of these arrangements are suggested as certain, however, and I do not think that Soyinka actually believes that this is the end of his novel or of his characters. Rather, it is simply the last page, the last paragraph, an interval, as the last chapter itself has been.

> End of interval; and the bell recalled them, distant and shrill like a leper's peal. But they stood unbelieving. By Sekoni's Wrestler Simi waited, Kola poised near her in confusion. Egbo watched her while she walked towards him, eyes ocean-clams with her peculiar sadness . . . like a choice of a man drowning, he was saying . . . only like a choice of drowning. (p.273)

All of this has been nothing more than an intermission because Soyinka's interpreters will go back to hear the rest of Joe Golder's concert and when the concert is over they will continue living their lives exactly as they have before. Little has happened; nothing has really changed.

I have belabored the narrative thread of Soyinka's story and yet in many ways it is the least significant aspect of his novel—that is, for what happens or does not happen to his characters. Technically, the structure is something altogether different from that of any previous African novels, with much more experimentation (in a Western sense) than in Camara Laye's *Le regard du roi* or even James Ngugi's *A Grain of Wheat*. At times, this obscurity is more harmful than beneficial to the novel itself, and it becomes extremely difficult to grasp Soyinka's meaning. Time is obscured almost completely except for occasional references to specific blocks of time, usually between chapters. The flashbacks are often spatial instead of temporal, and the imagery has a tendency to cluster around one given character but overlap upon others. Soyinka's ubiquitous references to water are the most obvious examples of this, beginning with the initial flashback relating the drowning of Egbo's parents to the final paragraph just quoted where Egbo watches Simi walk toward Kola, associating her movement and their relationship not only with drowning but with the infinite number of choices and decisions a person must make in his life. As Egbo listens to Joe Golder's concert, for example, the following images rush through his mind:

The double spot bore a hole in the ground and Joe Golder stood with his feet in this circle of emptiness, Egbo thinking how they would take possession of the dyers' compound when the women were gone, standing on the rims of the enormous pots of the dyers, buried deep in black drenched sands. When the women were gone they would jump up and clutch the cross-bamboos and be suspended for a while. But at times the bamboo broke and a child fell into the dye-pot and a huge out-splash of dye flew out above the rims, and the child emerged shedding indigo tears, blackened to the eyeballs. The blackness swallowed Joe Golder now before his eyes, and Egbo heard the shriek of the child's terror once again and the blackened hands that flailed desperately for hands to touch his and lips to meet his and clean waters to lave him and the waters did. Indigo fountains rose and swirled his feet. Joe Golder seeking blackness ever, walked in the backyards of old women through criss-crosses of bamboos so low it seemed a place for hanging dwarfs, and he went crouched and humpbacked through crossing jet-stained bamboos chipped and knotted, hung on wooden crocks, and the dye-clothes dripped unwrung. There were black rains from dwarf skies, and clean quicksands beneath his feet were drenched in this one dye of his choice. Joe Golder pressed his foot anywhere and springs uprushed of dye and old women's long straddled piss, straddled across the rims of their own dye-pots, and black pap frothing through black bubbles from cornices from black lava deep in the bowels of seasoned pots deep in rim levels with the ground, oh I've played among them Egbo said where old women dye their shrouds, and grief is such women, old as the curse from snuff-lined throats. Joe Golder uprushing dye from quicksands stepped through the torn mouth of sunken cauldrons and wet shrouds swirling heavy in the wind, frothing indigo lather. They wrapped his feet and bore him round and round and down and down and the black bubbles were huge as Olokun's angered eyes bubbling, Egbo-lo, e-pulu-pulu, E-gbo-lo, e-pulu-pulu, E-gbo-lo . . . (p.268)

Spatially, Egbo's train of associations is triggered by Joe Golder's appearance before him, but Egbo's thoughts flow through a number of differing times. The enormousness of the women's dye pots reminds him of the breadth of the river where his parents drowned and the childhood cum adult fear of his own drowning which has been used as a leitmotif throughout the novel. Egbo recalls his own screaming at times when he has remembered his parents' death, as the black waters have threatened to gobble him up too. Joe Golder's search for his African heritage (blacker than his own one-fourth Negro blood) is connected to Egbo's own fears of drowning, and Golder's femininity is paired off with Egbo's masculinity. (Soyinka is making it quite clear what he feels about Afro-Americans coming to Africa to find their heritage.) And yet this passage is just one of literally dozens of others which relate to the water imagery of the novel: rain, rivers, the sea, drowning, Simi who is connected to the Mammy Watta myth and fertility, baptism, Lazarus' church in the lagoon, drinking, inebriation. As the water flows along, often controlling their lives by its rushing power and current, often nearly destroying them, so flows the contemporary society of the interpreters. The picture of Nigerian society is altogether that of a nation not yet certain of itself—waiting for the final wave to batter it apart.

The transitory nature of the foundations of Soyinka's Nigerian society are also stressed in the novel's repeated references to the place of art in an emergent society. Modern African societies have had to move so quickly to keep up with the times that their budgets and energies have been spent almost entirely on the utilitarian aspects of development: schools, roads, communication, electric power plants. Like his Ghanaian counterpart, Ayi Kwei Armah, Soyinka laments this tendency yet realizes at the same time the decisions which have led to such practices. All of Soyinka's interpreters are artists who have for the most part had their artistic intentions thwarted by public necessity. Only Sekoni is able to turn his energies completely to art, and then only after the failure of the power station and his co-workers have branded him insane. Kola, it is true, is an artist by choice and profession, since he paints what he wants and teaches at the university. Yet, of all of Soyinka's interpreters, Kola alone realizes that he is the lesser artist, and so he tells Monica the night he finishes his pantheon, which he has worked on for fifteen months:

> "You must know by now that I am not really an artist. I never set out to be one. But I understand the nature of art and so I make an excellent teacher of art. That is all. This canvas, for instance. Egbo started me on it, unwittingly of course, and in fact he should be labouring it out, not me. For one thing he is closer to the subject, really close you know, and he is sufficiently ruthless. But at least I can record, my intimations of all these presences have been too momentary and they come in disjointed fragments, that is why I have taken so long. . . ."
> (pp.247–248)

And he adds about Sagoe, " 'Even Sagoe has a sort of seventh sense, a kind of creative antenna with which he pursues his vocation' " (p.248).

Kola hints at the theme of Soyinka's novel: it is religion, ritual, the quest for the finer sensitivity which is missing from contemporary African society and above all the artistic side of it. Until these sensitivities are restored, until people have regained their faith in religion and art—bribery, corruption, religious quackery and pretense will reign. And the African intellectual will remain an interpreter instead of a creator.

What characteristics brand Wole Soyinka's *The Interpreters* as a distinctly African novel? No doubt this is a question which is asked by Africans more frequently than by non-Africans. The Western reader is already familiar with the kind of experimentation found in *The Interpreters*—in the Western novel of the twentieth century it is hard to miss this kind of thing. In answering the question, then, one is inclined to conclude that it is content only which will ultimately identify the African novel from any other novel—the inside point of view of an African culture as seen by an African himself, for it is slowly becoming obvious that it is in this direction that African fiction is moving as the second generation of writers becomes further and further removed from traditional African society, and as African oral literary materials are slowly forgotten. As we noticed with Lenrie Peters' *The Second Round*, we have already reached the point where an African writer may create a work which contains nothing that may be regarded as culturally exclusive. The time is approaching when the African novelist will be regarded as a writer first and as an African second.

Such is the way that Ghanaian Ayi Kwei Armah tends to regard himself: as a novelist only incidentally African. On occasion Armah has gone to rather great pains to make it clear that he is writing literature first, and that the Africanness of his writing is something of less great importance. With few exceptions, Armah's two novels—and especially the second one—would seem to support this theory, for there are very few "Africanisms" in his work, and his protagonists become alienated men—lonely, isolated individuals confronting a thoroughly dehumanized society in which everyone else seems insane, although it is usually Armah's insular protagonists who, because of their determination to dance to a different drummer, become the accused criminals or madmen. Being thus, Armah's novels fall into the mainstream of current Western tradition, and his protagonists are not very different from a whole line of Western literary anti-heroes: Julian Sorel, Huckleberry Finn, Stephen Dedalus, or Ralph Ellison's Invisible Man.

Like the unnamed protagonist in Ellison's work, Armah's protagonist in *The Beautyful Ones Are Not Yet Born* (1968) is also unnamed, simply referred to as "the man." In addition, like Ellison's Invisible Man, Armah's Man goes on a journey through hell, though unlike Ellison's protagonist, who only slowly comes to the realization that it is his society that is out of joint, Armah's Man knows all along that his society has lost its values and that he is the lone center of value in a society which has long since traded its soul to the devil. It is this awareness from the very beginning that makes the Man's voyage so excruciatingly painful.

The journey itself begins and ends with a bus ride; the Man is riding to work. The emphasis is not, however, on the Man but on the bus itself, the driver, the conductor, and the other passengers, because *The Beautyful Ones Are Not Yet Born* is not so much a novel about a person as it is a novel about a society: post-independent Ghana in the days prior to Nkrumah's fall. Thus it is possible here to think of the situational or communal theme returning to African fiction—with the protagonist now definitely *outside* of the situation or the community, that is, the hero as voyeur. The bus the Man is riding is falling apart; the matches that the drives uses to try to light his cigarette will not light (a subtle reference to indigenously produced goods which do not work like their imported counterparts); the money that the conductor handles is old, rotten, and rather odoriferous. Only after this rather detailed description of his environment does the emphasis shift to the Man himself: sleeping in the back of the bus, a stream of spittle running from his mouth. The Man's initial appearance in the story is slightly incongruous with the later rather pristine character he is presented as being.

As the Man leaves the bus, Armah begins his graphic description of the Man's hell: a modern wasteland transported to contemporary Africa. Refuse, waste, filth, debris, excrement become the overriding images of his novel. There is a brief explanation of the graft and corruption involved with the introduction of waste receptacles in the city, followed by a description of one of the containers under discussion:

> It took no time at all for them to get full. People still used them, and they overflowed with banana peels and mango seeds and thoroughly sucked-out oranges and the chaff of sugarcane and

most of all the thick brown wrapping from a hundred balls of *kenkey*. People did not have to go up to the boxes any more. From a distance they aimed their rubbish at the growing heap, and a good amount of juicy offal hit the face and sides of the box before finding a final resting place upon the heap. As yet the box was still visible above it all, though the writing upon it could no longer be read.[3]

The Man continues his walk to The Block where he works as a controller for the Ghanaian railroad system, constantly aware of the filth and decay around him: "The touch of the banister on the balls of his fingertips had something uncomfortably organic about it" (p.11). The life history of the banister is then given as Armah begins a quasi-scatological description of the Man's working environment:

> Apart from the wood itself there were, of course, people themselves, just so many hands and fingers bringing help to the wood in its course toward putrefaction. Left-hand fingers in their careless journey from a hasty anus sliding all the way up the banister as their owners made the return trip from the lavatory downstairs to the offices above. Right-hand fingers still dripping with the after-piss and the stale sweat from fat crotches. The callused palms of messengers after they had blown their clogged noses reaching for a convenient place to leave the well-rubbed moisture. Afternoon hands not entirely licked clean of palm soup and remnants of *kenkey*. The wood would always win. (pp.12–13)

The physical decay of his environment soon becomes linked to the moral decay of the society itself.

In the office itself, nothing seems to work. The communication system with the various stations frequently blanks out completely; it is a wonder that there are not more train accidents than there are. Even the pencil sharpener in the office is broken, and another controller states that he doubts if he will ever see the money he has just won in the state lottery. The day is unbearably hot—the only respite for the Man is a short break when he walks down to the harbor, breathing in the fresh air. When he returns, the other controllers have left, and a visitor tries to bribe the Man so he can get his lumber loaded on a train. But the Man refuses to accept the bribe, to play the national game, feeling as a consequence that *he* is the guilty one, the criminal:

> The man was left alone with thoughts of the easy slide and how everything said there was something miserable, something unspeakably dishonest about a man who refused to take and to give what everyone around was busy taking and giving: something unnatural, something very cruel, something that was criminal, for who but a criminal could ever be left with such a feeling of loneliness? (p.31)

Later at night, as he is going home, the Man encounters an old schoolmate, named Koomson, now a big man—a politician in an expensive car, his wife wearing a wig. The encounter itself is brief enough, but gnaws at the Man's conscience, and when he reaches home and mentions the meeting to his wife and the bribe he has refused, his wife calls him an "Onward Christian Soldier" and a chichidodo for refusing to accept the bribe: " '. . . the chichidodo is a bird. The chichidodo hates his excrement with all its soul. But the chichidodo only feeds on maggots, and you know the maggots grow best inside the lavatory' " (p.44).

After dinner, the Man leaves his family and goes to visit his only friend: identified simply as the Teacher. The style of Armah's novel suddenly shifts to that of the informal essay as the Man analyzes his depression, his inability to play the national game in spite of familial pressures. He explains his feelings to the Teacher:

> "I feel like a criminal. Often these days I find myself thinking of something sudden I could do to redeem myself in their eyes. Then I sit down and ask myself what I have done wrong, and there is really nothing."
>
> "You have not done what everybody is doing," said the naked man, "and in this world that is one of the crimes. You have always known that." (p.53)

But the comfort and understanding he has always found in the Teacher is no longer what it was; and the Man realizes that the Teacher too is slowly being destroyed by the society around him. The Teacher says he died long ago.

The style of the longest chapter in the book (Chapter Six) is rhetorical—the Man debating with himself the validity of his present actions. The tone is more that of an essay than of fiction or autobiography, as the Man—still at the Teacher's—reflects on the happier moments of his youth. The reminiscences are the most memorable part of Armah's novel, relating the childhood experiences of stealing the white man's mangoes, and, later, as an adolescent, of smoking *wee* (marijuana) with Kofi Billy and Sister Maanan, at a time prior to independence. But even these memories become tainted with violence and terror. The white man's dogs chase him as he steals the mangoes, Kofi Billy hangs himself, and Maanan goes mad, as the whole society begins to break away from its roots. "Even the women were becoming mean. In the market there was nothing they wanted to give, and they were careful about money in a way that brought the sickness home to all of us" (p.75). Materialism becomes the new religion, money the new god.

Materialism and Westernization danced arm in arm with the continuation of political corruption. Independence brought little change. Armah asks how long Africa will be cursed with her leaders. "We were ready for big and beautiful things, but what we had was our own black men hugging new paunches scrambling to ask the white man to welcome them onto our backs" (p.79). And the new African leaders simply became darker shadows of the white men:

There is something so terrible in watching a black man trying at all points to be the dark ghost of a European, and that was what we were seeing in those days. . . . How could they understand that even those who have not been anywhere know that the black man who has spent his life fleeing from himself into whiteness has no power if the white master gives him none? . . . We knew then, and we know now, that the only real power a black man can have will come from black people. We knew also that we were the people to whom these oily men were looking for their support. (p.80)

Independence, thus, brought little change at all: "There is no difference. . . . No difference at all between the white men and their apes, the lawyers and the merchants, and now the apes of the apes, our Party men" (p.88). Armah shifts his attack directly to the President of Ghana—Nkrumah:

Life has not changed. Only some people have been growing, becoming different, that is all. After a youth spent fighting the white man, why should not the president discover as he grows older that his real desire has been to be like the white governor himself, to live above all blackness in the big old slave castle? And the men around him, why not? What stops them sending their loved children to kindergartens in Europe? And if the little men around the big men can send their children to new international schools, why not? That is all anyone here ever struggles for: to be nearer the white man. All the shouting against the white man was not hate. It was love. Twisted, but love all the same. (p.91)

The rhetorical style increases to a near frenzy as the Man returns to his home, realizing that the Teacher, too, feels the same frustrations as he.

Work has become almost unbearable. Everywhere around him there is nothing but filth: going to work, the man slips on vomit; the description of the lavatory at work makes de Sade's concern with excrement read like the musings of a child just completing toilet training. Everywhere black people are trying to be white.

The office fills up as the day clerks enter, first the small boys and messengers, then the other clerks. About nine-thirty the Senior Service men come in each with his bit of leftover British craziness. This one has long white hose, that one colonial white white. Another has spent two months on what he still calls a study tour of Britain, and ever since has worn, in all the heat of Ghana, waistcoats and coats.   (p.108)

Walking by the sea is the only thing that gives the Man any respite, and he wonders why the ocean too is not much dirtier than it is.

The story suddenly shifts to a more prolonged encounter with Koomson. The Man's wife, Oyo, has agreed to sign the papers for a boat, since by law politicians cannot own property: the state is supposed to be socialistic, but the corruption by the politicians has made it thoroughly capitalistic. Sunday morning, when the Man takes his children to his mother-in-law's, he is again reminded of the family pressures which have worn away almost the last of his energy. The children, in their innocence, jabber about big, shiny cars, television sets, and other luxury goods that other families have. His mother-in-law constantly reminds him that he is not a good provider. And in the evening, as the final preparations are made for a visit from Koomson, the man watches his wife painfully straighten her hair:

> "That must be very painful," he said. Immediately, he was wishing he had not said it.
>
> Oyo put the comb back among the coals, then lifted up her head and said, "Of course it is painful. I'm just trying to straighten it out a bit now, to make it presentable."
>
> "What is wrong with it natural?"
>
> "It's only bush women who wear their hair natural."
>
> "I wish you were a bush woman, then," he said.   (p.128)

The conversation is reminiscent of a similar comment made in *The Autobiography of Malcolm X*, and the reader is made depressingly aware of the similarity between contemporary Ghanaian life, as presented in this novel, and the lives of black people in the United States. Both groups have been forced to bleach their identities into a lighter shade of the white man's world. Oyo's final comment on her hair is that if she had a wig, there would be no problem. " 'If you had a wig,' the man muttered, 'I'd be in jail' " (p.128).

Koomson and his wife, Estelle, arrive. Armah comments, "It was awful, was it not, that the rich should have this effect on the poor, making them always want to apologize for their poverty. . . ." (p.130). Estelle does not want to drink the local beer the Man offers her, and she says, " 'Really, the only good drinks are European drinks. These make you ill' " (p.130). And Koomson imbibes enough so that he needs to go to the toilet, but the toilet in the complex where the Man lives is so foul that once Koomson sees it, he changes his mind. The following weekend Oyo signs the papers for the boat, the Man refusing to touch them. There is, of course, no real change in their lives. Occasionally Koomson sends them some fresh fish, but the registration of the boat in Oyo's name has not brought the riches she and her mother expected. The Man realizes, "The net had been made in the special Ghanaian way that allowed the really big corrupt people to pass through it" (p.152).

The denouement, to what has been a relatively unstructured story, is sudden, but not unexpected, nor does it really alter anything. If anything, it only heightens the timelessness of Armah's tale, for this is a story which will be told again and again, now of this country, now of another one. At work, presumably some months later, the Man learns that there has been a coup, and when he gets home later that day, he finds Koomson there, fleeing the police and the military who have taken over the government. The Man knows, however, that there will not be very much of a change. "In the life of the nation itself, maybe nothing really new would happen . . . there would only be a change of embezzlers and a change of the hunters and the hunted" (p.160). Koomson is sitting in the darkened livingroom; Armah cannot resist repeating a motif central to his novel: "His mouth had the rich stench of rotten menstrual blood. The man held his breath until the new smell had gone down in the mixture with the liquid atmosphere of the Party man's farts filling the room" (p.161). Out in the hall, Oyo tells her husband, " 'I am glad you never became like him'" (p.163). It is the one real note of change in the story—the relationship between the Man and his wife. Then the sound of the police van is heard and the Man reailzes the only escape is through the latrine which leads into an alley behind the housing complex.

The descent through the latrine hole symbolically represents the lowermost echelons of hell. Ironically, this is the same filthy lavatory that nauseated Koomson the time he first visited the Man and his wife. And now he and the Man must climb through the latrine-man's hole, through the foul wetness itself. For a moment, it appears that Koomson is too fat to crawl through the hole at the back of the latrine, that Koomson's high living has got the best of him. After stripping him of his coat, however, the Man manages to push him through. His own escape is easy enough, and then as if they were passing through the colon of a gigantic monster, the two of them walk "along the latrine man's circuit through life" (p.168), heading toward the ocean and Koomson's boat registered in Oyo's name.

After more bribery, the two of them reach the boat; and then the Man—when it appears that Koomson's escape will be possible—jumps overboard and swims to the shore. Symbolically, the Man has been cleansed by the sea—he who needs purification less than all of the others, he who has been tainted only by his association with Koomson. It is a significant passage of the narrative and we are reminded that the Man has had the desire for cleansing and the subsequent longing for rebirth in each of his walks along the sea. And, indeed, when he awakens on the beach the next morning, it looks as though it will be more than a day of reckoning: "When he awoke he felt very cold in the back, though already the sun was up over the sea, its rays coming very clean and clear on the water; and the sky above all open and beautiful" (p.177). In the distance, the Man notices a lone figure slowly advancing, and what the reader may have thought would at least be a quasi-optimistic ending whips back again to a continuation of the status quo. The Man believes he recognizes the figure as Maanan, now quite mad:

> The woman laughed at the name, with a recognition so remote that in the same cold moment the man was certain he only deceived himself about it. Then she walked away toward the distant town, away from the sun with her shadow out in front of her coloring the sand, leaving the man wondering why but knowing already that he would find no answers, from her, from Teacher, or from anybody else. (p.178)

Walking home, the Man sees a police barricade in the distance, and playing the role that he has played all along—that of the witness, the voyeur, but not the participant—the Man watches a bus as it is stopped by a policeman for a road check:

> The driver understood. Without waiting to be asked for it, he took out his license folder from his shirt pocket, brought out a cedi note from the same place, and stuck it in the folder. Then, with his back turned to the people waiting in his bus, the driver gave his folder, together with the bribe in it, to the policeman.
>
> The policeman looked with long and pensive dignity at the license folder and at what was inside it. With his left hand he extracted the money, rolling it up dexterously into an easy little ball hidden in his palm, while with his right he made awkward calculating motions, as if he were involved in checking the honesty of the document he held. In a moment he walked with the driver to the bus, looked cursorily into it, then gave the all-clear. (pp.179–180)

On the back of the bus the Man notices the following inscription:

THE BEAUTYFUL ONES

ARE NOT YET BORN *

Nothing has happened; nothing has changed. The police are the same; bribery and corruption are still the national game.

---

* Lorries in Africa typically have a slogan painted on the back of them, sometimes with words misspelled or grammatical errors.

The Man knows too well that this is all that he can expect: "Oyo, the eyes of the children after six o'clock, the office and every day, and above all the never-ending knowledge that this aching emptiness would be all that the remainder of his own life could offer him" (p.180). And he walks slowly home.

The Beautyful Ones Are Not Yet Born is a richly evocative work and its publication placed Ayi Kwei Armah in the forefront of the new generation of African writers. In his depiction of a society on the brink of suicide, Armah has created a deeply disturbing picture of the foibles of all decadent political systems—a decadence which has nothing to do with age—of all late bourgeois worlds where morals and values have been lost and even the man of good intentions begins to doubt his sanity, begins to feel that he is the guilty one for not being corrupt. It is a novel which burns with passion and tension, with a fire so strongly kindled that in every word and every sentence one can almost hear and smell the sizzling of the author's own branded flesh. Reading it for the first time, one is almost led to believe that its young author might have burned himself out in the mere process of its creation, but seemingly Armah had not yet sunk to the lowest levels of hell—that near fatal drowning was reserved for his second novel, *Fragments* (1970), which because of its autobiographical nature, its nearness to certain events in Armah's own life, strikes the reader with an even harsher reality than the earlier work as it probes more deeply into the cranium of the artist/intellectual in contemporary African society, and into the near impossibility of being an artist in Africa today.

The structural complexity of *Fragments* is hinted at in the title and in the dedication: "for AMA ATA & ANA LIVIA." Ama Ata is the Ghanaian writer, Christina Ama Ata Aidoo, an old friend of Armah's. Anna Livia is a character in James Joyce's *Finnegans Wake*. The content or story will be African; the structure (made up of fragments or little pieces like a puzzle) will show an indebtedness to Joyce, though not nearly the amount of obscurity present in Soyinka's *The Interpreters*. Armah does, however, make use of shifting points of view in *Fragments* and of extensive passages of introspection bordering on stream of consciousness. His story here is hardly more plotted than that in his earlier novel though the conflict is much more personalized. Baako, a writer, returns to Ghana after five years overseas and a recent nervous breakdown. Pressured by family and societal conventions, he soon suffers from a second breakdown, more serious than the first because this time it is his own family and country that lead to the collapse.

There are two other important characters in *Fragments* besides Baako—his grandmother, Naana, and a young Puerto Rican psychiatrist, Juana, who becomes Baako's lover. They represent a kind of stability and tradition which is rapidly being destroyed—Naana, whose grasp on traditional culture has made her at one with the world; Juana, whose practicality is based on the spirit of Western individualism—for, if anything, Armah's picture of contemporary Ghana in *Fragments* is more appalling, more an exposé of corruption than that in *The Beautyful Ones Are Not Yet Born*. The novel begins with a chapter devoted to each of these women, the first entitled "Naana."

> Each thing that goes away returns and nothing in the end is lost. The great friend throws all things apart and brings all things together again. That is the way everything goes and turns round. That is how all living things come back after long absences, and in the whole great world all things are living things. All that goes returns. He will return. (p. 11)

This opening paragraph of *Fragments* injects us into the mind of Baako's blind grandmother. She is at peace with her world, like Diallo in *Le regard du roi*, and she knows that Baako will eventually return home. Her belief in the inevitability of Baako's return is in sharp contrast to the fears of her daughter, Baako's mother—Efua. In the jumbled time sequence of this chapter, we participate through Naana's blind eyes in a parting scene with Baako, the day he had left for overseas, five years ago. Because of the awareness born of her own isolation, Naana has had a premonition and a fear that her favorite grandchild too is suffering from loneliness and isolation resulting from more than physical displacement. She thinks, "Sometimes I know my blindness was sent to me to save me from the madness that would surely have come with seeing so much that was not to be understood" (p.23). The tradition she represents is that of a Ghana now almost completely lost, completely forgotten.

The second chapter, "Edin" * which means "What is your name?", shifts the point of view to that of the omniscient writer, and presents a rather oblique picture of Juana. Taking a break from work one afternoon, she drives toward the sea and encounters along the road a group of men killing a rabid dog. It is a pathetic incident, especially the depiction of the whimpering child who owns the dog, crying that the dog is his best friend in the world. The dog is beaten to a mangled pulp on the pavement, foreshadowing the way Baako's own family will treat him when he has another relapse. After the incident, Juana drives the rest of the way to the beach where she sees a prophet and his followers worshipping. (Unlike Soyinka's prophet, this one of Armah's has more thoroughly succumbed to the lures of capitalism: after the revival, he drives away in a Mercedes.) Juana gives a ride back to the city to one of the women who attended the revival—unknown to her this is Efua, Baako's mother. The latter explains to Juana that she will follow the prophet if she gets what she wants. " 'The prophet has promised me something, if only I have faith and follow him' " (p.57). It is here that we see the difference between Efua and Naana;

* Armah's chapter titles are apparently corruptions of Akan. He has said that he no longer remembers his African language.

Naana knows that Baako will return—it is inevitable; Efua has lost faith not only in Baako's return but also in faith itself. (Later, after Baako does return and she has gotten what she wants, she conveniently stops going to see the prophet.) The chapter ends with Juana and Efua introducing themselves to each other.

Chapter Three, "Akwaaba" ("welcome"), brings the prodigal son back to his homeland. As it begins, Baako is in an airport in Paris, waiting for his flight. The narrative shifts for a time to the flight to Accra, as the emphasis is placed on another passenger, named Brempong, an obnoxious Ghanaian whose only concern is in showing off the possessions he has acquired in Europe. As he tells Baako, " 'There are important things you can't get to buy at home. Every time I go out I arrange to buy all I need, suits and so on . . . I got two good cars on this trip' " (p.73). Later he tells Baako, " 'When a Ghanaian has had a chance to go abroad and is returning home, it's clear from any distance he's a been-to coming back' " (p.76). Baako, of course, has brought back nothing, except a guitar and his manuscripts. The gaudiness of the scene—approaching religious parody—is continued in the airport in Accra. A mob of people are waiting for Brempong, their new Christ, whom they refer to as their "white man," and they anoint him by pouring an expensive bottle of drink over his shoes and then giving him an expensive cloth to walk on. In contrast to Brempong, Baako is met by no one at the airport. He has not told his family of his arrival.

Baako spends the night in a hotel, and his surroundings cause a nauseous feeling to come over him. This feeling will return again and again as the pressures of conformity begin to strangle him. Baako's feelings of nausea resemble Roquentin's similar experiences in Jean-Paul Sartre's novel, *Nausea*, and the descriptions of certain objects resemble those of filth and disgust in some of the passages of *The Beautyful Ones Are Not Yet Born*. In the morning, Baako goes to a bank to see an old friend, and almost immediately he is bombarded with impressions of change. The girls at the bank now wear wigs; no one can understand why Baako has not brought a car back to Ghana with him. Even his mother, whom Baako later meets at the school where she works, asks him when his car will arrive so her bones may rest.

As the fourth chapter begins, "Awo" ("birth"), presumably it is some weeks later. Baako is living at home with his grandmother, his mother, and his sister, Araba, and her husband. At the beginning of this chapter, Baako, unemployed, rushes his pregnant sister to a hospital because her labor pains have begun. There is a brief delay when the nurse will not admit her to the new maternity ward—reserved for VIP's and Senior Officers only—so Araba has her child in the older ward. The narrative returns to Baako and his inability to get a job as a script writer for Ghanavision because he has not bribed the proper people. Aided by Ocran—one of his old teachers—he later manages to secure this position. In a brief discussion on the potentials of art in an emergent nation, Baako explains the importance of film for communicating with the illiterate masses. Ocran warns him that no one in Ghana takes art seriously: " 'What can you expect? The place is run by this so-called elite of pompous asses trained to do nothing. Nothing works' " (p.122).

The chapter ends with Baako's having another attack of nausea. Even Araba's child, born prematurely, is considered in terms of material gain. Efua suggests the child's "outdooring ceremony" be held the Sunday after the child's birth, that is, five days later, because it falls after pay day—the only time the guests will be generous with their money. Baako warns of the hasty venture—it may be detrimental to the child's health, but he and Kwesi, Araba's husband, have little say in the matter. Only blind Naana, of all the women, is against the outdooring, but no one pays any attention to her: " 'Five days. The child is not yet with us. He is in the keeping of the spirits still, and already they are dragging him out into this world for eyes in heads that have eaten flesh to gape at'" (p.143). She further tells Baako, "'. . . he must be protected. Or he will run screaming back, fleeing the horrors prepared for him up here'" (p.144).

Chapter Five, "Osagyefo" (the name given to Nkrumah, literally "leader"), and Chapter Six, "Geyfo" (seemingly a corruption of the previous word), bring Baako and Juana together. Baako initially meets Juana because he seeks her out professionally; he expresses his fears to her about his writing and the fact that he does not fit into the typical pattern of the been-to, grabbing for material comfort. Shortly after their initial meeting, in the most satiric scene of the novel, the two of them attend a "literary evening" at the Drama Studio. There is a good bit of humor here at the expense of Akosua Russell, the grande dame who runs the literary society (mostly for her own profit), for even here—in what should be the purity and comradeship of art—Baako learns that corruption is common and that very little creation takes place.* Later that night, Baako and Juana make love on the beach. Armah's descriptions of physical love are often as graphic as D. H. Lawrence's—most untypical of African writing.

The ensuing chapters are devoted to the growing love between Baako and Juana, and Baako's increasing disillusionment with his job at Ghanavision. Although he works hard on his scripts, they are not filmed. All film is used to exalt the country's important leaders. As the director tells him, "'A nation is built through glorifying its big shots'" (p.193). At work, and everywhere he goes, Baako runs into corruption.

---

* Several characters in *Fragments* are satiric portraits of well-known Ghanaian artists. Akosua Russell is Efua Sutherland; the "epic poem" she reads to the group, "The Coming of the Brilliant Light of the New Age to Amosema Junction Village," is a parody of Sutherland's "New Life at Kyerefaso." Armah's director of Ghanavision is based on another Ghanaian artist, George Awoonor-Williams, who now calls himself Kofi Awoonor.

Eventually, it is too much; he realizes that he is just another part of a gigantic system designed to make the big shots richer and the poor people poorer. In such a system, there is no place for the artist at all. After a final attempt to get one of his scripts filmed fails, Baako quits his job and burns his manuscripts. The specific script he had tried to have filmed was about slavery—human cargo. Baako realizes that a new kind of slavery is choking the nation—the slavery to material possessions, a concern with objects—symbolizing how wide the gap has become with the unseen world.

Although the temporal element is not completely clear, some time after quitting his job, as related in the ninth chapter, called "Dam" ("madness"), Baako has another temporary breakdown. Juana has gone back to Puerto Rico for her annual leave. It is clear by now, of course, that like the Man in Armah's earlier novel, Baako is an island of sanity in an ocean of madness, for he is the one who has failed to give in to the dominant system of life. In one of the most disturbing scenes in the novel, where Baako is ill with fever yet continuing to write in his notebooks, Armah brilliantly sums up the dilemma of the writer in contemporary Africa, growing up in a society which is still essentially analphabetic and has not yet been able to throw off its suspicions of the written word: when Baako's mother asks him what he is writing, he replies:

> "Something that occurred to me, a thought, that's all," he said.
> "For whom?"
> "Myself."
> "You wrote it to yourself," she said slowly, her voice musing. Thinking he had made himself plain enough he added nothing to help her. "But that is a little like having a conversation with no one, talking alone to yourself."
> "Well, if you want . . ." he said.
> "Baako," she asked, "is that the way it was before you came, when you were ill?"
> "Is that what?"
> "Did you write things to yourself?" (p.228)

As the fever continues, Baako's family turns against him and tries to place him in a mental institution. For a time he is successful in thwarting their plans, but eventually, because they take advantage of his exhaustion from the fever, his uncle Foli and three other men chase him through the streets, proclaiming to the bystanders that he is mad—rabid. " 'Stay far from him. His bite will make you also maaaaad!' " (p.245). As he is being tied up, he hears the crowd talking about him:

> "Some enemy he made has done him this."
> "It was himself, they say."
> "Books."
> "Ah, yes. Books."
> "Books."   (p.247)

Only Naana protests the family's treatment of Baako, but her words are ignored.

In the remaining four chapters—covering the period when Baako is in the insane asylum—the narrative is interrupted by flashbacks or shifts in the point of view. Chapter Ten, named after Baako's mother Efua, relates an incident where she had shown Baako an unfinished house she had begun building when he was overseas. It was her intention that Baako would return and complete it for her. Chapter Eleven, "Iwu" ("death"), flashes back to the outdooring ceremony for Araba's child. The child died three weeks later, presumably because of exposure. In Chapter Twelve, "Obra" ("life"), Juana returns to Ghana, and with the help of the artist, Ocran, she prepares for Baako's release from the asylum. And the last chapter, which completes the cycle, is again named after Baako's blind grandmother, Naana, and is related from her point of view.

> I have lived too long. The elders I knew and those who came traveling with me, they are all on the other side, and I myself am lost here, a stranger unable to find a home in a town of strangers so huge it has finished sending me helpless the long way back to all the ignorance of childhood.   (p.279)

Out of her faith in the unseen world there can be hope for Baako too:

My spirit is straining for another beginning in a place where
there will be new eyes and where the farewells that will remain
unsaid here will turn to a glad welcome and my ghost will find
the beginning that will be known here as my end.   (p.280)

Naana's thoughts suggest that for Baako, too, the only release
will be exile to a place where there will be new eyes, new
faces. The events in *Fragments* record those which precipitated
Ayi Kwei Armah's own mental relapse when he returned to
Ghana after studying abroad. As it is suggested in Naana's
poignant dialogue with herself, Baako/Armah later exiled himself from his native land, and has since continued his writing in
the United States and in Europe.

Ayi Kwei Armah is the most skilled prose stylist in Anglophone Africa today, a painter whose medium happens to be
prose. His novel, wrenched from his soul, belongs on the
honored shelf with a whole world tradition of autobiographical
novels such as André Gide's *Les faux monnayeurs*, James
Joyce's *Portrait of the Artist as a Young Man*, Thomas Wolfe's
Look Homeward, Angel. In his depiction of the stifled artist in
contemporary Africa, and specifically of the writer, Armah
has turned to a theme almost as old as Western fiction itself
but a theme entirely new in African literature. How odd this
is, we may think—those of us who are used to reading novels
about struggling writers and other artists. We forget, however,
that in spite of the fact that the canon of contemporary African
literature now includes several hundred volumes of creative
work, the printed word is still something relatively new in sub-
Saharan Africa, and the theme of the thwarted novelist has
been able to surface only now that a second generation of
writers have begun their careers and African nations are beginning to close the illiteracy gap.

The arts in contemporary Africa have received only the
most cursory attention, and the plight of the artist, as both
Wole Soyinka and Ayi Kwei Armah have shown us, can indeed

be a tragic thing. Misunderstood by family and friends, working in a medium which seems of little importance among national priorities, the writer must overcome almost insurmountable odds. Unlike the West, Africa has no grants or awards to give, no chairs at universities for writers in residence, no quarterlies, and few other publications which print serious work, and almost no publishing houses willing to print materials of a creative nature.* At this writing, there is still no African writer who lives solely on the income he derives from his work.** It is, however a startling fact that there has been as much creativity as there has been, that there are already half-a-dozen African novelists whose works deserve serious consideration and who have attained a level of distinction comparable to that of the most talented writers now living in the West—with whose writing it seems inevitable ensuing African fiction will be compared. How surprising, we might conclude, that with Wole Soyinka and Ayi Kwei Armah, the African novel as a literary genre now moves into the main stream of Western tradition, yet how even more surprising, we might think, that this did not happen long before now.

* The East African Publishing House in Nairobi, Kenya is an exception, though until very recently their publications have been somewhat infrequent.

** The time for this is rapidly approaching, with the most likely possibilities being Chinua Achebe, Cyprian Ekwensi, and Wole Soyinka.

10

Conclusion:

The Emergence of African Fiction

THERE WAS A TIME—AND A NOT VERY DISTANT time at that—when the literary image of Africa was created almost entirely by non-African writers. Some of these writers were fairly objective and sympathetic in their treatment of the African experience, others used Africa as a kind of backdrop where white characters were permitted to work out their neuroses in rather stock patterns—usually the white man either found a meaning for life in Africa or he regressed to what the author felt was a previous atavistic state. Still other non-African writers ruthlessly depicted Africa in primitive patterns which, if nothing else, symbolically reflected the colonial rape that the continent itself was physically undergoing. In a period of barely twenty-five years, however, the situation has entirely changed. It isn't so easy for the European or the American to write about Africa any more now that the African novelist has appeared on the scene. The novels by Kenyan writer, James Ngugi, which depict his country in the time of the Mau Mau rebellion, have set the record straight for us about that tragedy. We no longer have to believe such claptrap as Robert Ruark's *Something of Value*. A growing number of South

African short story writers and novelists have balanced the picture that they felt was one-sided in Alan Paton's *Cry, the Beloved Country*. And, if nothing more, the literary image of the white trader who goes insane in Africa has come to an end. As Paul Theroux has written,[1] and as Ayi Kwei Armah's second novel has shown, it is the African who goes mad now. The age of literary distortion of Africa has come to an end.

Except for isolated antecedents, the African novel is, as we have pointed out, barely twenty-five years old. But that is an age measured only by time, and as we have already noticed, Africa's time is often quite different from that of the West. A little like Camara Laye's king, the African novel is both very young and very old; maturity was forced upon it just as African societies themselves were undergoing the labor pains of old age within a few short years after they gained independence. What the Western novel became in a leisurely course of three hundred years, the African novel was forced to become in a mere generation and a half. And the novels which we once thought so typical of African fiction—*The Palm-Wine Drinkard, Things Fall Apart*, even *Mine Boy*—are now beginning to seem a part of the past. For the felt experience of African life has gone far beyond the pictures presented in these works to encompass entirely new perspectives in societies which in a few short years have moved from analphabetic to literate, from largely rural to increasingly urban, from communal to individual. And the fiction itself has mirrored these evolutions in its own patterns. Situational plots are being replaced by works which concentrate on character individuality. Description, and treatment of time and space are becoming more typically Western. Experimentation tends now toward Western techniques which replace the traditional conscious or subconscious incorporation of oral literary materials into the text. With some novels it is even difficult to tell whether or not the writer is an African.

The African writer himself has almost always been a microcosm of the accumulated experiences of his society. If we think of fiction as growing out of the collective experience of the society in which the writer lives—out of the reservoir of ideas and experiences of the total consciousness of the society itself—then the African writer has, indeed, been the historian of his continent's increasingly widened outlook on life, moving from a limited, virtually closed-off societal view of the village and the clan to an ever widening world view. We have already noted the five general subject areas of African fiction. Although these subjects did not necessarily appear in African fiction one after the other, the basic situations within the societies did occur in this sequence, as the works of at least one writer (Chinua Achebe) illustrate. That is, when his own experiences (and those of his society) were essentially limited to traditional African village life and the initial conflicts with Western religion and colonialism, the novel which resulted could only be one such as *Things Fall Apart*. After his society itself had undergone a more direct confrontation with Western education and urbanization, then only could Achebe write *No Longer at Ease*, illustrating, as it does, these conflicts with Westernization. Then, as Achebe's society sped past independence and was confronted with the increasing problems of political and economic stability, and these new problems become a part of the collective consciousness, a novel such as *A Man of the People* could appear. Achebe's own work at the moment does not illustrate the fifth subject of African fiction—the increasing concern with an individual life style—but other African writing does. We have already noticed, too, how it has essentially required a second generation of African writers before the theme or subject matter of the novel could become inner rather than outer directed. In sum, the broadening experiences of the African writer have constantly reflected the most contemporary problems confronting African societies.

Categorization is always a dangerous game. Experiences themselves defy this sort of thing—each writer is unique and so are his experiences. Where experiences are translated into fiction there are a thousand or a thousand thousand results. The categories and the generalizations in this study resulted because of necessity and practicality, and they admittedly have their shortcomings. For it is the tendency to defy being typed which most strongly marks African writing today—especially the African novel. While it is probably safe to say that some of the early examples of the influences of the oral tradition upon the novel form will slowly decrease in frequency as these materials themselves are forgotten, and that as a consequence the African novel will become increasingly experimental in a Western instead of an African way, at the same time it is impossible to predict what the future of African fiction will be. Already on the horizon appear novelists whose works bear little similarity to one another: Wole Soyinka, Ayi Kwei Armah, Ezekiel Mphahlele, Yambo Ouologuem, and Okot p'Bitek to name only five. Soyinka and Armah are at times similar in their attitudes, but in technical respects their novels are worlds apart. Ezekiel Mphahlele's *The Wanderers* and Yambo Ouologuem's *Le devoir de violence* are as different from one another and the novels of Soyinka and Armah as they could possibly be. Ugandan writer Okot p'Bitek has already written two books which his publishers refer to as "a new African form of English literature and language" and which some critics have called novels and others poems. And yet these are only five novelists from five different African countries, and as soon as we begin thinking in terms of numbers we notice that there are barely two hundred African novels (in European languages) which have been written since World War II. And we notice, also, that in some areas of Africa the novel is still virtually unknown, that there are not only ethnic groups that are not represented at all but entire nations from which a single novelist has yet to appear; and that for many other African countries the novel is still pretty much a one man show. This study itself has relied heavily on fiction from

Nigeria—simply because more fiction has come from Nigeria than from any other country in tropical Africa. Who knows what the scene will be once a similar amount of fiction appears from Kenya, Uganda, Tanzania, the Ivory Coast, Togo, and Gabon?

We are left to conclude that African fiction in the future will reflect only one tendency: diversity. With the multiplicity of African experiences and the pasts of roughly a thousand different ethnic groups south of the Sahara that are not always very similar, it would be literally impossible to expect that there could be only one direction for African fiction. This has certainly not been so in the past; there is no reason to expect that it will be so in the future. Life is not that simple. Clearly it is this ability to continually startle, to constantly remain fresh and alive which most typically identifies African fiction. In spite of the fact that the novel is not an indigenous African form, ever since its African beginnings it has been the most healthy and the most exciting literary genre. Already half-a-dozen African novelists have achieved worldwide esteem and recognition for their accomplishments. And yet, even in numbers, the African novel has only begun—it is still very young. The publishing industry in Africa is just beginning to get its footing; the African reading audience is still in a formative stage. As in the past, only one thing is certain: there will never be one typical form for African fiction. Ultimately, as with African life itself, there will be changing patterns.

Notes

1. Critical Approaches to African Fiction

1. For a more detailed account of Mofolo's work, see: Daniel P. Kunene, *The Works of Thomas Mofolo*. Occasional Paper No. 2. (African Studies Center, University of California, Los Angeles, 1967); and Janheinz Jahn, *Muntu* (New York: Grove Press, 1961), pp.196–199.

2. O. R. Dathorne, "The Beginnings of the West African Novel," *Nigeria Magazine*, No. 93 (June 1967), 168–170.

3. Amos Tutuola, *The Palm-Wine Drinkard* (New York: Grove Press, 1953), pp.7–8.

4. Dylan Thomas, "Blithe Spirits," *The Observer*, Sunday, July 6, 1952, p.7.

5. Anthony West, "Shadow and Substance," *The New Yorker*, XXIX (December 5, 1953), 207.

6. Ibid.

7. Lee Rogow, "African Primitive," *Saturday Review*, XXXVI (October 17, 1953), 30.

8. Ibid., p.44.

9. Rye Vervaet, "Adebisi's Odyssey," *New York Times Book Review*, November 2, 1958, p.41.

10. Ibid.

11. Harold R. Collins, *Amos Tutuola* (New York: Twayne Publishers, Inc., 1969), pp.43–44.

12. Ibid., p.44.

13. Gerald Moore, *Seven African Writers* (London: Oxford University Press, 1962), p.39.

14. Ibid., p.57.

15. West, p.207.

16. *Times Literary Supplement*, Friday, June 20, 1958, p.341.

17. Milton S. Byam, *Library Journal*, LXXXVI (June 1, 1961), 2118.

18. Keith Waterhouse, *New Statesman*, LX (September 17, 1960), 398.

19. Ronald Christ, "Among the Ibo," *New York Times Book Review*, December 12, 1967, p.22.

20. Hassolt Davis, "Jungle Strongman," *Saturday Review*, XXXXII (January 31, 1959), 18.

21. *Time*, LXXXVIII (August 19, 1966), 84.

22. Gerald Moore, "English Words, African Lives," *Présence Africaine*, No. 54 (1965), 94–95.

23. Ibid., p.95.

24. Taban lo Liyong, *Africa Report*, X (December 1965), 43.

25. Ibid.

26. *The Christian Century*, LXXVII (June 8, 1960), 697.

27. Moore, "English Words, African Lives," p.95.

28. John Hughes, *The Christian Science Monitor*, March 31, 1960, p.17.

29. Mbelle Sonne Dipoko, *Présence Africaine*, No. 30 (1966), 248.

30. Liyong, p.43.

31. Davis, p.18.

32. Milton S. Byam, *Library Journal*, LXXXIV (March 15, 1959), 860.

33. Jean-Paul Sartre, "Orphée noir," in Léopold Sédar Senghor, *Anthologie de la nouvelle poésie nègre et malgache de langue française* (Paris: Presses Universitaires de France, 1948), p.IX; Jean-Paul Sartre, *Black Orpheus*. Trans. S. W. Allen (Paris, no date), pp.7–8.

34. Ibid., Sartre, p.XV; and Allen, pp.17–18.

35. Ibid., Sartre, p.XXXIII; and Allen, p.47.

36. See Jahn's *Muntu* (New York: Grove Press, 1961) and *Neo-African Literature* (New York: Grove Press, 1969).

37. Chinua Achebe, "The Role of the Writer in a New Nation," *Nigeria Magazine*, No. 81 (June 1964), 160.

38. Chinua Achebe, "English and the African Writer," *Transition*, No. 18 (1965), 29.

39. Cyprian Ekwensi, "African Literature," *Nigeria Magazine*, No. 83 (December 1964), 294.

40. Cyprian Ekwensi, "Problems of Nigerian Writers," *Nigeria Magazine*, No. 78 (September 1963), 217.

41. Cyprian Ekwensi, "African Literature," p.299.

42. J. P. Clark, "Our Literary Critics," *Nigeria Magazine*, No. 74 (September 1962), 80.

43. Denis Williams, "The Mbari Publications," *Nigeria Magazine*, No. 75 (December 1962), 69.

44. Anaïs Nin, *The Novel of the Future* (New York: The Macmillan Co., 1968), pp.155–156.

2. *Chinua Achebe's* Things Fall Apart: *The Archetypal African Novel*

1. Chinua Achebe, "The Novelist as Teacher," *The New Statesman*, LXIX (January 29, 1965), 162.

2. Chinua Achebe, *Things Fall Apart* (Greenwich, Conn.: Fawcett Publications, Inc., 1969), p.7. Subsequent page references will appear in the text.

3. Taban lo Liyong, *Africa Report*, X (December 1965), 43.

4. Joyce Cary, *Mister Johnson* (New York: Harper and Row, 1969), p.1.

5. J. Carnochan and Belonwu Iwuchuku, *An Igbo Revision Course* (London: Oxford University Press, 1963), p.28.

6. Victor C. Uchendu, *The Igbo of Southwest Nigeria* (New York: Holt, Rinehart and Winston, 1965), p.103.

7. Eldred Jones, "A Comment on 'Things Fall Apart,'" in *African Literature and the Universities*, ed. Gerald Moore (Ibadan: Ibadan University Press, 1965), pp.91–95.

8. Chinua Achebe, "The Novelist as Teacher," p.162.

9. "Conversation with Chinua Achebe," *Africa Report*, IX (July 1964), 19.

10. Ibid.

3. Pamela *in Africa: Onitsha Market Literature*

1. Donatus I. Nwoga, "Onitsha Market Literature," *Transition* No. 19 (1965), 26–33. Subsequent page references will appear in the text.

2. Nancy J. Schmidt, "Nigeria: Fiction for the Average Man," *Africa Report*, X (August 1965), 40.

3. For a more detailed account of the Onitsha "Kennedy" pamphlets, see my article: "The Kennedy Myth in Nigeria," *The Colorado Quarterly*, XVI (Summer 1967), 39–45.

4. For further examples of the functional (read "didactic and educative") tendency of traditional African tales, see Ulli Beier, ed., *The Origin of Life and Death* (London: Heinemann Educational Books, 1966). All of the eighteen tales in this collection end with some variant of the "moral lesson."

5. Robert Scholes and Robert Kellog, *The Nature of Narrative* (New York: Oxford University Press, 1966), p.56.

6. Thomas Iguh, *The Sorrows of Love* (Onitsha: A. Onwudiwe & Sons, no date), p.iii. Subsequent page references will appear in the text.

7. J. U. Tagbo Nzeako, *Rose Darling in the Garden of Love* (Onitsha, no date), pp.28–29.

8. Speedy Eric, *Mabel the Sweet Honey* (Onitsha: A. Onwudiwe & Sons, no date), p.3. Subsequent page references will appear in the text.

9. Ulli Beier, "Public Opinion on Lovers," *Black Orpheus*, No. 14 (1964), 7.

10. Erich Auerbach, *Mimesis* (Princeton: Princeton University Press, 1953), pp.399–400. Subsequent page references will appear in the text.

11. Cyprian Ekwensi, *When Love Whispers* (Onitsha: Tabansi Press, no date), p.8. Subsequent page references will appear in the text.

12. Cyprian Ekwensi, *Jagua Nana* (Greenwich, Conn.: Fawcett Publications, Inc., 1969), p.14. Subsequent page references will appear in the text.

4. *Time, Space, and Description: The Tutuolan World*

1. See Janheinz Jahn, *A Bibliography of Neo-African Literature* (New York: Praeger, 1965), pp.62–63. Particularly telling are the French (*L'ivrogne dans la brousse*) and the Italian (*Il bevitore di vino di palma*) translations.

2. Harold Collins, *Amos Tutuola* (New York: Twayne Publishers, Inc., 1969).

3. Margaret Laurence, *Long Drums and Cannons* (London: Macmillan, 1968), p.147.

4. Maurice Nadeau, *The History of Surrealism* (New York: Collier Books, 1967), p.89.

5. Amos Tutuola, *The Palm-Wine Drinkard* (New York: Grove Press, 1953), p.9. Subsequent page references will appear in the text.

6. The "Complete Gentleman" story as noted above.

7. Again I refer to Harold Collins' book on Tutuola as the most refreshing study so far.

8. "Conversation with Amos Tutuola," *Africa Report*, IX (July 1964), 11.

5. *The "Situational" Novel: The Novels of James Ngugi*

1. John S. Mbiti, *African Religion and Philosophy* (London: Heinemann, 1969), p.108.

2. Mohamadou Kane, "The African Writer and His Public," *Présence Africaine*, No. 58 (1966), 28.

3. James Ngugi, *A Grain of Wheat* (London: Heinemann Educational Books, 1967), p.29. Subsequent page references will appear in the text.

4. Legson Kayira, *Jingala* (Essex: Longmans, Green & Co., Ltd., 1969), pp.50–51. Subsequent page references will appear in the text.

5. James Ngugi, *Weep Not, Child*, Intro. by Martin Tucker (New York: Collier Books, 1969), p.21. Subsequent page references will appear in the text.

6. James Ngugi, *The River Between* (London: Heinemann Educational Books, 1965), p.1. Subsequent page references will appear in the text.

7. An interview with James Ngugi in *Cultural Events in Africa*, No. 31 (June 1967), I.

6. *Characters and Modes of Characterization: Chinua Achebe, James Ngugi, and Peter Abrahams*

1. Chinua Achebe, *Arrow of God* (Garden City: Doubleday & Co., Inc., 1969), pp.160–161. Subsequent page references will appear in the text.

2. Chinua Achebe, *A Man of the People* (Garden City: Doubleday & Co., Inc., 1967), pp.42–43.

3. James Ngugi, *Weep Not, Child* (New York: Collier Books, 1969), p.21. Subsequent page references will appear in the text.

4. Dorrit Cohn, "Narrated Monologue: Definition of a Fictional Style," *Comparative Literature*, XVIII (1966), 97–112.

5. James Ngugi, *A Grain of Wheat* (London: Heinemann Educational Books, 1967), pp.141–142.

6. Ezekiel Mphahlele, *The African Image* (New York: Praeger, 1962), p.186.

7. Peter Abrahams, *Mine Boy* (New York: Collier Books, 1970), p.14. Subsequent page references will appear in the text.

7. *Assimilated Négritude: Camara Laye's* Le regard du roi

1. Léopold Sédar Senghor, "Comme les Lamantins vont boire à la source," in *Éthiopiques* (Paris: Éditions du Seuil, 1956), p.120; *Senghor: Prose and Poetry*, ed. & trans. John Reed and Clive Wake (London: Oxford University Press, 1965), pp.94–95.

2. Ellen Conroy Kennedy and Paulette J. Trout, "The Roots of Négritude," *Africa Report*, XI (May 1966), 61.

3. Mongo Beti, *Mission terminée* (Paris: Buchet/Chastel, 1957), pp.250–251; *Mission to Kala* (New York: Collier Books, 1971), p.213.

4. Camara Laye, *L'Enfant noir* (London: Cambridge University Press, 1966), p.75; *The African Child* (London: Fontana Books, 1959), p.63. Subsequent page references will appear in the text.

5. See my article, "Laye's Unfulfilled African Dream," *Books Abroad*, XXXIII (Spring 1969), 209–211.

6. Léopold Sédar Senghor, "Prière aux masques," in *Léopold Sédar Senghor*, ed. Armand Guibert (Paris: Editions Pierre Seghers, 1961), p.123.

7. Camara Laye, *Le regard du roi* (Paris: Librairie Plon, 1954), p.9; *The Radiance of the King* (New York: Collier Books, 1971), p.21. Subsequent page references will appear in the text.

8. William Fagg, *Nigerian Images* (New York: Praeger, 1963), p.33.

9. Janheinz Jahn, "Camara Laye: Another Interpretation," in *Introduction to African Literature*, ed. Ulli Beier (Evanston: Northwestern University Press, 1967), p.202.

10. Birago Diop, *Contes Choisis* (London: Cambridge University Press, 1967), p.102; Charles R. Larson, ed., *African Short Stories* (New York: Collier Books, 1970), p.62.

11. Ezekiel Mphahlele, *Down Second Avenue* (Berlin: Seven Seas, 1962), pp.218–219.

8. *Lenrie Peters'* The Second Round: *West African Gothic*

1. Austin C. Clarke, "Introduction," *This Island, Now*, by Peter Abrahams (New York: Collier Books, 1971), p.9.

2. Louis James, "The Protest Tradition," in *Protest and Conflict in African Literature*, ed. Cosmo Pieterse and Donald Munro (New York: Africana Publishing Corp., 1969), p. 109.

3. See my article, "Whither the African Novel?" *CLA Journal*, XIII (December 1969), 144–152.

4. Lenrie Peters, *The Second Round* (London: Heinemann Educational Books, 1966), p.11. Subsequent page references will appear in the text.

9. *The Novel of the Future: Wole Soyinka and Ayi Kwei Armah*

1. Ayi Kwei Armah, *Fragments* (New York: Collier Books, 1971), p.151. Subsequent page references will appear in the text.
2. Wole Soyinka, *The Interpreters* (New York: Collier Books, 1970), p.173. Subsequent page references will appear in the text.
3. Ayi Kwei Armah, *The Beautyful Ones Are Not Yet Born* (New York: Collier Books, 1969), p.8. Subsequent page references will appear in the text.

10. *Conclusions: The Emergence of African Fiction*

1. Paul Theroux, "Speaking of Books: My Travels with Joseph Conrad," *New York Times Book Review*, June 22, 1969, pp.2 and 26.

·٨·٨·٨·

Selected and Annotated Bibliography:
African Fiction

·٨·٨·٨·

THIS BIBLIOGRAPHY is in no way an attempt to be a complete listing of contemporary African fiction. Rather, I have listed those titles which I feel are the most important. For the sake of practicality, the most readily available edition has been listed below; and, in any case where that edition is a reprint, the date of the original publication has been included in parentheses following the title of the work. The emphasis is upon those works which are currently available in American or British editions—and, as a consequence, only those Francophone titles which have been translated into English are included.

Works of other than a novelistic nature (drama, poetry, autobiography, etc.) by the writers listed below have been omitted. (The reader should consult Janheinz Jahn, *A Bibliography of Neo-African Literature*, New York: Praeger, 1965; "A Supplementary Bibliography to J. Jahn's Bibliography of Neo-African Literature from Africa, America and the Caribbean," by Paul Paricsy, *Journal of the New African Literature and the Arts*, Fall 1967, pp.70–82; "Additions and Corrections to Janheinz Jahn's *Bibliography*," by Bernth Lindfors, *African Studies Bulletin*, September 1968 pp. 129–148.)

Most of the titles listed as Heinemann publications are available in the United States from the Humanities Press. Publications of the East African Publishing House are distributed in the United States by the Northwestern University Press. All of the Collier titles are part of the African/American Library, which includes works by black writers in the United States and the Caribbean. I have commented on those works of special interest and suggested a number of titles as suitable for public school use.

Abrahams, Peter (South Africa)
  Mine Boy (1946). New York: Collier Books, 1970. (Introduction
  by Charles R. Larson.)
  The story of a young mine worker in Johannesburg.
  Suitable for high schools. (See Chapter Six herein.)
  Wild Conquest (1950). Middlesex: Penguin Books (UK), 1967.
  A Wreath for Udomo (1956). New York: Collier Books, 1971.
  (Introduction by Stanlake Samkange.)
  One of the first African "political" novels and one of the best.
  The setting is West Africa, prior to independence.
  The Path of Thunder. New York: Harper & Brothers, 1958.
  A Night of Their Own. New York: Knopf, 1965.
  This Island Now (1966). New York: Collier Books, 1971. (Intro-
  duction by Austin C. Clarke.)
  Abrahams' first novel set outside of Africa—in the Caribbean.
  Again, with a political theme.
Abruquah, Joseph (Ghana)
  The Torrent. London: Longmans, 1968.
Achebe, Chinua (Nigeria)
  Things Fall Apart (1958). Greenwich, Conn.: Fawcett, 1969.
  The archetypal African novel, depicting a small village's initial
  exposure to the West, roughly between 1890 and 1900. In many
  ways the most significant piece of fiction by an Anglophone
  African writer. Suitable for high schools. (See Chapter Two
  herein.)
  No Longer at Ease (1960). Greenwich, Conn.: Fawcett, 1969.
  A sequel to *Things Fall Apart.*
  Arrow of God (1964). New York: Doubleday, 1969. (Introduc-
  tion by K. W. J. Post.)
  Achebe's most mature work to date. (See Chapter Six herein.)
  A Man of the People (1966). New York: Doubleday, 1967.
  (Introduction by K. W. J. Post.)
  Political satire—post-independent Africa. (See Chapter Six
  herein.)
Agunwa, Clement (Nigeria)
  More Than Once. London: Longmans, 1967.
Aidoo, Christina Ama Ata (Ghana)
  No Sweetness Here (1970). New York: Doubleday, 1971. (Short
  stories.)
Akpan. N. U. (Nigeria)
  The Wooden Gong. London: Longmans, 1965.
  A novella, written for the African primary school market.
Aluko, Timothy (Nigeria)
  One Man, One Wife (1959). London: Heinemann, 1967.
  One Man, One Matchet. London: Heinemann, 1964.

Political satire—a most readable novel, with a humorous intent.
Kinsman and Foreman. London: Heinemann, 1966.
Chief the Honourable Minister. London: Heinemann, 1970.
Amadi, Elechi (Nigeria)
The Concubine. London: Heinemann, 1966.
A rather over-drawn portrait of a Nigerian woman and her world.
The Great Ponds. London: Heinemann, 1969.
The story of a land dispute between two villages.
Armah, Ayi Kwei (Ghana)
The Beautyful Ones Are Not Yet Born (1968). New York: Collier Books, 1969. (Introduction by Christina Ama Ata Aidoo.)
Armah is one of the finest African prose stylists writing today. A ghastly story of corruption in post-independent Africa. (See Chapter Nine herein.)
Fragments (1970). New York: Collier Books, 1971.
A powerful account of a young Ghanaian artist's mental breakdown upon his return to Africa after studying overseas. (See Chapter Nine herein.)
Asalache, Khadambi (Kenya)
A Calabash of Life. London: Longmans, 1967.
Love and war in a small Kenyan village before the coming of the white man. Suitable for high schools.
Asare, Bediako (Ghana)
Rebel. London: Heinemann, 1969.
Awoonor, Kofi (Ghana)
This Earth, My Brother. . . , New York: Doubleday, 1971.
A lyrical novel by Ghana's most famous poet.
Balewa, Alhaji Sir Abubaker Tafawa (Nigeria)
Shaihu Umar. London: Longmans, 1967.
A traditional tale of Hausa life, translated from the Hausa. The book is frequently used in African primary schools.
Beti, Mongo (Cameroon)
Mission to Kala (*Mission terminée*, 1957). New York: Collier Books, 1971. (Introduction by Bernth Lindfors.)
Beti's forte is satire and a reversal of the usual. In this novel, young Jean-Paul Medza, having failed his *baccalauréat* exams, visits an up-country village and becomes re-educated into African life. The book is a perfect little gem.
King Lazarus (*Le roi miraculé*, 1958). New York: Collier Books, 1971. (Introduction by O. R. Dathorne.)
More satire—this time at the expense of Christianity—as an old chief becomes converted on his death bed.
Conton, William (Sierra Leone)
The African. London: Heinemann, 1960.

A rather mixed affair. When the hero is in England, getting his education, Conton's story is believable and alive. When he returns to Africa, the novel falls apart.

Dipoko, Mbella S. (Cameroon)

A Few Nights and Days. London: Longmans, 1966.
The story of a young African, studying in Paris. Sex, fun and games.

Because of Women. London: Heinemann, 1969.

Djioleto, Ama (Ghana)

The Strange Man. London: Heinemann, 1967.

Duodu, Cameron (Ghana)

The Gab Boys (1967). London: Fontana, 1970.
What can you say about a school certificate graduate who has no job?

Dzovo, E. V. K. (Ghana)

Salami and Musa. London: Longmans, 1967.
A story written for the African public school market.

Egbuna, Obi B. (Nigeria)

Wind Versus Polygamy. London: Faber and Faber, 1965.
Daughters of the Sun and Other Stories. London: Oxford, 1970.

Ekwensi, Cyprian O. (Nigeria)

People of the City (1954). Greenwich, Conn.: Fawcett, 1969.
One of the first novels of African urban life.

Jagua Nana (1961). Greenwich, Conn.: Fawcett, 1969.
Ekwensi's paean of an aging African sex queen. What more can be said? See Chapter Three herein.

Burning Grass. London: Heinemann, 1962.
The Fulani and their traditions; plus Ekwensi's typical concern with an African beauty.

Beautiful Feathers. London: Hutchinson, 1963.

Lokotown and Other Stories. London: Heinemann, 1966.

Iska. London: Hutchinson, 1967.
Post-independent Nigeria. The fast pace of life in Lagos. Plus a coup thrown in for good measure.

Fagunwa, D. O. (Nigeria)

The Forest of a Thousand Deamons. London: Nelson, 1968. (Translated by Wole Soyinka.)
Fagunwa's traditional Yoruba "novels" have influenced the work of Amos Tutuola.

Farah, Nuruddin (Somali Republic)

From a Crooked Rib. London: Heinemann, 1970.
Women's Lib in the Somali Republic.

Head, Bessie (South Africa)

When Rain Clouds Gather (1968). New York: Bantam Books, 1970.

Maru. New York: McCall Publishing Co., 1971.

Honwana, Louis Bernardo (Mozambique)
  We Killed Mangy-Dog and Other Stories. London: Heinemann, 1969.
  Translated from the Portuguese. Fascinating stories.
Ike, Chukwuemeka (Nigeria)
  Toads for Supper (1965). London: Fontana, 1965.
  University life. Lucky Jim in Eastern Nigeria.
Kachingwe, Aubrey (Malawi)
  No Easy Task. London: Heinemann, 1966.
Kane, Cheikh Hamidou (Sénégal)
  Ambiguous Adventure (*L'aventure ambiguë*, 1961). New York: Collier Books, 1969. (Introduction by Wilfred Cartey.)
  The disturbing account of a young student's growing disillusionment and confusion with his Islamic background because of his exposure to Western education in Africa and Paris. A brilliant novel, complex and philosophical.
Kayira, Legson (Malawi)
  The Looming Shadow (1967). New York: Collier Books, 1970. (Introduction by Harold Collins.)
  Dying traditions in an African village—witchcraft and murder. A fine novel for introducing traditional African life to high school students.
  Jingala. New York: Doubleday, 1969.
  The generation gap in Africa.
Kibera, Leonard and Samuel Kahiga (Kenya)
  Potent Ash. Nairobi: East African Publishing House, 1968. (Short stories.)
Kimenye, Barbara (Uganda)
  Kalasanda. London: Oxford, 1965. (Short stories.)
  Kalasanda Revisited. London: Oxford, 1966. (Short stories.)
  Enjoyable reading. For the most part, short, terse pictures of African village life.
Konadu, S. A. (Ghana)
  A Wonman in Her Prime. London: Heinemann, 1967.
  A lengthy portrait of an African woman.
LaGuma, Alex (South Africa)
  And a Threefold Cord. East Berlin: Seven Seas, 1964.
  Apartheid in South Africa. Fine writing.
  A Walk in the Night and Other Stories. London: Heinemann, 1967.
  LaGuma's stories are hard and tense—realism approaching naturalism.
  The Stone Country. East Berlin: Seven Seas, 1967.
  South African prison life.
Laye, Camara (Guinea)

The African Child (*L'enfant noir,* 1953). London: Fontana, 1959.
I have included Laye's first work here because some critics have called it a novel, instead of an autobiography. In any case, *The African Child* is one of the finest pieces of writing to come from Africa in the last twenty years. The Fontana paperbacked edition should be read if one has a choice. There is also an American edition called *The Dark Child,* published by Farrar, Straus and Giroux (Second Printing, 1969), but the translation is awful. The Fontana translation is by James Kirkup, who has beautifully translated all of Laye's books. *The African Child* is an excellent book for junior and high school students. (See Chapter Seven herein.)

The Radiance of the King (*Le regard du roi,* 1954). New York: Collier Books, 1971. (Introduction by Albert S. Gérard.)
The great African novel. The story of a white man confronting his destiny in tropical Africa. (See Chapter Seven herein.)

A Dream of Africa (*Dramouss,* 1966.) New York: Collier Books, 1971. (Introduction by Emile Snyder.)
A sequel to Laye's first work—set in post-independent Guinea. Because of the political overtones in the book, Laye had to go into exile in Sénégal.

Liyong, Taban lo (Uganda)
Fixions and Other Stories. London: Heinemann, 1969.
Brilliant short stories.

Mofolo, Thomas (Basutoland)
Chaka (1931). London: Oxford, 1967.
A chronicle of the South African warrior tyrant, Chaka. Translated from the original Sesuto.

Mphahlele, Ezekiel (South Africa)
In Corner B. Nairobi: East African Publishing House, 1967.
Fine short stories by the Dean of African Letters.

The Wanderers (1971). New York: Collier Books, 1972.
The first African novel with a Pan-African plot—South African exiles trying to make it in West and East Africa. One of the most important pieces of South African fiction.

Munonye, John (Nigeria)
The Only Son. London: Heinemann, 1966.
A young man's conflict with Western education and religion.

Ngugi, James (Kenya)
Weep Not, Child (1964). New York: Collier Books, 1969. (Introduction by Martin Tucker.)
Education in conflict with family ties and the rise of Mau Mau in Kenya, as seen through the eyes of a young school boy. An impressive piece of African writing—excellent for secondary schools. (See Chapters Five and Six herein.)

The River Between. London: Heinemann, 1965.
Traditional African village life in conflict with Western religion and education. (See Chapters Five and Six herein.)
A Grain of Wheat. London: Heinemann, 1967.
Ngugi's most impressive work—six villagers trying to come to grips with the Mau Mau rebellion. (See Chapters Five and Six herein.)

Nicol, Abioseh (Sierra Leone)
The Truly Married Woman and Other Stories. London: Oxford, 1965.
A fine collection of short stories by Africa's most skilled short-story writer. Suitable for high schools.

Nwapa, Flora (Nigeria)
Efuru. London: Heinemann, 1966.
A rather lengthy picture of an African woman and her problems.
Idu. London: Heinemann, 1970.

Nwanko, Nkem (Nigeria)
Danda (1964). London: Heinemann, 1970.
A delightful picaresque tale. One of the most memorable African characters.

Nzekwu, Onuora (Nigeria)
Wand of Noble Wood (1961). New York: New American Library, 1963.
A novel long on anthropology and short on plot and character.
Blade Among the Boys. London: Hutchinson, 1962.
Highlife for Lizards. London: Hutchinson. 1965.

Oculi, Okello (Uganda)
Prostitute. Nairobi: East African Publishing House, 1968.
The title is more titillating than the novel.

Ogot, Grace (Kenya)
The Promised Land. Nairobi: East African Publishing House, 1966.
The story of an unsuccessful migration.
Land without Thunder. Nairobi: East African Publishing House, 1968. (Short stories.)

Okara, Gabriel (Nigeria)
The Voice (1964). London: Heinemann, 1970.

Okpenwho, Isidore (Nigeria)
The Victims. London: Longman, 1970.

Ouologuem, Yambo (Mali)
Bound to Violence (*Le devoir de violence*, 1968). New York: Harcourt Brace Jovanovich, 1971.
A violent historical novel which begins in 1202 and ends in 1947. Absolutely brilliant in its philosophical overtones.

Ousmane, Sembene (Senegal)
  God's Bits of Wood (*Les bouts de bois de Dieu*, 1960). New
  York: Doubleday, 1970. (Introduction by A. Adu Boahen.)
  The story of the Dakar-Niger railroad workers' strike of
  1947–1948. An excellent novel by one of Francophone Africa's
  most successful writers. His only novel translated into English.
Oyono, Ferdinand (Cameroon)
  Boy! (*Une vie de boy*, 1956). New York: Collier Books, 1970.
  (Introduction by Edris Makward.)
  The downfall of a naive African houseboy, caught in the trap
  of white colonialism. Humorous on the surface, bitter under-
  neath. Excellent reading.
  The Old Man and the Medal (*Le vieux négre et la medaille*,
  1956). New York: Collier Books, 1971. (Introduction by John
  Pepper Clark.)
  Again, a picture of the African as a victim of colonialism.
Palangyo, Peter (Tanzania)
  Dying in the Sun. London: Heinemann, 1968.
Peters, Lenrie (Gambia)
  The Second Round. London: Heinemann, 1965.
  A beautiful novel; see Chapter Eight herein.
Rive, Richard (South Africa)
  African Songs. East Berlin: Seven Seas, 1963. (Short stories.)
  Emergency (1964). New York: Collier Books, 1970. (Introduc-
  tion by Ezekiel Mphahlele.)
  A story based upon the South African Sharpesville Massacre
  of 1960.
Rubadira, David (Malawi)
  No Bride Price. Nairobi: East African Publishing House, 1967.
Ruhumbika, Gabriel (Tanzania)
  Village in Uhuru. London: Longmans, 1969.
Salih, Tayeb (Sudan)
  The Wedding of Zein. London: Heinemann, 1968. (Two short
  stories and a novella.) Translated from the Arabic.
  Season of Migration to the North. London: Heinemann, 1969.
  Translated from the Arabic.
Samkange, Stanlake (Rhodesia)
  On Trial for My Country. London: Heinemann, 1966.
  An historical novel based on the clash between Cecil Rhodes
  and the Matebele King, Lobengula. Suitable for secondary
  schools.
Sellassie, Sahle (Ethiopia)
  The Afersata. London: Heinemann, 1969.
  A novella, long on African customs. Apparently written for
  the African public school market.

Serumaga, Robert (Uganda)
  Return to the Shadows. London: Heinemann, 1969.
Soyinka, Wole (Nigeria)
  The Interpreters (1965). New York: Collier Books, 1970. (Intro-
    duction by Leslie Lacy.)
    Soyinka's radically experimental novel about African intellec-
    tuals in contemporary Nigeria. One of the most significant
    pieces of African fiction. (See Chapter Nine herein. See also
    D. O. Fagunwa above.)
Tutuola, Amos (Nigeria)
  The Palm-Wine Drinkard (1952). New York: Grove Press, 1953.
    A fascinating piece of writing by the storyteller some critics
    feel is most typically African. The palm-wine Drinkard's
    search for his dead palm-wine tapster. Suitable for high schools.
    (See Chapters One and Four herein.)
  My Life in the Bush of Ghosts (1954). New York: Grove Press,
    1970.
  Simbi and the Satyr of the Dark Jungle. London: Faber, 1956.
  The Brave African Huntress (1958). New York: Grove Press,
    1970.
  The Feather Woman of the Jungle. London: Faber, 1962. (Short
    stories.)
  Ajaiyi and His Inherited Poverty. London: Faber, 1967.
Ulasi, Adsora Lily (Nigeria)
  Many Things You No Understand. London: Michael Joseph,
    1970.
    For once the Africans win in their struggle against the colonial
    government.
Uzodinma, E. C. C. (Nigeria)
  Our Dead Speak. London: Longmans, 1967.
Wachira, Godwin (Kenya)
  Ordeal in the Forest. Nairobi: East African Publishing House,
    1968.

Index

Abrahams, Peter, 162-66: as first generation African novelist, 242; *Mine Boy*, 162-66; *This Island, Now*, 228; *A Wreath for Udomo*, 114

Achebe, Chinua, 27-65; on an African writing in English, 23-24; anthropological description in, 42-44; character portrayal by, 33, 38, 148-55; civil service job, 243; communal experience in, 117; dialogue of, 33, 40; *A Man of the People*, 14, 16, 64, 114, 153-55, 244, 280; narration in, 19; *No Longer at Ease*, 119; oral tradition in, 34-37, 64, 151-52; plots of, 18, 63-64; popularity and influence of, 27-28; proverbs used by, 34-35, 64; reviews of, 12-14, 16-17; satire of, 153-55; sub-stories compared with Tutuola's, 97; time presentation, 106; *Things Fall Apart*, 12-15, 19, 27-65, 97, 106, 114-17, 122-23, 135, 137, 149-52, 157, 250, 280

The African, 18

The African Child (*L'Enfant noir*), 170-73

African fiction: *The Beautyful Ones Are Not Yet Born*, post-independence political decadence, 258-68; characterization in, 17-18, 147-66; as creating a new genre, 25-26; critics' views on, 3-26; as defying categorization, 7-8, 66-67; didactic endings of, 19, 60-61, 73, 111; as different

from Western, 7-13; diversity in, 148-49, 278-82; earliest, 3-4; *L'Enfant noir* autobiography of growing up in Guinea, 170-73; essence of, 20-21; ethnological material in, 13-17, 42-44, 121, 171, 224; *Fragments* alienated autobiography, 268-76; Franco-phone, 67-68, 167-226; of the future, 278-82; geographically oriented differences in, 148-49; *A Grain of Wheat* complex situational novel, 138-46; *The Interpreters*, novel of artist's place in post-independent society, 246-57; *Jagua Nana* market novella, 87-91; *Mabel the Sweet Honey* market novella, 75-82; *Mine Boy* South African autobiography, 162-66; négritude in, 22-23, 167-226; Onitsha market literature, 69-92; *The Palm-Wine Drinkard* Yoruba oral tales, 94-112; plot in, 18-19; post-independence, 243-77; reception in the West, 3-26; *Le regard du roi* with European main character, 173-226; of the second generation, 243-77; *The Second Round* horror story irrelevant to black culture, 229-41; "simplicity" of, 12-13; situational novels, 116-46; subject areas of, 113-20, 280; *Things Fall Apart* archetypal novel of colonial impact, 27-65; *Weep Not, Child* Kenyan independence novel, 121-35, 155-58; *When Love Whispers* market